Language, Space, and Cultural Play

This multimodal approach to linguistic landscapes examines the role of linguistic and semiotic regimes in constructing landscape affect. Affect, as distinct from emotion, is object-oriented and can be analyzed in terms of structures of language and signs which operate on individuals and groups in specific spatial settings. Analyzing a series of landscape types – including "*kawaii*," "reverenced," "romance," "friendly," "luxury," and "digital" landscapes – Lionel Wee and Robbie B. H. Goh explore how language plays a crucial role in shaping affective responses to, and interactions with, space. This linguistic and semiotic construction of different spaces also involves cultural contestations and modulations in spatial responses, and the book offers an account of the different conditions under which "affective economies" gain or lose momentum.

LIONEL WEE is Professor of Linguistics in the Department of English Language and Literature, National University of Singapore. He works on language policy, sociolinguistics, and new Englishes. His publications include *The Singlish Controversy* (Cambridge University Press, 2018), *The Language of Organizational Styling* (Cambridge University Press, 2015), *Markets of English* (2012), and *Language without Rights* (2011).

ROBBIE B. H. GOH is Professor of English Literature in the Department of English Language and Literature, National University of Singapore. He works at the nexus of semiotics, cultural studies, and narratology. His publications include *Protestant Christianity in the Indian Diaspora: Abjected Identities, Evangelical Relations, and Pentecostal Visions* (2018), *Contours of Culture: Space and Social Difference in Singapore* (2005), and *Christianity in Southeast Asia* (2005).

T0371553

Language, Space, and Cultural Play

Theorizing Affect in the Semiotic Landscape

Lionel Wee

National University of Singapore

Robbie B. H. Goh

National University of Singapore

CAMBRIDGE
UNIVERSITY PRESS

University Printing House, Cambridge CB2 8BS, United Kingdom

One Liberty Plaza, 20th Floor, New York, NY 10006, USA

477 Williamstown Road, Port Melbourne, VIC 3207, Australia

314-321, 3rd Floor, Plot 3, Splendor Forum, Jasola District Centre, New Delhi - 110025, India

103 Penang Road, #05-06/07, Visioncrest Commercial, Singapore 238467

Cambridge University Press is part of the University of Cambridge.

It furthers the University's mission by disseminating knowledge in the pursuit of education, learning and research at the highest international levels of excellence.

www.cambridge.org
Information on this title: www.cambridge.org/9781108459136
DOI: 10.1017/9781108559515

First published 2020
First paperback edition 2022

A catalogue record for this publication is available from the British Library

Library of Congress Cataloging in Publication data
Names: Wee, Lionel, 1963– author. | Goh, Robbie B. H., 1964– author.
Title: Language, space and cultural play : theorising affect in the semiotic landscape / Lionel Wee, Robbie B. H. Goh.
Description: Cambridge ; New York : Cambridge University Press, 2019. | Includes bibliographical references and index.
Identifiers: LCCN 2019032604 | ISBN 9781107136564 (hardback) | ISBN 9781108472203 (hardback) | ISBN 9781108559515 (epub)
Subjects: LCSH: Sociolinguistics. | Place (Philosophy) | Signs and symbols – Social aspects.
Classification: LCC P40.5.P53 W44 2019 | DDC 306.44–dc23
LC record available at https://lccn.loc.gov/2019032604

ISBN 978-1-108-47220-3 Hardback
ISBN 978-1-108-45913-6 Paperback

Contents

Figures

Acknowledgments

Chapter 3 is based on an article that Lionel Wee coauthored with Mie Hiramoto, which is scheduled to appear in volume 13, issue 1, of the journal *Sociolinguistic Studies*. Lionel thanks Mie for her generosity in allowing this joint piece of work to be used and *Sociolinguistic Studies* for permission to reproduce significant portions of the article.

Chapter 8 draws on Lionel Wee's "Mobilizing affect in the linguistic cyberlandscape: The R-word campaign," which appeared in *Conflict, Exclusion and Dissent in the Linguistic Landscape* (2015, pp. 185–206), edited by Rani Rubdy and Selim ben Said and published by Palgrave Macmillan. Lionel expresses his appreciation to Palgrave Macmillan for permission to reproduce this work.

Fieldwork that went into sections of Chapters 4, 5, and 7 was funded by HDRSS grants from the National University of Singapore (NUS; R-103-000-097-101 in 2012, R-103-000-108-133 in 2013, R-103-000-119-101 in 2014, and R-103-000-129-101 in 2015). Robbie is grateful to NUS for the generous research support.

1 Introduction

The study of linguistic landscapes focuses on what Spolsky (2009: 65) calls "public linguistic space," such as "the city streets and squares, roads and parks, railway and bus stations and stops." As the journal *Linguistic Landscape* makes clear in its *Aim and Scope*, the emphasis is on languages and how they "surround us everywhere … in flashy advertisements and commercials, names of buildings, streets and shops, instructions and warning signs, graffiti and cyber space." The reference to cyberspace is a recognition that linguistic landscapes are not limited to physical spaces but also include virtual spaces such as websites and chat rooms (though private messaging, much like private oral conversations in physical landscapes, are excluded).

While "linguistic landscape" remains the most commonly used term, other terms are used in order to reflect different research emphases. Gorter (2013: 191) has suggested using "multilingual landscapes" to highlight an interest in multilingualism. And "semiotic landscapes" (Jaworski and Thurlow 2010; Shohamy and Gorter 2008) is usually favored when there is a desire to emphasize the multimodal nature of landscapes, where the interest is on how language interacts with other modalities such as visual images, nonverbal communication, and the infrastructure of the surrounding environment. In this book, we use "semiotic landscape" because, as we argue below, affect is an important aspect of the landscape, and the study of affect requires attention not only to language but to other modalities as well.

Many landscape studies, whether specifically linguistic or more broadly semiotic, are concerned with distributional issues, that is, the relative distributions of particular languages in selected sites (Backhaus 2007; Ben-Rafael, Shohamy, Amara and Trumer-Hecht 2006; Coluzzi 2009; Mendisu, Malinowski and Woldenmichael 2016; Monnier 1989; Muth 2012; Tang 2018). This is a "quantitative-distributive" approach (Gorter 2013: 199). However, as Blommaert (2013: 41) points out, such an approach has its limitations:

Quantitative LLS, as the very first step, will draw attention to the existence and presence of languages in a particular space and can answer questions such as "how many languages are used in space X? " But the argument does not cut very deep, and what we get is a rather superficial, "horizontal," and distributional image of multilingualism. The fact that these languages are ingredients of multimodal signs, and that these signs occur in non-random ways in public space, is left aside.

To pursue our interest in affect in the semiotic landscape, we adopt a phenomenological orientation that understands the landscape to be ideologically loaded and, moreover, is interested in how this ideological loading may be aimed at regulating the patterns of interactions of those individuals or groups that happen to be located within the landscape, as well as the different possibilities of interpretations of the landscape (or structures of meaning) by different individuals and groups. The landscape is, in other words, a constellation of interpretable signs. There are many other works that also adopt more qualitative analyses (see, among others, Eastman and Stein 1993; Spolsky and Cooper 1991), although these may not necessarily see themselves as adopting a phenomenological orientation.

Our interest in a more phenomenological orientation is in line with other studies that are very much focused on attending to the ways in which ideologies pervade the landscape, such as Stroud and Mpendukana's (2009) study of the politics of aspiration in South Africa; Pennycook's (2008, 2010) analysis of the production of graffiti in urban areas or "graffscapes"; and Leeman and Modan's (2009) discussion of the commodification of language in Washington DC's Chinatown, to mention just a few.

The recognition of the ideological and sociopolitical content within land-scapes is, however, arguably far more well developed in other disciplines such as geography and urban studies. For Marxist geographers such as David Harvey (1989, 2009) and Edward Soja (1989), landscapes were the sites of contestations between different groups in which issues of class, wealth, power, and oppression were inextricably bound. This went far beyond merely asserting that landscapes were occupied by different socioeconomic groups often in tension with each other; landscapes themselves were understood to be written and structured by these relations. This was particularly true of the "postmo-dern" turn in Marxist geography from the late 1970s onward, with its "phe-nomenological" emphasis on "the subjectivity, intentionality, and consciousness of knowledgeable human agents engaged not only in making history but also in shaping the political culture of everyday life in modern capitalist society" (Soja 1989: 40–41). The "postmodern" turn in urban studies had a distinctive emphasis on the "city as text" (to use James Duncan's well-known phrase) and regarded the built environment itself as a system of symbols reflecting a "dominant ideology" and "cultural logic," a "problem of metaphors and thus of language" (Benjamin 1997: 44; Hutcheon 1988: 35; Jameson 1991: 6).

We will argue in this book that, as part of this phenomenological orientation with its concomitant emphasis on symbols and ideologies, it is also important to attend to digital landscapes (a point made by the journal *Linguistic Landscape* in its reference to "cyber space"; see above). And while it may be natural to understand the digital landscape to refer to cyberspace, or – to retain a connection to the prevailing terminologies of "linguistic landscape" and "semiotic landscape" – the "cyber landscape," it in fact needs to be seen as being much more than that. With the burgeoning of digital media and technologies around the turn of the twenty-first century, the notion of "landscape" and its phenomenological and interpretative dimensions have been even further complicated. Advanced film effects, especially CGI technology, meant a disruption of any notion of the physical landscape in itself; landscapes in films were modified by technologies, and within the overall narrative of the film, in order to create particular responses on the part of audiences. Yet audiences still responded to these filmic landscapes, and landscape features (trees, mountains, houses, and other natural and human features), as bona fide landscapes with an existence independent of their digital transformations. The most striking evidence of this is the rise of film- and TV-related tourism associated with hit shows like Peter Jackson's *Lord of the Rings* trilogy and *The Hobbit* films, and HBO's *Game of Thrones* series. The audience response created through these shows was strong enough to override the knowledge that many landscapes were digitally altered (some quite drastically so), and to give a significant boost to fan tourism to sites in countries like Iceland, Northern Ireland and Croatia (for *Game of Thrones*), and New Zealand (for *The Hobbit* and *Lord of the Rings*). At the same time, the development of purely digital landscapes in spin-offs such as video games based on the *Lord of the Rings* trilogy allowed other fans to interact with the landscapes as purely digital constructs, with no corresponding geophysical location. This phenomenon epitomized by the *Lord of the Rings* may best be described as the creation of a "blended" landscape, both physical and textual, with a digitally altered as well as extra-digital dimension (Goh 2014).

Beyond virtual reality is the increasing use of augmented reality (AR; another form of "blended" landscape), which is perhaps most recently exemplified by the overwhelming popularity of Pokémon Go, "the game that truly brought AR to the public at large" (Anderton 2016). As Anderton (2016) points out, AR is

technology that interacts directly with real world environments and supplements them with new content. Pokémon Go accomplishes this by making millions of people run around outside looking for cute little monsters that they can only see through their phone or tablet.

AR, then, raises interesting questions about how we can approach the landscape analytically, not least because it forces us to confront the issue of whether a clear demarcation between physical and digital landscapes is even feasible. Thus, given the rapid developments in digital technology and attempts to encourage their widespread adoption, a study of landscapes has to be prepared to address the interfaces between the physical and the digital. This means that even the notion of semiotic landscape, arguably, does not go quite far enough in capturing the impact of digital technology on the ways in which landscapes are modified and audience responses cultivated. This is because the semiotic landscape is still typically interpreted as being wedded to the idea of a physically demarcated piece of terrain – albeit now one that is acknowledged to be multimodal and saturated with ideologies.

For the moment, however, we simply want to highlight that implicit to varying degrees in all of the studies of ideologies in the landscape that were just mentioned is the undeniable influence played by the role of emotions or, more broadly, affect (we explain the distinction below). Emotions come to the fore perhaps most clearly in Stroud and Mpendukana (2009), when they show how in a particular South African township "sites of luxury" coexist uneasily with "sites of necessity." But they are also undeniably present in the production of graffiti, whose transgressive nature helps the graffiti artists project "pride" and "rebellion" (Pennycook 2008: 302). And they are also relevant in the commodification of Washington DC's Chinatown, which, as Leeman and Modan (2009: 340) point out, involves marketing the area as one that promises visitors an experience that is exciting, vibrant, and yet also authentically Chinese. In addition, religious affect has always been a significant factor in pilgrimages to specific religious sites, and it also plays a large role in things like religious heritage preservation and attitudes to the environment (Park 1994). Then there is the group-based affect, a "tribal identification" such as seen in sports fandom or nationalistic causes, that plays a significant role in such sites as Old Trafford stadium and Marylebone Cricket Club and battle sites such as Bannockburn and Gettysburg.

In making the earlier observations, we are certainly not suggesting that linguistics has not given any attention at all to emotions or affect. For example, in a landmark paper, Besnier (1990) observes that

a strict distinction among referential, social, and affective meanings rests on assumptions that are problematic, including ones such as the following: (i) meaning involves "a unidirectional mapping from a predefined reality onto arbitrary linguistic forms"; (ii) cognition and emotion "must be assumed to be dichotomous"; and (iii) "affective meaning is seen as the encoding of the speaker's emotions, which the interlocutor decodes in verbal messages by giving precedence to intentionality" (1990: 419–420).

Besnier (1990: 421) goes on to argue that affect must be understood as a "multichannel phenomenon" that can be conveyed both linguistically and by "nonverbal devices" (1990: 427) and that it can be a group affair (1990: 428), and, finally, suggests that affect might be fruitfully studied as a form of semiosis (1990: 428). We find very little in Besnier's remarks to disagree with, and in Chapter 2 we do in fact develop a semiotic account of affect.

Other, more recent, linguistic approaches to the study of emotions include the collection of papers in Harvey and Shalom (2002), which focus specifically on how language is used to convey romance, desire, and sexuality. That is, the main question driving these papers is how "our desires" can take on "linguistic form," especially since this involves trying "to understand an experience that overwhelms us and thereby threatens constantly to outmaneuver and outclass our verbal resources, the principal means at our disposal for ordering and making sense of our lives" (Harvey and Shalom 2002: 1). The collection is at bottom highly text driven, being concerned with how "the encoding of desire results in distinct and describable linguistic features and patterns" (Harvey and Shalom 2002: 3). And Schwarz-Friesel (2015), taking a critical cognitive linguistic approach, treats emotion and language as belonging to different mental subsystems. Schwarz-Friesel's interest lies in the ways that linguistic features can serve to convey emotion and evaluation, and she treats the emotion subsystem as providing the necessary evaluative component to what are otherwise apparently unemotional or un-evaluative ideational meanings. Aside from the fact that Schwarz-Friesel is focused on language and emotion as aspects of cognition rather than as material representations in a landscape, we find her sharp distinction between emotion or evaluation, on the one hand, and ideation, on the other hand, to be problematic (see the comments from Besnier 1990 mentioned earlier; see also the discussion in Reddy 2001: 14–15).

In a recent review, McElhinny (2010) highlights a number of research gaps that might be fruitfully approached from the perspective of language and affect, including the need for more historically sensitive analyses; the rise of terror and hate, and the corresponding importance of conviviality in public speech; and the use of language in affective labor. Some of these themes, such as conviviality in the public arena and affective labor, are clearly relevant to the study of semiotic landscapes. Nevertheless, it still has to be said that the focus in these works tends to be on the emotions or feelings of individuals and/or groups rather than on the ways in which social expectations regarding appropriate emotions or feelings come to be sited in different parts of a landscape.

Where landscape studies in particular are concerned, a more explicit attempt to focus on emotions can be found in the collection of papers edited by Rubdy and Ben Said (2015). However, the papers in this collection deal with a very restricted set of emotions and their triggers, namely "the dynamics of the linguistic landscape as a site of conflict, exclusion, and dissent often arising from mechanisms of language policy, language politics, language hierarchies, and the ethnolinguistic struggles engendered by them" (Rubdy 2015: 1). It is of course clear that the range of emotions in a landscape goes beyond those of conflict and dissent, with religious fervor, conviviality, and memorializations being just a few that come immediately to mind. And it is equally clear that many of the emotions involved need not be the result of language policy issues even if language does play a role in the communication and management of emotions.

Because emotions are either treated as separate from referential or ideational meanings, or only implicitly recognized in many of the works on landscapes, or given due attention only when they involve conflicts that can be related to matters of language policy, we think it is not inaccurate to state that serious sociolinguistic theorization concerning the general ways in which emotions come to be emplaced in particular landscapes is still in its infancy, notwith-standing works such as by Peck, Williams, and Stroud (forthcoming) and Wee (2016). And we should point out that any attempt at such a theorization is in fact somewhat belated because the "affective turn" in social and critical theory (Clough 2007) took place more than a decade ago. What might be broadly described as the critical study of emotions has resulted in a number of key studies, handbooks, and overviews (Barbalet 1998; Berlant 2011; Brennan 2004; Hochschild 1983; Lewis, Haviland-Jones, and Barrett 2008; Reddy 2001; Rutherford 2016; Scheff 1990; Stets and Turner 2006; Turner and Stets 2005).

What this means is that even though theorizing in sociolinguistics and land-scape studies is only just beginning to appreciate the significance of the ideas that constitute the affective turn and to draw upon them, there is also great potential for sociolinguistics and landscape studies to inform these critical studies of emotions. Of course, just because there has been a shift toward greater interest in the study of affect elsewhere does not mean that socio-linguistics, too, has to follow suit. It is the purpose of this introductory chapter, therefore, to make the case as to why the affective dimensions of semiotic landscapes (including the impacts of AR and cyber landscapes) should be of interest to sociolinguistics. It is to this issue that we now turn our discussion.

Emotions and Affect: A Matter of Orientation

Let us now clarify the difference between "emotion" and "affect." The distinc-tion is not always made, which means that the two terms are sometimes used interchangeably, (see also Hochschild 1979: 551; Smith-Lovin 1995). However, we will now argue that it is affect rather than emotion that is in fact of greater relevance and analytical value in the study of semiotic landscapes.

Whereas emotions refer to the "culturally given labels that we assign to experiences" of individuals or groups, affect is much more general and instead refers to "any evaluative (positive or negative) orientation toward an object" (Robinson, Smith-Lovin, and Wisecup 2006: 181, 183; see also Jasper 2014: 64; Massumi 1995). Since any such evaluative orientation can also be described using emotion labels, it is useful to think of a cultural label as amenable to being studied as an emotion or as a form of affect. The focus on emotion might be better suited to a social psychological study, whereas the focus on affect would highlight the interaction between environmental factors and the individual. So, one could, for example, study hysteria as an emotion by focusing on an individual's psychological state. But one could also study hysteria as a form of affect by exploring how the environment might facilitate its spread across a crowd.

Emotions are typically assumed to reside "within" the entity that is feeling the emotion. This entity is often taken to be the individual and, in some cases, the group, where the latter is then conceptualized as a single entity because the individual members are all seen to be sharing the same emotion or to be in the same emotional state. This way of thinking about emotions as being internal to the feeling entity (be it the group or the individual) shifts the focus away from the role that the surrounding environment and the objects that help constitute the environment play in shaping or affecting the emotions of the entity in question. And in the case of a posited group-level emotion, it also raises the question of how it is that the individual members come to share the same emotional state. Here, it is important to recognize that from the perspective of a single individual, the presence of other comembers of the group is undeniably also part of that individual's environment (Massumi 2002; Sedgwick 2003).

This shift of focus away from the environment is avoided if we think in terms of affect rather than emotions (Brennan 2004). This is because affect involves an orientation toward an object, and this serves in turn to emphasize that affect is fundamentally relational in nature. This relational nature is captured in the fact that we often speak of "being affected" by something and, in psychological studies, a person with "low" or "flat" affect is usually someone who is emotionally detached or unresponsive to her surroundings. The outward orientation of affect is also evident in its etymology from the Latin *afficere*, which in turn contains the root *facere* ("to do" or "to perform"). Indeed, Wissinger (2007: 232; see also Tomkins 1962, 1991) reminds us that affect is "social in that it constitutes a contagious energy, an energy that can be whipped up or dampened in the course of interaction." Thinking in terms of affect is therefore much more appropriate if we are interested in better understanding semiotic landscapes because the notion of affect is always contextual or environmental.

Thinking in terms of affect also allows us to focus on a variety of phenomena that are not always clearly identifiable via specific emotion labels. For example, there are states or capacities that are not obviously emotions even though they do have emotional dimensions, such as being alert or being patient. Emotions are typically thought of as relatively short-lived and spontaneous (*I'm feeling happy today; The knock on the door startled me*). They are not usually thought of as cultivatable even though they can be (*I want to be a happier person; I want to be less anxious all the time*), as Frankfurt (1988) points out. In such cases, emotions also blur into other states or capacities that are not usually thought of as emotions (*He is a highly resilient person; John is one of our most vigilant security guards*). Thinking in terms of affect then has the advantage of allowing us to capture the range from prototypical emotions to states and capacities because the analytical focus is on the orientation toward objects in the environment, and such an orientation can encompass a myriad of reactions and responses.

Having discussed the distinction between emotion and affect, we now consider how a focus on the latter bears on and helps to illuminate the study of semiotic landscapes.

Affect and Semiotic Landscapes

Because affect is relational, an affect-analytic perspective helps to shift the focus from questions about the internal states of individuals or groups toward the structuring of the environment and in particular how that structuring is aimed at regulating or managing the public display or materialization of affect. From a landscape perspective, this is useful as it allows us to confront more sociologically oriented questions like the extent to which certain ideologies might be materially emplaced as part of the semiotic landscape. In other words, the semiotic landscape should not merely be seen as the context in which individuals and groups experience or express emotions, but, importantly, also as contributing to these very experiences *qua* affect. The semiotic landscape has to be acknowledged as structuring the affective affordances and positionings of individuals and groups. Massey (2005) emphasizes that the social and the spatial are mutually constitutive, that is, social structures are emplaced to produce "spatialities" rather than simply being located within pre-given spatial markers.

Affect in the semiotic landscape, then, needs to be appreciated as a kind of spatiality. For example, Wee (2016) shows how the Arlington National Cemetery represents a site where a specific kind of affective regime is cultivated, namely one where honor and respect are to be accorded to the servicemen who died for their country. There are signs on the cemetery grounds that request "Silence and Respect," as well as visitors' rules that explain that because the cemetery is "a shrine to the honored dead ... disorderly conduct ... boisterous language," among others, are prohibited (2016: 111–113). In both these cases, it is not as if the spatial exists prior to and separate from the social, or vice versa. Rather, the recognition of a site as "Singapore society" or "the Arlington National Cemetery" involves the coconstitutive structuring of the social and spatial.

Hochschild (1979, 1983) observes that emotions are subject to "feeling rules" and "display rules." The former specifies the kinds of feelings that are considered appropriate in particular situations and the latter how these feelings should be overtly expressed. Socialization into a particular culture means learning the associated feeling rules and display rules, so that individuals then attempt to manage their own emotions in ways that accord with the normative expectations imposed by such rules. Individuals learn the feeling and display rules governing when and how to come across as cheerful, angry, supportive, or welcoming, among others. Particularly in the various service industries that have been studied as a result of Hochschild's pioneering work, the results are what Hochschild describes as "emotion work," such as evocation, where the actor tries to bring about "a desired feeling which is initially absent," and suppression, where the actor tries to remove "an undesired feeling which is initially present" (1979: 561). Successful emotion work then allows the actor to be legitimately described (both by herself and by her interactional others) as possessing the appropriate emotion, that is, by having her internal state be describable by invoking the relevant cultural-specific label. However, semiotic landscapes do not always make use of culture-specific labels to manage the kinds of emotions or behaviors that might be expected or considered appropriate to a particular site. Indeed, inhabitants in a given site may be experiencing a wide range of emotions and the specification of appropriate emotions may not even always be relevant to the remit of how a particular semiotic landscape has been structured. This is to say that not all sites attempt to regulate emotions to the same explicit degree as the Arlington National Cemetery. But all sites, implicitly or otherwise, do have normative expectations regarding appropriate social conduct, where the concomitant emotive dimension oftentimes remains implicit and is therefore better captured in terms of a general evaluative orientation or affect rather than via the invocation of specific labels. For example, "third places" (Oldenburg 1997) such as public libraries and cafes do not explicitly specify what kinds of emotions would be appropriate. But as communally sociable places where individuals from differing backgrounds can be expected to congregate and relax, violent expressions of anger or even excessively loud demonstrations of jubilation are not always welcome. The issue, at least where "third places" are concerned, then, is less a matter of policing any particular emotion by invoking a culture-specific label than one of very broadly regulating positive affect.

Finally, since the concept of affect also captures states and capacities that are not prototypically considered emotions, it is useful in analyzing the activities and goals of urban spaces as these try to accumulate various kinds of symbolic capital. For example, cities may want to be seen as convivial or business-friendly, and specific environments or neighborhoods may want to present themselves as pedestrian-friendly or dementia-friendly. These are less about specific emotions than about encouraging a positive or supportive orientation toward corporate interests or dementia sufferers and their families. They clearly involve attempts at structuring the semiotic landscape in ways that, hopefully, come to be construed as possessing the relevant symbolic capital. And while emotions are still relevant, these have now to be understood as emplaced so that the desired ambience is brought about. So, instead of speaking about an individual or couple feeling romantic, we need to ask, for instance, how a setting comes to be seen as romantic. This emplacement of affect, of course, brings us right back to the very first point of this section, namely the relational nature of affect.

The Organization of the Book

Having made the case for why affect needs to be studied as part of our attempts to better understand the ideological structuring of semiotic landscapes, the next question that needs to be addressed is how this can be done in a theoretically coherent way that can lead to insightful analytical payoffs. This is the focus of Chapter 2, *Theorizing Affect in the Semiotic Landscape*, which draws on the concepts of an affective regime (Wee 2016) and an affective economy (Ahmed 2004a, 2004b), among others, to show how these can combine to provide a framework for understanding both the materialization and circulation of affect. The theorization of affect that we proposed is based largely on Peirce's notion of semiotics. The value of this framework is that it integrates the analysis of affect as part of a more general process of semiosis rather than treating it as a unique or distinctive phenomenon. The framework thus serves to provide a concrete theorization of Wissinger's (2007; see above) description of affect as socially "contagious energy." In the absence of concrete theorization, Wissinger's description, despite its aptness, remains a colorful metaphor. But the actual mechanisms by which affect is materialized, circulates, and becomes "whipped up or dampened" need to be more systematically articulated, and Chapter 2 does exactly that.

The utility of the framework is then illustrated over the next six chapters. The chapters are arranged in such a way as to progressively deal with cases where affect becomes more nebulous and implicit, but is nevertheless still relevant to the semiotic landscape. In this regard, Chapter 3, Kawaii *in the Semiotic Landscape*, begins the illustration with what might be considered a relatively transparent attempt at regulating affect: the use of figures that are considered *kawaii*, a Japanese term meaning "cute" or "adorable." An examination of how *kawaii* figures are employed by various municipal authorities in Tokyo brings to light just how affect works when linguistic and nonlinguistic modalities are combined. This is a fairly straightforward case of affect in the semiotic landscape for at least two reasons. One, the concept of *kawaii* is already clearly one that is loaded with affect given its association with notions of cuteness and adorability. As we will see, Japanese society socializes its speakers into treating *kawaii* characters as vulnerable and deserving of gentle, even tender, treatment. Two, the use of *kawaii* in public signage, especially in the form of cartoon figures, brings to light and helps exemplify Ahmed's (2004a, b) claim that affect circulates via the use of characters that tend to evoke specific cultural stereotypes.

Chapter 4, *Reverencing the Landscape*, looks at the ways in which sites such as places of worship construct affective responses of reverence, respect, and awe. The multimodal nature of these sites is particularly instructive, being in many cases a combination of architecture and spatial organization, linguistic signposting or instruction, and communal behavior ("ritual," broadly understood). In an age where secularism and post-secularism are in contestation, many of these religious semiotics and affects leach out into nonreligious public sites, while at the same time aspects of nonreligious popular culture creep into some religious sites as well (Beaumont and Baker 2011; Graham 2013). Thus, reverence as a semiotic affect can also be seen in quasi-religious sites and landscapes such as memorials to persons or events of consequence to a nation or community (holocaust memorials, Mandela's cell in Robben Island prison), certain sites of office or power (the presidential residence "the Istana" in Singapore; the Palace of the Parliament in Bucharest), even certain popular and grand natural phenomena (Niagara Falls, Uluru). Reverence as an affect is commonly found in group interactions with semiotic landscapes – that is to say, there is a communal or ritualistic dimension by which a group with shared affinities (religious, nationalistic, sporting, etc.) reinforces the affect of reverence in a particular semiotic landscape. While it is generally true that affect (being a semiotic structure outside of the individual) operates on multiple participants, this is different from saying that there is a particularly communal affect that operates in the case of reverence – that relies on and reinforces the affect that a particular group (*qua* group) feels toward a semiotic landscape. Conversely, there are affects that tend to individualize the experience of a semiotic landscape, even though (again) more than one individual can be the subject of this affect.

Chapter 5, *Romancing the Landscape*, describes the ways in which a set of "romance" signs create a landscape as the site of an individual adventure, journey of growth, and path to fulfillment. The romance archetype, as theorized by Northrop Frye, is an enduring genre that has shown "little change over the course of centuries," and whose "essential element of plot ... is adventure" (Frye 1976: 4, 2015: 186). The structuring of romance affects is not only prolific in literature and folk tales, as Frye observes, but has all kinds of implications for geophysical landscapes as well: from touristic discourses which describe specific destinations as sites of "romance" and "adventure," to film narratives which intersect with tourism by leveraging on viewer fandom to popularize certain film locations, to the semiotics of amusement parks and other attractions.

Chapter 6, "Friendly Places," addresses a different issue regarding affect and semiotic landscapes, that of boundaries. That is, how are the boundaries established between one site where a particular kind of affect is being fostered and another site where some other affect is either encouraged or where the affect fostered by the former site is no longer a relevant concern? Or, to phrase the issue more succinctly: How are the limits or contours of an affective regime carved out and established? The chapter begins with a brief consideration of various attempts to demarcate specific sites as "friendly," including the third places identified by Oldenburg (1997). The discussion of third places is useful because it gives us a sense of what the semiotics of conviviality might look like. Once identified, the array of semiotic resources in third places can serve as a conceptual point of departure for examining the boundaries where the third place conviviality no longer holds, or where other kinds of convivialities might instead prevail, such as sites that claim to be "family friendly" or "gay friendly." The latter half of the chapter then comprises a detailed case study of a "dementia friendly" neighborhood in Singapore.

While "friendly" places show the ways in which accessibility, safety, and welcome feature in urban planning and the branding of certain commercial spaces, this sits in dialectical tension with another powerful force in the habitus: that of exclusivity and extreme desirability. Chapter 7, The Affective Regime of Luxury and Exclusivity, examines the ways in which areas such as luxury housing projects and enclaves are structured as luxurious, desirable, and valuable by virtue of being unattainable by the general public. The nature of such "Veblen goods" is primarily to confer preeminent status upon the owner; as such, they have to be strictly demarcated as being both desired by the majority of people, and also distinctly out of their reach (Rudzitis, Marcouiller, and Lorah 2011: 130). The dialectical tension between strong desire and distinct unattainability relies on a complex semiotics combining some of the elements of conviviality (safety, acceptance, comfort, and well-being) with quite different elements of awe, superiority, and rejection. The affect of luxury is not confined to prestige housing, but is also deployed in other sites such as exclusive clubs, premier travel spaces (luxury yachts, first-class compartments of airplanes), and even to a certain extent in sites associated with "elite" membership such as in education, shopping, and popular culture fandom.

Chapter 8, Affecting the Digital Landscape, focuses on communication that takes place via new communicative technologies, particularly social media.

The chapter begins with a review of Wee's (2015) discussion of the R-word campaign, which analyzes some of the strategies and techniques that are being used to mobilize affect on the Internet. This is followed by an analysis of cyberbullying, and attempts to combat it by calling for a "safer, friendlier Internet." The Safer Internet Day is a global initiative that aims to promote "the safe, responsible, and positive use of digital technology," and in Singapore, this has been taken up by the government's Media Literacy Council. The key issue being examined in this chapter is the relationship between online behavior and the real world, since it is the presumed demarcation between the two domains that allows cyberbullies to act as they do. In this regard, the chapter ends with a discussion of the increased use of virtual and augmented realities, as possible ways of more effectively encouraging responsible online behavior by getting social media users to better appreciate the connectivities that can and do exist between the world online and the world offline.

Chapter 9, *Conclusion*, addresses the broad question of what it means to talk about a semiotic landscape in the era of late modernity, given the complexities observed and arguments presented in the preceding chapters. It identifies three possible lines of future research that we believe are likely to only gain in significance and urgency: the digitalization of third places, the experience economy, and the dynamics of affective regimes. As digital technology changes the ways in which we communicate, this too will influence the nature of social interaction in third places, with concomitant consequences for their status as "friendly/convivial" sites. The experience economy refers to the commodification of experiences. Providing consumers with memorable or interesting experiences is increasingly a competitive factor. A focus on the experience economy as a line of inquiry follows from our earlier discussion in Chapter 5 of how semiotic landscapes are romanticized. Finally, we have emphasized throughout our book the analytical value of the concept of an affective regime. An interesting question that follows would be the ways in which affective regimes cohere or conflict with one another. Further investigation into this issue would shed greater light on how some affective regimes enjoy a wider impact than others.

2   Theorizing Affect in the Semiotic Landscape

Introduction

In Chapter 1, we made the argument that if our interest is in how emotions are regulated or managed in the semiotic landscape, then it is conceptually more suitable to think in terms of affect. This is because affect is much more inclusive (it allows us to address emotions but from a broader perspective that can also handle states and capacities that are not typically thought of as emotions); it is less culture-specific (thus allowing us to avoid the dilemma of cross-cultural comparisons that comes from using culture-specific emotion labels); and it is relational (which serves as a useful reminder to constantly keep in mind the structuring and affordances of the "-scaped" environment). All of this, however, raises the question of how affect can be theorized in such a way as to take into account its relation to the semiotic landscape.

Our aim in the present chapter is to provide just such a theoretical account. We will introduce a number of theoretical concepts, but undergirding the theorization of affect is Peirce's (1958, 1980) notion of semiosis. We therefore begin with Peirce's ideas about semiotics.

The Semiotics of Peirce

Peirce defines semiotics as "the analytic study of the essential conditions to which all signs are subject" and "what would be true of signs in all cases" (Peirce 1998: 327). This allows Peirce to treat as signs (and hence, as relevant to semiotics) linguistic as well as nonlinguistic phenomena, including what might be described as natural signs (e.g. certain cloud formations that signal a coming storm) and nonhuman signs (e.g. animal communication).

This is an important point. It is worth noting because it opens the way for a unified treatment of both linguistic and nonlinguistic signs, rather than assuming that there is something significantly different or special about the

14

former that distinguishes it from the latter.[1] The reason why this is important is that the semiotic landscape is populated with both kinds of signs working together. But Peirce's idea of semiotics is invaluable beyond its willingness to treat linguistic and nonlinguistic signs on a unified basis. A key feature of Peirce's semiotics is the conception of the sign as a triadic relation between sign, object, and interpretant, as opposed to, say, Saussure's work, which focuses on the signifier–signified dyad (Deely 1990: 115). Peirce, in one of his clearer explications, points out that "it is very easy to see what the interpretant of a sign is: it is all that is explicit in the sign itself apart from its context and circumstances of utterance" (Peirce 1955: 276). Thus, while the interpretant is itself yet another sign (Sebeok 1994: 12), it is a sign that comes about as a result of the interaction between an earlier sign and the activities of a user of this earlier sign. It is the notion of an interpretant that crucially allows relations between signs to be understood as an ongoing, possibly never-ending, process of semiosis, where signs do not merely exist but give rise to yet further signs (cf. Deely 1990: 23).

Peirce elaborates on this initial insight by establishing four conditions that are needed for a sign to count as a sign (Liszka 1996: 18–19): (i) a sign must correlate with or represent an object, that is, "all signs have a directedness toward objects, or at least purport to be about something"; (ii) the sign must correlate or represent its object in some capacity or manner; (iii) the sign must (at least potentially) determine its interpretant, that is, "a sign must have the ability to create another equivalent or more developed sign, in some interpreter, which articulates the original"; and (iv) the triadic relation between sign, object, and interpretant is an "irreducible interrelation through which each component gets its sense," that is, each individual component (sign, object, or interpretant) is recognizable as such only because of the totality of the triad. We can separate out or isolate a sign, or its object, or its interpretant – but we can only do so because this very act of isolating a component is itself a process of semiosis that inevitably relies on the "irreducible interrelation."

---

[1] This is by no means a trivial matter, since there are semiotic approaches that sometimes emphasize the self-contained nature of sign systems, particularly the linguistic sign system. This is perhaps most prominent in Saussure's (1983) attempt to establish what he called the discipline of "semiology." For Saussure, language is a "special type of sign system" (1983: 15–16) because it best illustrates principles such as the arbitrariness of the sign (1983: 100), and he argues that "language is form and not substance, its elements have only contrastive and combinatorial properties" (1983: 61). There are of course differences of opinions as to what Saussure may have actually intended, since most interpretations of his ideas come from lecture notes compiled by his students. Nevertheless, contemporary interpretations of Saussure do attribute to him a treatment of the linguistic sign system as closed and self-contained (see, for example, Brennan 2004; Norris 2004).

Peirce's notion of the interpretant provides an explicit explanation for what we mean when we say that affect is a matter of evaluative orientation toward some object in the environment (see Chapter 1). The affective orientation is the interpretant that arises from an encounter between a user and the object, resulting in yet another sign. Such a move may seem strange if we are used to thinking of signs as conveying information and the understanding or interpretation of signs as a cognitive process where cognition is assumed to be in a mutually exclusive relationship to emotion. This misconception that cognition and emotion are somehow mutually exclusive, and where the latter is also oftentimes construed as undermining the former, is, rather unfortunately, a fairly prevalent assumption. But it is unfounded, as Jasper (2014: 8, italics added) points out:

> Emotions have a bad reputation, since the philosophers who tend to write about them prefer to talk about abstract thoughts instead of the messy act of thinking, ideas over feelings, products over processes. They have portrayed emotions as the opposite of thinking, as unfortunate interferences that lead us to do dumb things. *Only recently have psychologists shown that emotions also send us signals and help us process information, evaluate our situations, and begin to formulate paths to action. Far from always disrupting our lives, emotions help us carry on.* They are functional, sometimes even wise. They are a part of sensible actions as well as regrettable ones. They are neither good nor bad, but simply normal. Emotions are part of culture because we learn when and how to display them, and what to call them (fear versus anger, for instance). They also permeate cognition: emotions bring stories to life, make us care about collective identities, help us hate villains or pity victims. *Cognition and emotion are inseparable.*

Likewise, Williams and Bendelow (1998: xv) observe that "Despite their obvious importance to a range of issues within the social sciences, emotions, like the body to which they are so closely tied, have tended to enjoy a rather 'ethereal' existence within sociology, lurking in the shadows or banished to the margins of sociological thought and practice." Williams and Bendelow (ibid.) trace the "roots of this neglect" to a tradition of Western thought, which they describe as

> a tradition which has sought to divorce body from mind, nature from culture, reason from emotion, and public from private. As such, emotions have tended to be dismissed as private, "irrational," inner sensations, which have been tied, historically, to women's "dangerous desires" and "hysterical bodies."

The fact that cognition and emotion are in actuality inseparable means that when it comes to semiosis and the interpretant, any attempt to identify a purely cognitive sign in contrast to a purely emotive or affective sign is simply wrongheaded. Indeed, as we already noted in the preceding chapter, all analyses of how various ideologies pervade the semiotic landscape to varying degrees of explicitness have to acknowledge that there is an emotive dimension present. This is why a study of affect in the landscape is critical. It is no exaggeration to say that a failure to attend to the unavoidable presence of affect will mean that our understanding of the landscape remains incomplete.

And our insistence that cognition and emotion are not separable in semiosis is entirely consonant with Peirce's (1980) "inclusion rule." Even though Peirce (1980) distinguishes between three types of signs (icon, index, and symbol), he is at pains to stress that there is no such thing as a pure symbol.[2] An icon bears similarities or resemblances to the object that it represents. A map of a particular area or a photograph of an individual would be icons of their respective objects. An index represents its object not because of similarities but because of contiguity. The sign, in this case, bears a spatiotemporal connection to the object it represents. A sign such as "No Parking Here" is indexical in that the area where parking is prohibited is understood to bear some proximity to the sign's own location. Finally, a symbol represents its object via the establishment of some convention or habit. Linguistic signs such as the English word "cat" and the Malay word *kucing*, both of which describe a particular kind of feline, are examples of symbols.

Liszka (1996: 46, citing Peirce 1980, Vol. 2) elaborates on the inclusion rule as follows:

[T]he inclusion rule suggests that there is no such thing as a pure symbol, for example, since it will always include an index and icon. It may be the case that the included sign serves as the vehicle by which the principal sign conveys information or refers to its object. The fact that a symbol includes an index allows it to refer, and the fact that it includes an icon allows it to signify.

In other words, for Peirce, processes of interpretation cannot rely only on a purely arbitrary or purely symbolic relationship between the sign and that which it represents. For a sign to work as a sign, it has to be capable of being interpreted, and this interpretation has to be constrained or directed in some way – which is why any symbol will, according to Peirce, also include an index and an icon. However purely arbitrary the symbol may appear at first blush, once we start trying to make sense of the symbol, we are necessarily also drawing upon its indexical and iconic aspects, as Hoopes (1991: 12, italics in original) explains:

---

[2] Peirce's distinction between these three types of signs concerns what he calls the "second division" (1955). The "first division" concerns a distinction between "qualisigns," "sinsigns," and "legisigns." We do not find the first division particularly useful given that (and this line of reasoning extrapolates from the inclusion rule) every legisign requires a sinsign and every sinsign involves a qualisign or even several qualisigns (1955: 101–2). Indeed, there is a point where Peirce may be said to have been overly enthusiastic in his attempt to identify different sign types, so much so that the distinctions being proposed are really slicing the salami far too thinly (Atkin 2013).

The meaning of the sign is not necessarily arbitrary but may be as logical as the thought that interprets it. While some contemporary literary theorists tell us that signs are arbitrary, verbal representations of their objects and as free to depart from them as "rose" from its flower, Peirce pointed out that many interpretants predicate real relations between signs and their objects. He called such signs indices, and one of his favorite examples was the interpretation of a weathercock as accurately signifying the direction of the wind because of its having a real relation with the wind. Moreover, even arbitrary symbols such as the stop sign are nevertheless not arbitrarily interpreted. A stop sign might just as well be triangular in shape if that were the arbitrarily chosen convention, but its interpretant would still be the thought of stopping. A driver might of course arbitrarily interpret the stop sign to mean "floor it!" In doing so, however, he would put himself at *real* risk.

Thus, the symbol is just one of three possible kinds of signs, and more importantly, a purely symbolic sign is simply not workable. A sign gains its meaningfulness and interpretability from being an icon and an index. The sign as symbol merely allows just about anything to be recruited or utilized to stand for some object. But for any actual understanding of just what object the sign happens to be standing for to take place, the sign must also be an icon and an index. To see why this is so, consider the following example. The variable X is prototypically used to stand for some unknown. In this sense, X is a symbol. However, for any use of X to be meaningful – that is, so that it can give rise to an interpretant – it necessarily requires some contextualization of X. For example, X can be an unknown value in a quadratic equation; it can stand for the unknown identity of a murderer; it can mark the as-yet-to-be-determined location of some buried treasure. These various contextualizations of X then imbue the variable with the properties of an icon and an index as well as those of a symbol. Crucially, in the absence of the first two kinds of properties, X as a pure symbol is simply uninterpretable.

It might be argued that surely a mathematical sign such as X is a pure symbol, that there is nothing iconic about it. This would be wrong. Peirce (1980: 281, 531) explains that "likeness" may be "extreme," as in the case of a photograph, or it may be subtle, as with mathematical symbols. Peirce explains (1980: 179):

Particularly deserving of notice are icons in which the likeness is aided by conventional rules. Thus, an algebraic formula is an icon, rendered such by the rules of commutation, association, and distribution of the symbols.

An icon represents by resembling, but it would be a mistake to adopt an oversimplified notion of what it means to resemble. Resemblance is not always or necessarily pictorial. For example, the "X" used in a given equation resembles other "X"s and hence is recognizable as a token of the letter "X," and the latter further recognized as a member of the alphabet, and there is in turn an appreciation of the convention of using letters of the alphabet (such as "Y," "Z," "A," and "C" for that matter) in mathematical equations. This is iconic resemblance at a subtler level than that found in a photograph.

All this is highly relevant to the study of semiotic landscapes because signs qua index and icon now bear some relationship to a world beyond the signs themselves. This is a relationship that anchors the signs to specific sites and that consequently constrains the kinds of interpretants that could arise, because how the signs are interpreted can have actual material consequences. In this regard, Hoopes (1991: 12, italics added) makes the point that Peirce's semiotics opens up the possibility of treating individual cognitive signs and social institutional signs as a unified phenomenon (see also the discussion of Willis 1990, below):

[B]y adopting the viewpoint of Peirce's semiotic, it is possible to avoid either gnawing the old bone of the relation of thought to behavior or else isolating intellectual activity from society. Once intellectual activity is understood to be "real" behavior, its possible importance can be weighed fairly against other "real" elements in society. Conversely, social institutions such as government, political parties, corporations, labor unions, voluntary associations, and so on may be regarded as thought, once a thought is understood to be, not an idea known immediately within a mind, but rather, an interpretive relation. Once thought is understood as a process of sign interpretation, a great range of social phenomena too large to be comprehended within any individual mind may nevertheless be best understood as the result of a process of intelligence. *Institutions and organizations are semiotic syntheses, so to speak, of the thoughts of a great many people.*

To summarize the discussion thus far, Peircean semiotics provides us with a theoretically coherent way of thinking about affect as an orientation toward an object in the semiotic landscape. Moreover, it has the merit of not imposing sharp boundaries or distinctions between linguistic signs and nonlinguistic ones, between cognition and emotion, or between individual and institutional processes of sign interpretation. Keeping this in mind, we can now turn to the idea of an affective regime.

The Semiosis of Affective Regimes

Wee (2016: 109) defines an affective regime in the following manner:

[T]he set of conditions that govern with varying degrees of hegemonic status the ways in which particular kinds of affect can be appropriately materialized in the context of a given site . . .

Because an affective regime operates at the level of the site, even in the absence of any particular individual, that is, even when a given site happens to be uninhabited or unoccupied, it is still meaningful to speak of an affective regime associated with that environment. This is because the site itself can be structured in ways that are intended to evoke particular dispositions regardless of whether anyone happens to be present.

Some affective regimes may be explicitly concerned with encouraging particular affects (as in signs at memorials that request respect from visitors). Other
affective regimes may be less directly concerned with specific affects, but they
nonetheless have the effect (intended or otherwise) of encouraging some
affects while discouraging others (such as the use of CCTVs, which typically
alerts individuals that they are in an area that is under surveillance but leaves
unspecified – and hence up to the individuals to infer for themselves – just what
kinds of behaviors are to be considered appropriate or inappropriate to that
specific area). The idea of an affective regime is thus one particular instantiation of material calibration, which refers to *the ways in which activities and
technologies (including language) are – to varying degrees – aligned so as to
bring about desired states of affairs*. Material calibration is not necessarily
geared toward governance or surveillance. The desired state of affairs can vary
depending on the specific goal of the actor responsible for the calibration.
A graffiti artist may have the goal of ensuring that her work is prominently and
regularly displayed on various urban surfaces. The use of spray paint, the
choice of surface, and an identifiable signature or style would then constitute
her alignment of activities and technologies. Governance and surveillance are
not likely to be part of the graffiti artist's desired state of affairs. But there are of
course other actors for whom the decisions about how to align activities and
technologies are motivated by the governance and surveillance of affect, such
as the Arlington National Cemetery, discussed below (see also preceding
chapter).[3]

It is important to appreciate that in all affective regimes, the affects clearly do
not reside in any of the material conditions themselves but emerge from the
interactions between these conditions and the individuals who encounter
them.[4] This is the case even when the semiotic landscape may have been
carefully structured to "over-determine" the appropriate affect, such as, say,
the Disney theme park's emphasis on being "a happy place." To insist on
a purely materialist notion of the affective regime is to subscribe to the fallacy
of deterministic landscapes, as if the interpreting subject had no choice but to
feel and behave in a particular way in a particular semiotic landscape. The
possibility of affective dissent or divergence (where a particular interpreter
chooses to respond in an uncommon way to the landscape) indicates the degree
of interpretative freedom that still resides in the subject in response to material

---

[3] The concept of material calibration coheres well with Scollon and Scollon's (2003, 2004, 2007)
    notions of geosemiotics and nexus analysis. For them, the meaning of a sign, then, has to be
    understood in relation to its materialization in particular locations and contexts. However,
    material calibration is not intended as a form of ethnography (though it could certainly be used
    as such), which is where it diverges from the interests of the Scollons (Scollon and Scollon 2004:
    9, 2007: 608).
[4] This is a point that Brennan (2004) emphasizes in her own account of affect, although she is
    ultimately interested in the physiological shifts that come about (2004: 5).

conditions. The corollary to this point is the reality of interpretative contestation: the struggle by different groups to insist on different significations of the same landscape – differences motivated by differences in culture, politics, economics, and other factors. A common manifestation of interpretative contestation in the semiotic landscape occurs when Aboriginal or First Nations groups insist on a spiritual interpretation of a site that clashes with the interpretations and interactions of other groups such as colonial settlers, tourist agencies, filmmakers, property developers, and others. This can be seen, among other sites, in places like Uluru in Australia and Mount Ngauruhoe in New Zealand (Figueroa and Waitt 2011; Goh 2014).

In this regard, it is useful to understand that affective regimes are broader or more inclusive than cultural scripts. The latter are highly influential and widely used in sociological accounts of how individuals manage their emotions. They represent particular normative sociological phenomena that specify the ways in which individuals and/or groups are expected to respond when encountering the affective regimes that are emplaced in different kinds of environments.[5] For example, Hochschild's (1983: 56) descriptions of how individuals may be expected to display particular emotions in different situations (e.g. grief at a funeral, happiness at a birthday party) are essentially appeals to cultural scripts. Thus, Hochschild suggests that we recognize a feeling rule (1983: 57) by "inspecting how we assess our feelings, how other people assess our emotional display, and by sanctions issuing from ourselves and from them." The focus is almost entirely on the reactions of individuals (self and others) in different situations, and even the discussion of the public aspect and placing of feelings concerns the reactions of individuals and their awareness of the sociocultural norms governing the kinds of emotions that they are expected to feel and to display (1983: 67). The rules are therefore generally taken as given; they are presented as preexisting normative structures or scripts that to varying degrees constrain the behaviors of particular individuals.

Whereas Hochschild emphasizes the performance of emotional labor and the possible sense of alienation that results from having to conform to feeling and displaying rules, Collins (1987, 2004) argues that rituals perform a valuable function in contributing to the sustainability of social solidarity. For Collins, the key to understanding social life is to focus on "the situation," which he defines (2004: 3) as "momentary encounters among human bodies charged up with

---

[5] This should also make it clear that we are not treating affective regimes as only being found in urban environments. Certainly, rural environments, too, contain affective regimes. And perhaps most significantly, it is important not to treat the urban–rural divide as a sharp one, such that the processes and phenomena associated with one kind of environment are assumed to somehow automatically become irrelevant when we move to the other. Such an assumption risks essentializing the distinction, whereas, as Lefebvre (1991, 1996) reminds us, it is probably more useful to take note of points of contact, convergence, and tensions between relatively more rural versus relatively more urban environments.

emotions and consciousness because they have gone through chains of pre-vious encounters." This definition of a situation emphasizes that individuals always enter any new situation already bringing with them the effects of past situations, and it has opened Collins up to accusations that he is downplaying or even denying the agency of individuals. In response, Collins (2004: 5) deflects such criticisms by arguing as follows:

The individual is the precipitate of past interactional situations and an ingredient of each new situation. An ingredient, not the determinant, because a situation is an emergent property. A situation is not merely the result of the individual who comes into it, nor even of a combination of individuals (although it is that, too).

That is, the individual is not a determinant of any situation. This is a countercriticism that cautions against overplaying the power or effectiveness of individual agency. And neither does the situation itself represent a fixed outcome. As an emergent property, the situation is itself an ongoing and developing phenomenon. Collins theorizes situations in terms of interactional ritual chains, where the emotional energy derived from one situation can be ritualistically carried over to other situations because there is among indivi-duals "a situational propensity toward certain cultural symbols" (2004: 32, 118). In other words, for Collins, situations are ritualized, and rituals create cultural symbols. These cultural symbols, if they are part of successfully ritualized situations, then become "charged up" or "recharged" with "renewed sentiments of respect" (2004: 38):

Along with this, individual participants get their own reservoir of charge. The "sort of electricity" that Durkheim metaphorically ascribes to the group in its state of heightened excitement is stored in batteries: one component of which is the symbol, and the other pole of which is the individual. Participation in a ritual gives the individual a special kind of energy, which I will call emotional energy. (2004: 38)

Collins (2004: 39) further states:

This socially derived emotional energy, as Durkheim says, is a feeling of confidence, courage to take action, boldness in taking initiative. It is a morally suffused energy; it makes the individual feel not only good, but exalted, with the sense of doing what is most important and most valuable. Durkheim goes on to note that groups hold periodic assemblies to revivify this feeling, drawing again on his point that sentiments fade out over a period of time if they are not resuscitated by another experience of collective effervescence.

For Collins, individuals are predisposed to seek this emotional energy so that, where possible, subsequent situations will tend to be shaped by this goal, thus leading to the "interaction ritual chains" that forms the title of Collins's works (1987, 2004). According to Collins, this emotional energy is highly valued by individuals because it provides them with the sense of being morally exalted. And because it is derivable from participation in group-based activities, it has the effect of strengthening group solidarity by increasing the individuals' desire to continue as group members in order that they can repeat and reexperience that sense of moral exaltation.

An affective regime is a broader-enough concept that it can accommodate Hochschild's observations on emotional labor and the normative pressure to display the kinds of behaviors that are conventionally seen to index the desired emotions. An affective regime can also certainly cover the kinds of ritual situations that Collins describes, where emotional energies are transmitted so as to foster among group members a sense of being morally exalted. This is because an affective regime can contain within it different and possibly even conflicting emotions. For example, a city's intention to reduce cases of road rage and to encourage more courteous driving can be seen as an attempt to create a particular affective regime. In trying to do so, CCTVs can be installed, fines can be raised and even jail terms imposed for road rage leading to assault, public banners and media campaigns can be mounted to emphasize the importance of being considerate when on the road, and traffic officers themselves can stop and "reward" drivers who have been noticed to have shown courteous behavior to other drivers and pedestrians. But this is not to say that all individual drivers will respond positively (or will respond with equal positivity) to such an intent. Moreover, specific parts of a city (different districts, neighborhoods, communities, or interest groups) may or may not react supportively to such an endeavor. So, the notion of an affective regime can accommodate within it conflicting emotions. In addition, a specific neighborhood may even decide to introduce local refinements – in effect, a more specific version of the larger affective regime – in order to more effectively encourage road courtesy within that neighborhood itself. As well, other cities may – if they are impressed with and inspired by the success of these measures – attempt to impose similar affective regimes. The notion of an affective regime is thus amenable to analysis at multiple scales, at the level of the city as well as below and above, as we will illustrate in the rest of the book.

For now, given that our goal is to establish the value of Peirce's ideas to the theorizing of affect, we concentrate our discussion on a localized example of an affective regime, using the example already mentioned in Chapter 1, the Arlington National Cemetery (ANC). Wee (2016) demonstrates via an analysis of linguistics signs in the ANC – for example, a plaque with the words "Silence and Respect" sits near the tomb of the Unknown Soldier (2016: 111) – that there are very explicit attempts by the cemetery's management to regulate the kinds of affect considered appropriate to the site. The ANC is a burial ground for memorializing members of the US military, and it stresses the kind of affective regime it wants to foster in its mission statement, which emphasizes the importance of showing dignity and honor for the dead, and respect and compassion for their families, and situating these concerns in relation to a larger sense of gratitude for the sacrifices made to the nation (2016: 110). These concerns are also reflected in the structuring of the physical landscape of the cemetery. Its austere and well-maintained headstones surrounded by well-tended greenery are aimed at evoking a sense of somber remembrance and appreciation for those who died for their country. The ANC's affective regime is therefore already well emplaced in terms of its physical layout even in the absence of any actual visitors.

We can use Peirce's ideas to concretize the ways in which the ANC's affective regime works. The affective regime in the ANC makes use of both linguistic and nonlinguistic resources to ensure that they work together to help project and encourage the desired affect. For example, a plaque that calls for "Silence and Respect" shows the ANC's serious commitment to the desired affect because it is presented in muted colors and carved out of stone and metal. The choice of colors (as opposed to say bright yellow or pink) conveys the seriousness with which the ANC guards the preservation of the desired affect. The use of stone and metal (as opposed to say the use of paper or cardboard) conveys the ANC long-term commitment to the same affect, and through the material connotations of the sign indicates the permanence or at least durability of such notions as respect, honor, and bravery. Taken holistically, the plaque *qua* Peircean sign has both linguistic and nonlinguistic dimensions – an inevitable concomitant to appreciating the materiality of language, which is itself a necessary consequence of studying the landscape.

The same plaque is also both directive (Mautner 2012) and affective in nature. The sign is directive in that it aims to exercise control over the site; it is in this sense a tool of social management and, moreover, one that draws upon the legal institution for its backing (Mautner 2012: 190–191). That is, the ANC makes it very clear that its rules regarding proper conduct have the legal backing of the US government so that violators may be barred from conducting memorial services and ceremonies within the cemetery for two years. But of course, the specific reason why the sign has the particular directive that it does is because it is concerned with the governance of affect, where silence and respect are considered normatively appropriate to the site of the ANC and its particular mission of demonstrating gratitude to those who served their country. The plaque, then, is neither purely cognitive nor purely affective. It is both.

And while there is undoubtedly a sense in which the design of the plaque and the use of language are symbolic, once established as recognized conventions of English and as adhering to a tradition of how plaques ought to look, the specific ANC plaque now becomes interpretable because it resembles other similar signs, that is, it is also an icon. And of course, the plaque is also an index because it is its location that helps visitors understand that the expectation of silence and respect applies to being on the ANC grounds and not beyond.

Finally, for the affective regime to have any chance of encouraging or cultivating the desired effect, there must be shared understandings between the ANC's management and the visitors to whom the affective regime is targeted about how to conventionally interpret the semiotic resources being utilized. This brings us to a point that we will pursue in greater detail when we consider specific case studies in the later chapters – that there is a kind of "grounded aesthetics" (Willis 1990: 21) at work here. Willis's aim (1990) was to argue that symbolic creativity can be found in everyday life. His point was that the creative use of semiotic resources is not just limited to institutions of "high culture" but can be found even in more mundane everyday life activities, although these may then also be rein-forced – "selected, reselected, highlighted" – by less ground-up processes such as TV and (increasingly) social media (Willis 1990: 21). We take Willis's insight as a point of departure to show how the affective regimes found in various semiotic landscapes draw on and are to varying degrees contiguous with the use of resources outside those landscapes. That is, it is because there are at least some shared understandings of the creative uses of semiotic resources that an emplaced affective regime can have some hope of bringing about the desired affect. This is of course consistent with the point that Hoopes (1991: 12, see above) makes concerning Peircean semiotics, which is that it allows for the treatment of individual signs and institutional ones on the same basis. That is, from a Peircean perspective, individual interpretants cannot be completely arbitrary or purely symbolic because there are actual consequences to how signs are interpreted.

These observations are all also consistent with the idea of affect as an evaluative orientation toward an object. We have focused on a single and localizable object such as the plaque so that the points we are making emerge as clearly as possible. Both the visitors to the ANC and the ANC management share (or are assumed to share) the same kind of orientation toward the cemetery and the specific objects emplaced there. Of course, the ANC manage-ment does not necessarily assume that all visitors would automatically have the same orientation. This is why the ANC management's attempt to cultivate the appropriate affective regime is not restricted to the actual site of the ANC. The ANC's website has a section on "Visitors' Rules," which details the kinds of behaviors and language use that are acceptable as well as those that are prohibited, thus giving visitors the opportunity to prepare themselves to act appropriately when they do arrive at the ANC. In this way, via the use of "Visitors' Rules" on its website as well as the use of language and other modalities on the actual cemetery grounds, the ANC tries to achieve an interpretability convergence between the individual visitor and institutional processes of sign interpretation where institutions and organizations are themselves to be seen as the "semiotic syntheses ... of a great many people" (Hoopes 1991: 12, see above).

The Affective Economy

We have seen how Peircean semiotics dovetails nicely with the notion of an affective regime. At this point, it is worth considering the arguments of Ahmed (2004a, b), which aim to provide a rich theorization of affect in terms of a circulating affective economy. Ahmed points out that emotions cannot be treated as a private matter of individual feelings (2004b: 117), emphasizing instead that (2004b: 120–121)

> emotions work as a form of capital: affect does not reside positively in the sign or commodity, but is produced only as an effect of its circulation ... Affect does not reside in an object or sign, but is an affect of the circulation between objects and signs ... Some signs, that is, increase in affective value as an effect of the movement between signs: the more they circulate, the more affective they become, and the more they appear to "contain" affect.

Ahmed's main claim is that emotions circulate by adhering to specific cultural stereotypes or figures such as the asylum-seeker, the international terrorist, or the chav. This is because emotions are necessarily always "about" something, "they involve a stance on the world, or a way of apprehending the world" (Ahmed 2004a: 7), and such cultural stereotypes or figures are the kinds of things that emotions tend to be about. In her discussion of hate (racist) speech, for example, Ahmed (2004b: 119) suggests that "hate is economic; it circulates between signifiers in relationships of difference and displacement," and specifically, this circulation is possible because of the evocation of figures such as "mixed-race couplings" and "the damaged bodies of the white woman and child." In this way, Ahmed suggests that emotions serve to bind the individual reader/ viewer who apprehends the figure while also imbuing that figure with a correlative emotion.[6] For example, the reader/viewer may feel hate or indignation when perceiving someone else categorized under the figure of "terrorist." Finally, there are material consequences, as when the reader/ viewer is moved to produce texts or engage in social practices that might be considered "hate speech" or discriminatory in other ways. And as these material consequences get repeated over time, the emotions that

---

[6] While Ahmed does not make distinction between emotion and affect, it is clear that she is actually talking about the latter (see the discussion in Chapter 1 of how emotion and affect are different).

relationally bind the reader/viewer to the cultural stereotype are intensified or strengthened, thus increasing in affective value.

Ahmed is right that cultural stereotypes or figures do evoke emotions or affect of various sorts so that as the former circulate, then so do the latter. However, affect does not always circulate via recognizable stereotypes, nor does it always involve intense emotions. Affect does not always increase in intensity as it circulates; it can also get dampened; and of course, affect can circulate under much more mundane circumstances where it works prosaically to sustain a sense of community or conviviality (Wissinger 2007). It would be odd to say that in the kinds of third places that Oldenburg (1997) describes, for example, there is no affective economy in place.

In addition, Ahmed's treatment of the circulation of affect has also been criticized for leaving out the interpretations that human actors bring to the affective economy. This is the point that Wetherell (2015: 155) makes when she remarks that "the place and the power given to 'emotion' in her [Ahmed's] work, defined as untethered movement, is hard to understand and justify." Wetherell (2015: 159, italics added) elaborates on her criticism of Ahmed as follows:

Emotion has fled the problematic locations of "inside" and "outside" for sure, but what has also disappeared is the practical human relational work involved in an episode of affect . . . *Affect, once more, seems to swirl, move, and "land" like a plastic bag blowing in the wind.* Once again, affect becomes uncanny. What human social actors (always in the process of formation) do to themselves, to their objects, and to each other fades from view as *the movement of affect becomes the dominant actor.* Paradoxically, we end up with something which functions rather like a basic emotions view. The analyst focuses on some conventional emotion type – hate, fear, anger, love (she might, for instance, track hate across racist web-sites) and examines how it constitutes subjects and objects and relations between them. The negotiation and parsing of affects as complex, live, often highly troubled, ongoing categorizations of human action disappears once again.

There is, as Wetherell observes and emphasizes, a need to ground the analysis of emotions and affect in the concrete activities of human actors and their environments. Wetherell (2015: 160) suggests that it may be more productive to think in terms of affective practice, which is intended to focus our attention on "particular lines of activity" that culminate in "a moment of recruitment, articulation, or enlistment when many complicated flows across bodies, subjectivities, relations, histories, and contexts entangle and intertwine together to form just this affective moment, episode, or atmosphere with its particular possible classifications." This is a point that of course holds with especial pertinence if our interest is in the semiotic landscape. The specific environmental affordances of different landscapes and the kinds of human actors that are expected to inhabit or encounter these landscapes – these all need to be taken into account so as to better highlight what Wetherell describes as the "negotiation and parsing of affects." Here is where we find it valuable to once again return to the process of semiosis, with signs giving rise to yet other signs as their interpretants, where the specific interpretants that come about are the result of the "complex, live, often highly troubled, ongoing categorizations of human action" (Wetherell 2015: 159, see also above) and other phenomena by humans. This way of thinking about the circulation of affect situates it squarely as part of the quotidian processes of everyday human interaction, including the use and transmission of language and other cultural texts. In particular, it requires us to think more carefully about two questions. One, how does language work in conjunction with nonlinguistic resources vis-à-vis the circulation of affect? Two, how can the circulation of signs (linguistic and otherwise) lead to changes in the ways in which they are understood?

To answer the first question, it is useful to consider Goffman's (1981) notion of a production format. This is because attention to these roles can provide for a finer-grained appreciation of the mechanisms by which affect is regulated. But for this to be possible, Goffman's production format also needs to be modified because it is too language- and human-centered. Goffman's main point is that to just think of language production in terms of a "speaker" is too simplistic since agentive responsibility for what is being said or produced can be distributed and so does not always reside with the speaking entity. In his concept of the "production format," Goffman (1981) therefore proposes to distinguish between the animator, the author, and the principal. The principal is the entity whose ideas and views are being conveyed via the language being used or produced. The author is the entity who composes the text. The animator is the entity or "sounding box" through which the language is actually emitted. In the case where all three roles converge, the entity that speaks or writes is also responsible for the actual words being used and the words reflect that same entity's point of view. This is the default assumption in communication, where, for example, if Speaker A says, "I am cold," the words are assumed to be chosen by A herself and they presumably reflect her actual state of being cold. The roles can diverge when, for example, a pop singer performs a song composed by someone else. In that case, the singer is the animator, the composer is the author, and (given that the song would typically represent a fictionalized scenario) the principal would be the fictional persona from the "song-world."[7]

---

[7] The fact that the roles of animator, author, and principal can cross real and fictional worlds is not a problem. The discourse analysis of reference and points of view has long recognized the need to acknowledge interfaces across multiple realities (Bamberg 1997; Fauconnier 1994). As Fauconnier (1994: 12–15) points out in his discussion of examples such as "In Len's painting, the girl with blue eyes has green eyes" and "In reality, the girl with brown eyes has blue eyes":

In presenting the fundamental symmetry of these reference phenomena, I have continued to use the terms *reality* and *real object*. But this cannot be right ... So what we have been calling

Goffman was specifically concerned with language use, but of course, if we are interested in affect, then language is just one of many semiotic resources that can be used. While speakers can and do convey emotions linguistically ("I am not happy about this"), it is the accompanying paralinguistic cues and devices that can either reinforce or even undermine the linguistically conveyed messaged. That is, should there be any conflict between the emotions conveyed linguistically and those conveyed paralinguistically, it is the latter that are typically taken to be the more sincere or more genuine indicator of the speaker's emotion. Thus, the use of an emoticon such as a smiley face, for example, can serve to convey that the speaker is joking when she says, "I am not happy about this." There is an asymmetry here in that the linguistically expressed message is not taken as undermining the affect that is indicated via the smiley face (Kaye, Malone, and Wall 2017). This is because nonverbal communication is generally considered to be more believable than talk (Jaworski and Galasiński 2002: 633). Other similar examples include the use of extra letters in text messages like *hiiiiiii* and *how are youuuuu* (Doll 2013), and signs of laughter such as *LOL* or *haha* (McWhorter 2013). In these examples, the repeated letters, *LOL*, or *haha*, are used as pragmatic markers to convey paralinguistic information rather than to send a linguistic message.

To answer the second question, we can turn to Silverstein's (2003) concept of indexicality (itself inspired by Peirce), which provides just such a characterization of how the use of signs can lead to changes in meanings as they circulate. Silverstein's (2003) indexical order captures how a first-order indexical can give rise to a second-order indexical and so on. In this way, newer meanings may be created based on existing ones so that there can be different orders of indexicality resulting in the formation of an indexical field, "a constellation of meanings that are ideologically linked" (Eckert 2008: 464). For example, Eckert (2012) discusses Labov's (1963) study of how the diphthong /ay/ marks the speaker as coming from Martha's Vineyard. This would constitute a first-order indexical. But while some Vineyarders had been lowering the nucleus of the diphthong so as to converge more closely to the pronunciation of the mainlanders, others reversed this pronunciation trend so as to avoid a lowering of the nucleus. This would constitute a second-order indexical, where the speaker is not just projecting her identity as a Vineyarder but as a specific kind of Vineyarder, as someone who is arguably more authentic than those other

---

"reality" must itself be a mental representation: the speaker's mental representation of reality. In accounting for the *linguistic* phenomena under scrutiny, it is not our (immediate) concern to tell whether (or to what extent) such representations may be accurate; nor is it our concern to find the philosophical, psychological, or neurological nature of reality beliefs, and pictures. We are looking only at ways of talking about them, in principle a different issue. (1994: 15, italics in original)

Vineyarders whose pronunciation more closely resembles that of the main-landers (Eckert 2012: 88). And, of course, there is no reason why the indexical order should stop only at two so that multiple indexical orders are not only possible but typical.

This growth in indexical orders leads Eckert (2008) to introduce the notion of an indexical field so as to highlight that a linguistic feature can be associated with "a constellation of ideologically linked meanings, any region of which can be invoked in context" (Eckert 2012: 94). An example of an indexical field is found in Campbell-Kibler (2007), who shows that the velar variant (as in "talking") tends to be associated with intelligence, formality, and sophistication where the nonvelar version (as in "talkin'") tends to be associated with the absence of these attributes (see also Eckert 2012: 97). Another example comes from Eckert (2008: 469), who notes that the indexical field of /t/ release can include meanings such as "being a school teacher," "being British," "being formal," "being emphatic," "being exasperated,' "being educated," "being elegant," and "being a gay diva." Some of these are social types ("British," "school teacher," "gay diva"), others are relatively stable attributes ("edu-cated," "articulate"), while yet others are stances that can change quite quickly and easily ("exasperated," "emphatic"). More importantly, these categories should not be taken as representing hard distinctions within the indexical field. Rather, the relations between them are highly fluid (Eckert 2008: 469), which is why it is useful to speak of an indexical potential (Eckert 2012: 97), where in any instance of the feature being used a number of the categories could be activated rather than just a single determinate category. And speakers may not always have a clear or determinate sense of which specific category/ categories is/are being "activated" by the use of the feature. The notions of indexicality and indexical orders are not just relevant to linguistic data but can also apply to images, including, of course, the kinds of cultural stereotypes that Ahmed focuses on. In this way, these notions help specify the mechanisms by which affect circulates while also allowing for changes to affect as different human actors (inevitably) negotiate and parse the signs that they encounter.

The above being said, Wetherell's discussion and critique of Ahmed, how-ever, does not explore the normative expectations that govern affective prac-tices, i.e., the expectations that may lead particular affective practices to be viewed as appropriate or even transgressive. This is why we are focusing on affective regimes in this book. Our interest is in how the semiotic landscape is being structured so that particular indexical meanings of signs are encouraged, especially those that pertain to the display of affect. Institutional actors that have jurisdiction over a given landscape will make use of specific signs and other resources in order to encourage some kinds of affect while discouraging others. The strategies or devices for affect modulation may include, as we have just seen in the discussion of the ANC, appeals to legal statutes. They may also include, as we will see shortly in Chapter 3, the use of particular cartoons or characters that are culturally associated with positive affect.

We now close our discussion by addressing the issue of how affect can be enhanced or dampened as it circulates. This is helpful as it serves to bring together the various ideas just discussed. The cultural symbols that are used to create an affective regime can include people as well as nonsentient entities such as language, clothing, and various infrastructural arrangements. And in any given landscape, these symbols are present to varying degrees. This means that while it is entirely possible, theoretically, to track the interpretants of an individual sign (following its chain of semiosis, so to speak), the interpretants are in actuality also the results of influences from other signs and the interactions among the many sign complexes. That is, other signs in the semiotic landscape may serve to reinforce the indexical meaning of a particular sign while yet other signs may serve to undermine that meaning.

Affect is just one dimension of a much more heterogeneous economy – a point that Bourdieu was at pains to emphasize when he identified other kinds of capital (symbolic, cultural) in addition to the economic. This means that any dampening or, conversely, any enhancing of affect is not necessarily just about or due to affective considerations *per se*. And even where a particular semiotic landscape is consistently structured so as to promote a particular affective regime, this is no guarantee that there might not be resistance. This is why the ANC, for example, has to also appeal to legal statutes to try to ensure compliance from visitors to its site.

Consider, as another example, and one that shows clearly what can happen when a sign circulates, the use of phrases that are intended to convey some of the attributes prized by enterprise culture (Du Gay 1996; Keat 1991). As Wee (2015: 41–42) points out, examples of such phrases include *thinking outside the box* (to convey creativity or initiative), *moving/going forward* (to convey purposefulness or the anticipation of future developments), and *taking it to the next level* (to show a commitment to constant improvement, innovation, and excellence). Some of these phrases have become overused (cf. Kramsch 2007: 60), with the result that there has even been a backlash, as in the case of *thinking outside the box* and *moving/going forward*. An example of how *moving forward* is used is, "Housing values are escalating at a steady pace in most major markets ... We expect this will remain the trend moving forward" (www.remax-wes tern.ca/news/com ... 012-says-remax; accessed June 5, 2013). Seacombe (2011) complains about the ubiquity of the phrase *going forward*, citing "nonsenses" such as "He's coming back to help going forward"; "We cannot back down, going forward"; "Problems for England's backs, going forward." The backlash against these phrases is reported by Barrow (2013):

Management jargon such as "thinking outside the box" and "going forward" are among the worst annoyances for office workers today.

Today a new survey of more than 2,000 managers reveals the most irritating habits of Britain's deskbound staff.

We want to emphasize that the use of such phrases is not just "informational" or "cognitive" as opposed to "affective." As already emphasized, there has been a false separation between cognition and emotion. Rather, these phrases also carry an affective dimension because speakers use them in order to (hopefully) create a positive impression of themselves as dynamic and entrepreneurial individuals. But precisely because of their overuse, that is, their "over-circulation" in the affective economy, there has been a growing negative reaction to the use of these phrases as clichéd and formulaic. Hence, the affective value of a sign can become the victim of its own popularity through excessive circulation and consequent contestation.

It cannot be sufficiently stressed that affect, its economy, and "fields" of practice function at the complex intersection of a number of factors, not merely the individual subject, the linguistic context, and the material conditions. Even within similar categories of affective regimes, different sites may deploy different factors to result in differing affects. For example, while practically all churches may fall within the category of "reverence" affects, there will be a significant difference between the so-called traditional "High" churches (typically Catholic, Orthodox, or Anglican in tradition), which deploy factors in their affective regimes to enhance reverence and solemnity throughout all aspects of the service, and, on the other hand, the more informal and newer "independent" churches (often Pentecostal in background) where a lesser degree of reverence is created, and is usually reserved for the special work of the "Holy Spirit" rather than for the entire service. Affects like "kawaii" and "luxury" can be adroitly done in some cases, and over-done (and thus creating an affective backlash, a judgment of failed affect) on the other. Since affective regimes, as structures, can be calibrated and adjusted – a process which requires semiotic judgment as well as assessments of human psychology and behavior – the study of affect has wider implications for areas of human behavior such as marketing, public relations, tourism, religion, politics, and other aspects of the governance of everyday life.

Conclusion

In this chapter, we have articulated a framework for understanding how affect is materialized in the semiotic landscape, drawing primarily on Peirce's notion of semiotics and complementing it with concepts such as the affective regimes, the affective economy, and the indexical field. We now move on to illustrate the analytical payoffs that accrue from the use of this framework, looking at several illustrative examples where complex interactions of factors in an affective regime are in play.

3   *Kawaii* in the Semiotic Landscape

Introduction

The Japanese adjective *kawaii* variously describes attributes such as "cute," "adorable," and "lovable," and it is typically used to describe animated characters, infants, animals, and natural objects – things that can be construed as small, delicate, and immature (Burdelski and Mitsuhashi 2010: 66; Kinsella 1995: 220). Entities culturally character-ized as *kawaii* are also perceived as being adorable, lovable, and delicate, and tend to foster fondness or affection (Burdelski and Mitsuhashi 2010: 66, 78; Starr 2015).

It is of course possible to treat *kawaii* as a label for a specific emotion. But doing so raises the issues that we described in Chapter 1. We therefore focus on the affective dimensions of *kawaii*: its relational properties and the kinds of orientations that it encourages.

Discussions of *kawaii* culture have typically focused on its influence on Japanese aesthetics (Bremner 2002; Kincaid 2014), its commodification (Allison 2006; Kinsella 1995), and its role in childhood socialization into gendered identities (Burdelski and Mitsuhashi 2010), drawing attention to *kawaii* as a key component of Japanese material culture. Manifestations of *kawaii* are observable in fashion items, stationary, cartoon characters, and communicative practices, including ges-ture, posture, a writing style that emphasizes rounded symbols, emojis, and voice qualities. Thus, in Figure 3.1, the website sugarsweet.me, which sells "Cute Kawaii Products Online" (accessed January 25, 2016) uses what might be described as *kawaii* fonts – characterized by fine lines, rounded characters (and therefore the avoidance of sharp angles or edges), random insertions of hearts, and smiley faces – even for more business-like expressions such as "Free Shipping," "Talk with Us," and "Latest Products." The importance of the font is illustrated in the examples below of public signage (www.freejapanesefont.com/kawaii-handwriting-font-download; accessed January 14, 2015). Also, the preferred colors are usually pastels or bright.

In the case of speech, a squeaky voice also serves to project a *kawaii* cultural aesthetic (Bremner 2002). Individuals who want to be *kawaii* are also

34

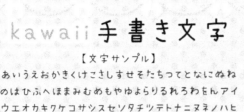

Figure 3.1 *Kawaii* fonts and colors

encouraged to smile and giggle more, to "lighten" their voices in order to "sound less harsh" ("How to be Kawaii" [with pictures], www.wikihow.com; accessed January 25, 2016).

These manifestations of *kawaii* are usually treated as relatively isolable units that happen to be imbued with *kawaii* attributes. Concomitantly, this means that the question of how *kawaii* entities or other features that are associated with *kawaii* aesthetics might be integrated into the broader sociocultural environment has tended to remain under-explored. Precisely because of this, the study of *kawaii* in the semiotic landscape has the potential to enrich both our understanding of *kawaii* culture and the ways in which affect may be semioticized as part of the lived environment.

We organize our discussion of *kawaii* in this chapter into three parts. In the first part, we review the meanings typically associated with *kawaii* to show that, when recontextualized in relation to specific situations, there are changes to the meanings that need to be accounted for. In this regard, we situate the various meanings as part of the indexical field (Eckert 2008) of *kawaii. In the second part, we describe three examples of kawaii* in the semiotic landscape: a public reminder to residents of Tokyo about a tax payment deadline, a bus stop sign, and a tourist information poster. Then, following our discussion in the first part of the chapter, we highlight some of the major issues raised by *kawaii* for the study of affect in the semiotic landscape.

The Indexical Field of *Kawaii*

As we have already noted, *kawaii* describes an attribute of the entity (as being, among other things, "cute," "adorable," and even "vulnerable") while also evoking a particular interactive stance toward that entity. In other words, because the *kawaii* entity is considered adorable and/or vulnerable, it has to be cared for or treated with gentleness. In fact, in an interesting series of experiments, Nittono et al. (2012: no page numbers) show that there are actual behavioral correlates to *kawaii*, claiming the following:

> That is, the tenderness elicited by cute images is more than just a positive affective feeling state. It can make people more physically tender in their motor behavior …
> The present study shows that perceiving cuteness not only improves fine motor skills but also increases perceptual carefulness …
> *Kawaii* things not only make us happier, but also affect our behavior. This study shows that viewing cute things improves subsequent performance in tasks that require behavioral carefulness, possibly by narrowing the breadth of attentional focus. This effect is not specific to tasks related to caregiving or social interaction.

Thus, the *kawaii* is affective in that it not only induces in the perceiving individual a feeling of tenderness toward the "cute things." It also results in an enhanced sense of care, attention, and even physical tenderness that the individual may give when interacting with these things categorized as *kawaii*.

The various meanings of *kawaii* thus constitute an indexical field in that the lexical item is conceptually associated with "a constellation of ideologically linked meanings, any region of which can be invoked in context" (Eckert 2012: 94, see Chapter 2). For example, the indexical field of *kawaii* includes attributes that can be considered fairly prototypical (such as being "cute," "adorable") and others that are less so (such as being "vulnerable"), as well as interactive motor programs (such as being protective toward the *kawaii* entity or simply being more careful in how one interacts with it). The combination of attributes and interactive motor programs highlights the affective nature of *kawaii*. Because *kawaii* entities are not merely bearers of attributes but evoke in the reader/viewer attitudes and interactional stances that are supposed to be protective or gentle in nature, it is clear that the default cultural expectation in the case of *kawaii* is one of positive affect.

The indexical field is of course not fixed. Rather, it is dynamic. And this not at all surprising since Peircean semiotics would lead us to expect that the meanings that constitute the field will continue to shift and change as speakers use and interpret language in various ways. For example, in Japan, *kawaii* aesthetics have been appropriated for governmental use. The nationwide phenomenon of local governments" branding themselves with *yuru-kyara*, "loose or wobbly character" mascots, shows how the indexical field of *kawaii* is strategically enacted by political bodies to help them achieve their various goals (see Occhi 2012). *Yuru-kyara*, a short form for *"yurui* characters," represent their regions as *kawaii* ambassadors and are created by regional municipal offices to promote tourism and local products. Some nationally popular ones include: Kumamon, the black bear, of Kumamoto prefecture; Hikonyan, the samurai cat, of Hikone city; and Mikyan, the mandarin orange dog, of Ehime prefecture. The civic governments use these mascots in their local PR materials and even sell commercial goods. Furthermore, the *yuru-kyara* characters all use social media outlets under their names and, through these platforms, regularly release promotional information regarding the region they represent, thus creating a synthetically personalized (Fairclough 2001) friendship with their followers in a similar manner as the synthetic sisterhood reported by Talbot (1995).[1]

Consider yet another example involving the use of *kawaii*, this time one that takes place outside of Japan. Chuang (2011) notes that in Taiwan's mayoral and presidential elections between 1998 and 2004, the creation of a *kawaii*-inspired doll, known as the "A-Bian Doll," to represent the Democratic Progressive Party's (DPP) candidate, Chen Shui-Bian, seemed to provide him with a huge electoral advantage:

The A-Bian Doll III . . . a 14-inch cotton-stuffed doll priced at NTD120 (about GBP2), was a hit commodity for the DPP in 2004 . . . The doll has a small body, an over-sized head, doe eyes, a child-like smile, and a rosy-cheeked, chubby face. (2011: 5)

Chuang (2011: 6) quotes the manager of Bian-Mao Company, who explains that the design team deliberately drew upon *kawaii* aesthetics to design the doll:

The design team even went to Japan to study their successful commodities. According to studies of Taiwanese toy and fashion markets, and based on my business experience, Japanese *Kawaii*-style commodities are still the most popular sellers in Taiwan, rather than American or European. In fact, we invited different companies from Taiwan, Japan, and America to design sample commodities. Then we chose the current *Kawaii* style.

As mayoral and later presidential candidate, Chen Shui-Bian is certainly not aiming to project an image of someone who is vulnerable, in need of protection, or to be treated with care. These other meanings of *kawaii* are therefore less prominent or possibly even irrelevant. Instead, it would seem that it is the meanings of "cute" and "adorable" that are maintained in the case of the A-Bian Doll, serving to present the politician as someone who is likeable and unthreatening. As Chuang (2011: 10) observes, the doll (and related A-Bian accessories such as tableware, mouse pads, and alarm clocks) "diminished the

---

[1] The strategies employed by these local governments to promote their *yuru-kyara* characters are therefore not too different from what Sanrio Corporation does with their signature products. Sanrio is a company specializing in *kawaii* products and its most famous character is Hello Kitty (lesser known characters in their stable are Chococat and Jewelpet). Their products include school supplies, stationary, gifts, and even travel gear.

distance between Chen, his staff members, and the ordinary person." What is interesting is that these shifts in the indexical field do not change the fact that *kawaii* is strongly associated with positive affect. Despite having discarded attributes such as vulnerability or requiring protection, the A-Bian doll is still considered to be *kawaii*, mainly because it is able to project cuteness and adorability.

However, once we start looking at how the concept is used in the semiotic landscape, the indexical field of *kawaii* raises questions such as the following: What other shifts in the indexical field might take place when we focus on *kawaii* in the semiotic landscape? What kinds of stances or attitudes does the use of *kawaii* aim to evoke? And how is *kawaii* deployed in such a way that it coheres/interacts with non-*kawaii* elements in the semiotic landscape?

Kawaii in Metropolitan Tokyo

Let us now consider some specific examples of *kawaii* in the semiotic landscape that are situated in metropolitan Tokyo.[2] We will present quickly, with brief comments, three examples illustrating the use of *kawaii*. We will reserve a detailed discussion for only after we have provided a sense of what the examples look like.

Consider the first example, shown in Figure 3.2. This sign is a public reminder to residents of Tokyo that they need to pay the annual tax by June 1. Literally translated, the text reads as follows:

Payment deadline, June 1 (Monday)
Tokyo Metropolitan Government Bureau of Taxation Office
Bureau of Taxation

Accompanying the text are pictorial representations of the Bureau of Taxation mascots, with their names given as "Takkusu Taku-chan" for the boy and "Nôzei Non-chan" for the girl.

Consider now the second example, shown in Figure 3.3. This is a bus stop sign located near Shinjuku Gyoen area. The name of the stop is "Hanazono-chô" and below the name is information telling commuters that the bus is "Bound for Shinjuku-nishiguchi." Also on the sign is a pictorial representation of Minkuru, the city of Tokyo's transportation service mascot.

Figure 3.4 depicts the same bus stop that was shown in Figure 3.3, but it also shows a display case that is located just next to the bus stop. The mascot once again appears on top of the display case, and this time, its name, "Minkuru," is given.

---

[2] All the photographs presented and discussed here were taken by Mie Hiramoto between December 2014 and April 2015.

Figure 3.2 Reminder to Tokyo residents about the annual tax payment deadline

Figure 3.3 Bus stop sign 1

Finally, consider the third example, which features the mascot "Matatabi-kun." This is shown in Figure 3.5. Unlike the earlier two examples, the sign here contains English as well as Mandarin translations of the Japanese text as it is a sign created by the Tourist Information Center and targeted at foreign tourists. The sign is located at the Tokyo City Air Terminal (T-CAT) building in Nihonbashi. This building is a hub for major long-distance buses, including buses that are headed toward Haneda/Narita. These buses, equipped with large storage rooms, provide travelers with an easy and inexpensive alternative to

Figure 3.4 Bus stop sign 2

Figure 3.5 T-CAT coin locker banner

a train or a cab, and therefore the hub is frequented by both foreign visitors and locals who are hoping to go to Haneda/Narita.

At this point, having gotten an overview of our examples, we can make the following three observations. First, the use of a mascot appears to be quite a common strategy in the Japanese municipality. But of course, a mascot is, strictly speaking, an independent phenomenon from that of *kawaii*. Mascots can be live animals, fictional entities, or even inanimate objects as long as they are used to represent a group or organization. Mascots can have different kinds of emotional effects too, and these are not necessarily the same kinds of emotional effects typically associated with *kawaii*. For example, in the United States, there are angry-looking mascots that have been claimed to promote "aggressivity and even violence," as in the case of Herky the Hawk, the University of Iowa's athletic department mascot (Piper 2016). In contrast, Trousselard et al. (2014) suggest that an animal-mascot bond can be useful in helping soldiers who have experienced combat deal with posttraumatic stress disorder. And in a series of studies, Fryberg et al. (2008) claim that the relatively widespread use of American Indian mascots in the media can be harmful to the self-esteem of American Indians "because they remind American Indians of the limited ways others see them and, in this way, constrain how they can see themselves."

Even in Japan, there are cases of some *yuru-kyara* from different regional government offices that had to be replaced due to negative reactions toward them from the general public. This is mainly because these mascots were not perceived as being appropriately *kawaii*. That is, they were not construed as evoking a sense of tenderness or cuteness. Sento-kun, the young Buddha-like boy with deer antlers, created by Nara city in 2008, and Katsue-san, the starving peasant girl, put forward by Tottori city in 2014 are some instances of *kawaii* gone wrong. These mascots were deemed by the public to be too grotesque to suit *kawaii* aesthetics. Presumably, Sento-kun was simply seen as a human-animal hybrid rather than an actual *kawaii* character. And, possibly, the condition of starvation that Katsue-san highlights evoked distress rather than affection or tenderness.

What we have, then, in the case of the three examples of *kawaii* in the semiotic landscape, are mascots – some of which are humanized characters (Figure 3.2) while others are fictional (nonhuman) creatures (Figures 3.3 and 3.5) – that have been rendered in the aesthetics of *kawaii* so as to appear cute and unthreatening. The *kawaii* attributes include large heads, round eyes, and, in the case of the humanized characters, childlike clothes to emphasize their youth. In contrast, the fictional creatures have no clothes because they have no bodies, being composed mainly of a very large head and smooth rounded limbs.

Our second observation is that the use of *kawaii* aesthetics does not merely involve the presence of mascots. We also need to consider the writing systems and fonts which accompany the pictorial representations of the mascots. The boy's name, Takkusu Taku-chan, is written in *katakana*, the script most often used in Japanese to denote non-Chinese loanwords. In this case, *katakana* script is used because the word *takkusu* actually comes from the English word "tax." The *katakana* script is characterized by short, straight strokes and sharp angles, and these are at odds with *kawaii*'s predilection for soft and rounded shapes. Thus, there is an aesthetic mismatch between the requirement that *katakana* script be used because an English loanword is involved, on the one hand, and the preference for the soft, rounded, or curved forms associated with *kawaii* aesthetics, on the other. However, this conflict is somewhat phonetically and culturally mitigated by the name given to the mascot. Taku is a common Japanese name for boys, which has nothing to do with *takkusu*. But this allows for a cultural association to be exploited. When both *takkusu* and *Taku* are used in combination to name the mascot, there is now a play on the English word "tax" as well as the use of alliteration and repetition that is commonly seen when Japanese mothers talk to their young children. This alliteration serves as a diminutive in baby talk (e.g. Toda, Fogel, and Kawai 1990: 287), and this helps to render the entire name Takkusu Taku-chan cute or adorable.

Morphologically, the boy's name is also not suffixed with the diminutive -*kun,* which is typically used for boys, as might be otherwise expected. Instead, there is a different diminutive, -*chan*, and this further infantilizes the name or the form of address that it attaches to. In fact, -*chan* is more commonly used for very small children and for girls' names, e.g. a common Japanese nickname for Hello Kitty is Kitty-chan. Burdelski and Mitsuhashi (2010: 74) point out that by the age of five, boys are no longer expected to think of themselves as *kawaii* and are instead expected to develop qualities of being tough and cool. A boy who is still characterized as *kawaii* is thus perceived to be somewhat feminized (Burdelski and Mitsuhashi 2010: 67). Indeed, this other more feminine diminutive, -*chan*, is found in the girl's name, Nôzei Non-chan. Note as well that the girl's name also employs phonetic repetition, as we saw in the case of the boy's name, so as to sound cute. The word *nôzei* means "paying tax," while Non-chan is a common nickname for girls whose names start with the sound sequence [no], e.g. N̲oriko, N̲ozomi, N̲orie, and N̲obuyo. The result is a name where the first mora becomes repeated, as in *Nôzei Non-chan*. The use of *katakana* script is not required for the girl's name since, unlike in the boy's name, there is no non-Chinese loanword involved. This means that the girl's name can be written in *hiragana* rather than *katakana*. It is worth noting, however, that the word *nôzei* is usually written in *kanji*, 納税. The main difference between the *kanji* and *hiragana* scripts is that the latter is considered to be more informal and approachable. Thus, wherever possible, we see attempts in varying the choice of script used to print the mascots' names. *Katakana* is dis-preferred and *hiragana* preferred instead. But the use of alliteration and diminutives also serve to project cuteness or softness, and these are particularly useful if the *katakana* script cannot be avoided. When taken together with the pictorial representations of the characters, the overall sign aims to as far as possible evoke a sense of informality and cuteness consistent with *kawaii* aesthetics.

Likewise, consider the case of Tokyo's transportation service mascot, Minkuru (Figure 3.4). The use of puns in names is a common strategy of *kawaii* as it is consistent with the idea of being playful and cute. Minkuru, a mascot for the city bus service, also sounds like the phrase *minna ku̲ru* "everyone come together," and *minna-no ku̲ruma* "everyone's car." As with [takkusu] and [taku] in Takkusu Taku-chan "tax Taku-chan," and [noːzei] and [non] in Nôzei Non-chan "paying tax Non-chan," Minkuru's name also puns on the aforesaid Japanese phrases. According to Minkuru's introduction on the Tokyo Metropolitan Government Bureau of Transportation website, the mascot is an anthropomorphized bus; its merged face-body is modeled after the front panel of a bus, and attached to it are wheel-like legs (Tokyo Metropolitan Government Bureau of Transportation 2012). The mascot's name is also written in *hiragana* (Figure 3.4), which, as we have already pointed out, allows the font to conform more closely to the aesthetics of *kawaii*. The name in *hiragana*, みんくる, uses a decorative font design which highlights the round-edness and curves of the symbols.

As for the coin locker banner, it features Matatabi-kun (Figure 3.5), a mascot for the T-CAT. His name does not appear on this particular poster but it is given on the T-CAT official website, spelt in *hiragana*: またたびくん. Here, too, we find the cute, punlike elements associated with *kawaii*. As the acronym of the building name "T-CAT" contains the word "cat," the mascot is designed as a hybrid cat-airplane creature. His name, *matatabi*, means "catnip" when read as one word, but it can also mean "travel again" when read as two words: *mata* "again" and *tabi* "travel." These elements thus construct a cute-sounding and *kawaii*-like name for the cat character representing T-CAT. Although the cat looks like a calico (which are almost always female), Matatabi-kun is introduced as a boy in his profile website (Tokyo City Air Terminal n.d.), and this is expected due to the prevailing gender stereotype in Japan that pilots are often men. His gender is marked with an iconic blue pilot hat and his name is suffixed with *-kun*.

We now come to our third observation. We have seen from the above examples that *kawaii* can be used in the semiotic landscape in a number of ways, from representing a transportation service network to reminding residents about tax deadlines to providing information for foreign and local commuters. The use of a *kawaii* character like Minkuru to represent metropolitan Tokyo's transportation service constitutes what we might consider a case of symbolic capital. In the case of Minkuru, at least where the particular example shown in Figure 3.4 is concerned, the character's presence is mainly representational. That is, Minkuru does not speak nor is the character associated with the conveyance of any particular message. The visual presentation of the character of Minkuru is supposed to help cultivate in the public mind a perception of the transportation service as a municipal organization that is friendly and service oriented and one that the public might hopefully view with some degree of affection. This is perhaps critical given that Tokyo transportation, despite its efficiency, can also be brutally crowded during peak travel hours. In fact, during rush hours, staff are specially employed to physically push people into the so-called sardine trains in order to allow the train doors to close and for the trains to travel on time (Xie 2016). In addition, for decades and especially in metropolitan areas, Japan's buses and trains have become infamous due to the presence of *chikan* "gropers" during rush hours (Horii and Burgess 2012; Okabe 2004). Such occurrences are repeated daily, and make it all the more important that commuters are positively predisposed toward their travel experiences.

Unlike Minkuru, however, the other *kawaii* characters "speak" in that they are associated with the conveyance of specific advisories or pieces of information. Thus, recall that the boy and girl characters, Takkusu Taku-chan and Nôzei Non-chan respectively, are present in the public poster to help remind residents not to miss their tax deadline. It is also worth noting that as humanlike characters their mouths are drawn to be slightly open as though to suggest an act of vocalization. Likewise, in the case of Matatabi-kun of the Tourist Information Center poster, he indicates to the reader/viewer the locations of the coin lockers with the statement "There are coin lockers on the 1st floor"; however, whether he is vocalizing the message or not is unclear. Nonetheless, the statement (whether intended to be construed as an act of vocalization or not) is the linguistic correlate of Matatabi-kun's gesture, and it is worth noting that, compared to the many *kanji* letters in this banner, the coin locker (there are = あります, *arimasu*) line looks softer and, to that extent, more *kawaii* because it is all in *hiragana* script. This line could in fact have been written in *kanji* (有ります) instead of hiragana. And had that been the case, it would then have looked more rigid and more formal.

By way of closing this section, let us summarize how the foregoing three observations allow us to address the questions that were mentioned earlier on in this chapter. Two of those questions can in fact be answered together:

• *What shifts in the indexical field take place when we focus on kawaii* in the semiotic landscape?
• *What kinds of stances or attitudes is the use of kawaii aiming to evoke?*

In the case of Minkuru, the Tokyo transportation service mascot, there appears to be no significant shifts in the indexical field. Used as a form of symbolic capital, this is a relatively straightforward case of *kawaii* being used by an organization to foster a sense of affection.

But where the other two examples are concerned, things become somewhat more interesting. Whereas *kawaii* characters are typically supposed to be helpless and hence evoke in the reader/viewer a desire to protect, Takkusu Taku-chan, Nôzei Non-chan, and Matatabi-kun are in their respective signs being helpful or providing a service to the reader/viewer. This is not unlike the case of the Taiwanese A-Bian Doll, where *kawaii* aesthetics have been attached to a character representing a public servant. The only difference between these characters is that they are entirely fictional in the Japanese cases, while the A-Bian Doll represents an actual Taiwanese politician. Nevertheless, as with

the Taiwanese case, being helpless or immature is no longer a salient meaning to the reader/viewer. What is important is that the mascots are perceived as being likeable so as to reduce the social distance between the information being conveyed by the relevant organizations/individuals. We might also add that the common semantic field, whether or not "helpfulness" is indicated, is a disarming quality, a rendering of the mascot as nonthreatening and noncon-frontational. These are of course qualities that are equally welcome whether for commodification (as with the Hello Kitty products) or for political purposes (as with the A-Bian Doll and the Takkusu Taku-chan, Nôzei Non-chan, and Matatabi-kun characters). Particularly in the latter case, *kawaii*'s disarming quality can be said to have a "civic" affect, in promoting a disposition toward civil obedience, cooperation, and conformity toward the characters and the regimes or policies they represent.
• *How is kawaii deployed in such a way that it coheres/interacts with non-kawaii elements in the semiotic landscape?*
We have seen that, wherever possible, the text being used in association with the *kawaii* characters tends to be written in *hiragana* as *hiragana* involves softer and curvier lines (unlike the angularity of *katakana*) and is considered more informal (unlike *kanji*). The fact that *hiragana* is the first of all the orthographies to be taught to children, in the same manner that letters of the alphabet are first introduced to children learning English, also leads to the association of the script with cute, juvenile images. Where the names of the mascots are concerned, phonetic repetition and the use of a diminutive indicates that the referent is feminine or very young.

And because the *kawaii* characters often appear in conjunction with other semiotic elements that are highly official or that have their own semiotic constraints, the placement of the characters is noteworthy. For example, Minkuru is located next to the name of a specific bus stop, Hanazono-chô, and the bus stop itself has to be semiotically consistent with how bus stops in general are represented, which has no connection with *kawaii* whatsoever. To avoid any overlaps between the *kawaii* elements and the non-*kawaii* elements of the same sign, the *kawaii* characters and information relating to them (such as their names or information being provided by them) are bounded off. In the case of the Takkusu Taku-chan and Nôzei Non-chan, the boy and girl are placed in a blue zone at the bottom of the poster. In the case of Minkuru, the creature is placed to one side of the bus stop (Figure 3.3) and it is located directly above other information related to the bus stop (Figure 3.4). Similarly, in Figure 3.5, Matatabi-kun appears at the bottom of the poster in a white zone demarcated from the green zone directly above it.

It may be useful to briefly compare the mascots observed within urban landscapes with their *yuru-kyara* "wobbly" ambassadors' counterparts. The latter are created for promotional purposes, usually to promote a specific region, a local produce, or local wildlife. In this sense, the *yuru-kyara* are *kawaii* characters that are of importance unto themselves since they are intended as embodiments of the things that they are supposed to promote. The idea here is that the popularity of the character will help in turn to popularize the region, produce etc. that it represents. Some of the *yuru-kyara* have even attained celebrity status, making public appearances and interacting with their own fans through social media or their dedicated websites (Brasor 2008; McKirdy 2014). Each *yuru-kyara* may have a particular theme song, dance routine, or even a festival associated with it. This heavy emphasis on commodification means that there are character-driven merchandise, such as credit cards, stickers, and keychains, to be sold. In this sense, *yuru-kyara* are much more typical of *kawaii* figures in the commodification of Japanese culture. In contrast, the mascots found in the urban landscapes serve a more specific communicative purpose. Rather than being the *kawaii* embodiment of a specific thing such as a produce or animal, they serve instead to soften the relatively mundane message or information that is being conveyed on the public signage. Thus, unlike *yuru-kyara*, the *kawaii* mascots do not actively interact with their reader/viewer through social media or their websites. They do not have celebrity status nor do they push for the sales of their particular sets of merchandise. This, of course, does not mean that such scenarios are impossible; rather, they are not the primary reasons why the mascots have been created.

Keeping the foregoing in mind, we can now turn to the question of how the use of *kawaii* in the semiotic landscape carries implications for the study of affect.

Implications for the Study of Affect in the Semiotic Landscape

We have now seen that *kawaii* is not merely an aspect of Japanese culture that can be found in specific contexts, however commodified, or in the gendered socialization patterns of Japanese children. It is also made use of in the wider semiotic landscape, in domains such as transportation, tourism, and taxation, as part of the resources being used by municipalities to manage life in the urban environment. Moreover, the main reason that *kawaii* is drawn upon is because of its affective nature – in particular, the fact that it is part of a cultural model wherein entities can be characterized as adorable, cute, or unthreatening, and where, conversely, the reader/viewer can be encouraged or expected to treat them with affection or gentleness. This then raises the issue of how the framework that we outlined in Chapter 2 is able to account for the presence of *kawaii* in the landscape.

This is where Ahmed's notion of a circulating affective economy is particularly useful, though still subject of course to the caveat that all signs have to be interpreted. Recall that Ahmed's (2004a, 2004b) main claim is that emotions circulate by adhering to specific cultural stereotypes or figures such as the asylum-seeker, the international terrorist, or the chav. Bearing in mind the examples of *kawaii* presented in this chapter, we can say that the *kawaii* characters in the various signs correspond to the cultural stereotypes or figures that Ahmed claims particular emotions are "about" or adhered to. Locals who are familiar with Japanese culture and with *kawaii* culture and aesthetics in particular will have been socialized into apprehending these characters in an emotionally appropriate manner. As Miller (2010: 69) points out, *kawaii* is so naturalized in Japan that it is found almost ubiquitously across a wide range of different domains including regional tourism campaigns, religious scenes, etiquette guides, and public service posters. In the case of *kawaii*, as we have seen from the studies mentioned early on, this means responding to the characters with affection and even gentleness. In Peircean terms, a sign signifies only when it is interpreted, giving rise in the process to further signs or interpretants. Indeed, when a newly created *kawaii* character or mascot is encountered for the very first time, there may not be any explicit declaration that this is supposed to be a *kawaii* character (in fact, there usually isn't). But the Japanese are expected to appreciate that the character is intended to be *kawaii*. And they are further expected to understand that there are normative reactions to a *kawaii* character, such as seeing it as adorable and vulnerable. For all this to occur, the character has to be first interpreted as *kawaii* through a process of Peircean semiosis, including Peirce's inclusion rule, which asserts that there are no pure symbols. Each newly created *kawaii* character combines elements of symbol, index, and icon so that, even though it may be a completely new entity, its resemblance to other entities (through the deployment of a range of recurrent features, including large eyes, small bodies, and accompanying fonts) helps the character as a sign to "determine" the kind of interpretant it gives rise to. As Atkin (2013) points out:

[A]lthough we have characterized the interpretant as the understanding we reach of some sign/object relation, it is perhaps more properly thought of as the translation or development of the original sign.

. . .

the sign determines an interpretant. Further, this determination is not determination in any causal sense, rather, the sign determines an interpretant by using certain features of the way the sign signifies its object to generate and shape our understanding.

The widespread use of *kawaii* characters and affiliated aesthetics (such as pastel colors and rounded fonts) also provides a good illustration of Willis's (1990) argument about symbolic creativity, namely that such creativity is to be found not only in high institutions but also in the more mundane everyday activities of, for example, youth. Indeed, Willis focused a fair amount of his analytical attention on youth culture, and the case of *kawaii* constitutes particularly strong support for his assertion that youth culture is creative in its mobilizing of semiotic resources. Moreover, as the adoption of *kawaii* culture by government and other institutions shows, it is in the appropriation of such semiotic resources that these institutions hope to communicate not just linguistically but affectively. That is, the institutions are drawing upon a widespread and shared appreciation of *kawaii* aesthetics and, in so doing, are hoping to not only foster an understanding of the propositional content of their various messages but also a desired affective response.

However, we have also seen that Ahmed's account is unclear about just exactly what she has in mind when she speaks of affect circulating. As Wetherell (2015: 155) observes, there is a need to ground the analysis of emotions and affect in the concrete activities of human actors and their environments. This is a point that of course holds with special pertinence if our interest is in the semiotic landscape. Recall that the concept of an affective regime refers to the conditions that govern the ways in which affect is considered to be appropriately materialized in a given site. Thus, different landscapes, their particular human actors, and the specific environmental affordances, that is, the affective regimes that are emplaced in different sites – these all need to be taken into account so as to better highlight what Wetherell (2015: 159) describes as the "negotiation and parsing of affects." The case of *kawaii* in the semiotic landscape is consistent with this insight. The use of *kawaii* characters and fonts in public signs partakes of the broader Japanese society's understanding of what kinds of affective responses the notion of *kawaii* is expected to invoke, as well as more localized appreciations of what kinds of information can be expected from sites such as the Taxation Office, a bus stop, or Tourist Information Center. There is undoubtedly an affective regime at work in these landscapes but we now need to ask how the *kawaii* characters work in concert with the linguistic messages that are being conveyed in the signs.

To answer this, we return to Goffman's (1981) production format that we discussed in Chapter 2. The idea of a production format is particularly useful in accounting for the asymmetry in how interpretations are assigned to linguistic and nonlinguistic signs.[3] This is because Goffman's point is a cautionary one in that when looking at a single source of production, we have to be careful not to

[3] This is also why we prefer to use the term "semiotic landscape" over "linguistic landscape" (see the discussion in Chapter 1). As the *kawaii* examples show, the landscape is not merely linguistic and neither is it simply multimodal in the sense that linguistic and nonlinguistic resources are both present. Rather, the asymmetry points to the fact that when there are conflicts between the two, it is the nonlinguistic resources whose interpretations override those of the linguistic resources. It is the nonlinguistic (*kawaii* characters) that serve as a main constituents of the affective regime.

conflate the different roles involved. In the case of *kawaii* discussed in the preceding section, this is less of an issue because the *kawaii* characters have already been semiotically demarcated in the signs. And insofar as these characters are associated with particular pieces of information or vocalizations, they are better considered animators rather than authors or principals. Let us clarify what we mean by this. In his earlier formulations, Goffman (1972: 523) considered the animator to be human, and used the term "figure" to describe various inanimate objects that the animator utilizes. But in later work, Goffman (1981: 144) refers to the animator as a "talking machine." As Manning and Gershon (2013: 112) observe in their comments about the development of Goffman's ideas, "the animator, in opposition to the more stereotypically human speakerly roles of principal and author, is suggestively described using insistent nonhuman techno-morphic metaphors." While the *kawaii* characters are not "talking machines," they are certainly technological extensions of a human or organizational author and principal. For example, in the tax deadline reminder and the tourist information posters, it is the taxation department and the tourism information center that are both the author and principal of their respective signs. The characters of Takkusu Taku-chan and Nôzei Non-chan (in the case of the taxation department) and Matatabi-kun (in the case of the tourism information center) are animators, serving as "sounding boxes" or, perhaps more appropriately, as avatars of the messages from the authors and principals. And this is where affect becomes pertinent. The animators do not merely serve as conduits for the messages. As *kawaii* characters, they work in a manner akin to that of emoticons in messaging services. They provide a paralinguistic affective layering to the messages by softening any possible negative impact on the reader/viewer. And this softening is possible because, as with emoticons, there is an asymmetry between the nonlinguistic (in this case, pictorial representations) and the linguistic which helps to override any likely conflict stemming from the relatively impersonal nature of official materials.

The example of Minkuru, the Tokyo transportation service mascot, is a good case in point. Recall that Minkuru is presented simply as a character but he does not actually say anything, unlike the other *kawaii* characters. In this case, it appears difficult to categorize Minkuru as an animator, much less an author or a principal. But such a difficulty arises only if we make the false assumptions that an animator exists in isolation, and that animators must only convey linguistic information. The assumption that an animator can exist in isolation without any author or principal also being present is akin to the fallacy that there can be purely symbolic signs that are not also icons or indexes. The assumption that animators must only convey linguistic information rests on the false dichotomy between the purely emotional and the purely cognitive or propositional. These assumptions are easily dispensed with without doing conceptual violence to Goffman's notion of a production format. We need to only understand that the roles of author, animator, and principal should apply not just to language but to nonlinguistic information as well, and we need to be clear that these roles may not always be occupied by humans but, increasingly, may be occupied by fictional characters, digital avatars, among others.

Putting together the ideas of Goffman's production format and Ahmed's notion of a circulating affective economy, we can say that Minkuru can indeed be treated as an animator. Even if he does not say anything, as a *kawaii* character, Minkuru serves to convey the societally expected affect of being cute and unthreatening. This paralinguistic information, together with the fact that Minkuru does not simply appear alone or in isolation but *qua* mascot indexes the transportation service of Tokyo, serves to add an affective layering to whatever public understandings of the transportation service already exist in the minds of various commuters. As animators, the circulation of the *kawaii* characters is dependent on how they are being deployed by the authors and principals. And as these characters circulate in the sense of being more prominently displayed in multiple signs in public spaces, the expectation is that the kind of affect associated with them increases in value. The character of Minkuru is present at various bus stops to (hopefully) remind commuters that the transportation authority in Tokyo sincerely cares about their travel needs and comforts. In this way, the organization aims to foster among these many commuters *qua* readers/viewers the desired affect of having a positive orientation toward its various services and initiatives.

By way of closing this section, we would like to emphasize the main theoretical points arising from our discussion of *kawaii* for the understanding of affect in the semiotic landscape. The first point concerns the importance of affective regimes. Affective regimes are sited, and, therefore, they serve to conceptually ground any analysis of affect to specific locations. In this way, they act as a counter to any tendency to treat affect or emotions as free-floating signifiers. Even the *yuru-kyara*, who are certainly much more mobile than the public signage mascots that we have discussed, are not free-floating manifestations of affect. As *kawaii* creations that are intended to promote specific products, they are officially linked to the specific region or produce that they promote. And they are of course digitally sited in the sense of having their own websites where they can then interact with their fans. (For a detailed discussion of the issue of digital landscapes, see Chapter 8.) To be fair, it is probably not the case that Ahmed herself subscribes to the idea that there are completely free-floating signifiers. However, as Wetherell (2015) points out, by not giving sufficient attention to how signifiers (such as the cultural stereotypes that she focuses on) are actually sited, her work does run the risk of treating them as free-floating.

The second point to appreciate is that because affective regimes are sited, this means it is necessary to take into account the kinds of ideologies – both broader and less site-specific ideologies about language and emotions, as well as those that are more particular to the site being investigated. This means that we need to attend to how broader ideologies concerning, say, emotions[4] and language interact with more particular ideologies that have to do with the site in question.

Consider, in this regard, the common belief about the nature of emotions. Emotions are assumed to be more spontaneous and authentic than the information conveyed via language. The latter, in contrast, is assumed to be more deliberately and consciously crafted. This belief accounts for the asymmetry that we noted earlier on about how paralinguistic information tends to override linguistic information. This asymmetry is indicative of a general ideology. Hence, where there are conflicts between the two kinds of information, it is the paralinguistic that are taken as being the more reliable indicator of the speaker's actual state of mind and intentions.

This belief also leads to another likely outcome. If emotions are to be valued precisely because they are spontaneous and authentic, then (notwithstanding cases of emotional labor where service staff are expected as part of their job performance to present a particular persona of care and concern for the customer), it becomes odd to demand that an individual feels a specific emotion and, moreover, feels it authentically and spontaneously. Where the issue of affect in the semiotic landscape is concerned, this suggests the following:

(i) Affective regimes do not in general explicitly demand specific emotions from individuals. This is not to say that such cases do not exist. Rather, they are relatively rare and can be considered anomalous when they do occur.

(ii) Affective regimes may however prohibit specific emotional displays (as opposed to directly prohibiting the emotions themselves). These prohibitions are less concerned with the actual emotions an individual may feel. Rather, they are aimed at ensuring that inappropriate emotional displays do not occur because these may undermine the goals of the affective regime in question.

To illustrate these two points, consider the recent attempt by the Philippines government to require that the country's national anthem be sung "with fervor" such that violators could face fines of up to US$2000 as well as a year in prison (Octia and Berlinger 2017):

The country's House of Representatives has approved a bill requiring members of the public to sing the country's national anthem, Lupang Hinirang, "with fervor" whenever it is played publicly . . .

---

[4] We make reference here to "emotions" rather than "affect" since, from an emic perspective, established ideologies are more likely to concern the former than the latter. That is, it is more common to find emotions rather than affect serving as the cultural constructs that are the objects of public discourse and shared understandings.

The measure did not define how it would qualify whether or not a citizen sang the anthem with enough fervor.

Some other stipulations in the bill:

- All students at public and private schools would be required to memorize the anthem
- It should be played in accordance with its original composition, a 2/4 time signature when played instrumentally and a 4/4 time signature when sang. It should be played at a tempo between 100 and 120 beats per minute
- All people are required to stand and face the flag during the anthem, or the band and conductor if there is no flag.
- Casting contempt, dishonor, or ridicule upon the national anthem is considered a violation of the law.

    . . .

The goal of the bill is to instill patriotism and respect, Marlyn Alonte, one of the bill's sponsors, told CNN.

It is certainly not uncommon for a country to demand that proper respect be shown during the singing of its national anthem. Such demands tend to involve behavioral correlates (such as standing up, facing the flag) and may include prohibitions on other behaviors (no laughing or making of funny faces), in other words emotional displays rather than the actual emotions themselves. In this regard, the reason why the Philippines's measure has raised eyebrows is precisely because it is seen as directly demanding of its citizens a specific emotion, that is, an internal state that is generally assumed to be spontaneous if it is to count as authentic. This is why the Philippines's measure has been met with ridicule and even likened to "an authoritarian decree that might be issued in North Korea" (Octia and Berlinger 2017).

It is also instructive here to contrast the affective regimes found in the Arlington National Cemetery with those discussed in the present chapter. Our discussion of the Arlington National Cemetery (Chapter 1) showed that it is very explicit in its attempts to regulate the kinds of affect considered appropriate to the site. There are explicit calls for visitors to the Arlington National Cemetery to show dignity and honor for the dead, and respect and compassion for their grieving families. In the same vein, the cemetery makes equally clear what kinds of behaviors it considers to be disrespectful and inappropriate. All these behavioral stipulations are consistently situated in relation to a larger sense of gratitude for the sacrifices made to the nation. In the case of the Arlington National Cemetery, then, its affective regime draws on broader notions of patriotism, nationalism, and sacrifice as well as site-specific understandings about how the dead should be remembered and honored. Moreover, the goal of all the stipulations put out by the Arlington National Cemetery has less to do with trying to regulate the internal emotional states of individuals (as in the case of the Philippines national anthem measure) than with trying to ensure that those visitors who are sincere in wanting to pay their respects at the

Arlington National Cemetery are not unduly distressed or upset by the activities and presence of disruptive, boisterous, or disrespectful others. This, again, reinforces our point about why it is more relevant to focus on affect rather than emotions. From the perspective of the semiotic landscape, the main concern has less to do with the internal states of individuals than with how the behavioral displays of individuals might have a detrimental effect on the experiences of other visitors to the Arlington National Cemetery. In other words, the concern is about affect as contagion (Wissinger 2007), as part of a social circulation of signs.

The *kawaii* in the semiotic landscape differs from the Arlington National Cemetery in that the intended or desired affect is not explicitly stated, nor are there specific prohibitions against what kinds of behaviors are deemed unacceptable. In this regard, the *kawaii* landscapes can be considered to be more typical of many urban landscapes, where the emotional states of urbanites are treated as private, personal, and internal matters. It is of course true that the affective load in the case of *kawai* landscapes is being carried mainly by the visual representations of the various *kawaii* characters. But even here, the intended affect is implicit, relying on generalized understandings of what it means to be *kawaii*, rather than explicitly demanding that readers/viewers of the signs respond with fondness or affection. The general goal appears to simply be that readers/viewers accept or take note of the information being conveyed, if not with conviviality, then at least with some degree of civility.

Conclusion

In this chapter, we have investigated how *kawaii* in the semiotic landscape functions as a key component of modern Japan's material culture. In particular, we have presented three different *kawaii* data that are integrated into the broader sociocultural environment such as the signage of a public transportation system, the taxation office's public announcement, and the tourist information banner in metropolitan Tokyo. The *kawaii* landscapes are not particularly concerned with cultivating any specific affect (beyond the generalized sense of affection that the notion of *kawaii* is associated with in Japanese society), given their goals of conveying information to the general public. This contrasts with that of the Arlington National Cemetery, which, because it is intent on maintaining an atmosphere of respect on its grounds, takes specific measures to ensure that visitors to the site behave in a manner that is considered appropriate by the cemetery's management (see Chapter 1). In this regard, our discussion in the next chapter considers a number of cases that are quite similar to that of the Arlington National Cemetery, where there is a focus on the cultivation of site-specific forms of reverence.

4   Reverencing the Landscape

Perhaps one of the clearest manifestations of landscape affect is the ways in which "spiritual" significance becomes attached to certain landscapes, with the result that such landscapes become the locus of regular group actions ("rituals"), and may at times even be politicized into sites which galvanize extraordinary actions such as protests, demonstrations, and violent conflict. To inspire such strong human actions – whether the discipline to participate in regular rituals at the cost of personal inconvenience or the tipping over into acts of violence that risk harm to self and justify harm to others – the affect of "reverence" requires a deeply rooted foundation in something believed to be permanent and unchanging, something more than human. The metaphysical or numinous dimension of "reverence" is captured in its etymology (Latin *vereri*, meaning "to fear"), which ties reverence to an underlying fear of a force that is believed to be larger than and prior to humanity. Reverence thus also reinforces the sense of affect as being relational rather than purely internal and subjective – as consisting of a relationship between the subject and, in this case, the environment. When a particular group united by a common belief system invests a particular site with significance in respect of that numinous order, then that site becomes one of reverence, with attendant heightened feelings and consequential actions (Collins 2004).

We might consider reverence to be the primal or archetypal affective attachment to the landscape, even as some theorists have posited the sacral relationship with a spiritual order or "supreme being" to be fundamental to the conception of "all people," whether in the "rude" and "primitive" belief in gods who were "superior" versions of the human, or else in the more "advanced" belief in "vast and powerful ... beings who control the gigantic machinery of nature" (Bataille 1992: 35; Frazer 1960: 121–122). From the perspective of anthropology and human psychology, reverence for the landscape stems from this fundamental source and is tied to the landscape as a component of the "religious ritual" that relates man to gods (Frazer 1960: 121).

Such sites are thus very potent examples of affective regimes, where language, spatial indexicality, symbolism, visual signs, and other semiotic features are deployed to appeal to this underlying reverence or fear in human society.

Eliade (1959: 26) observes that "every sacred space implies a hierophany, an irruption of the sacred that results in detaching a territory from the surrounding cosmic milieu and making it qualitatively different." A system of signs is thus in place to effect this detachment of the sacred space from the profane. Eliade speaks of "a large number of techniques for consecrating space," including "signs" such as a miraculous event, or the work of an animal to indicate a particular spot; when the sacred site is revealed, different "rituals of consecration" are performed in order to mark and distinguish the sacred site from the mundane and profane surrounding world (Eliade 1959: 27–29, 32).

By examining certain categories of reverenced sites – from classical versions of the "holy ground" to holocaust memorials, sporting venues, and burial sites of great individuals – we can see the common semiotic features at work, which unite these sites as versions of "hierophany" (in Eliade's terms, 1959: 26), of the human connection with something perceived as being spiritual and thus infinite. The semiotics of reverence set the site in question apart from other ground (which may be contiguous or otherwise resemble the sacred space), conferring on it aspects of grandeur and permanence which echo its spiritual permanence. The narratives, symbolic fittings, and displays of the site detail (usually with hyperbolic and/or emotive language) the spiritual significance of the site – see, for example, our discussion below of Elvis's gravesite. Mass rituals or disciplines of the body – including linguistic behaviors – are often imposed on visitors, to impress on them the solemnity or grandeur of the site, thus making them (consciously or unconsciously) accede to the shared reverence. In keeping with the etymology of "reverence," in all this semiotic and performative reinforcement, there is often also an aspect of fear (admittedly with a range of intensities): an instilling of the imperative to comply or obey for fear of punishment, a sense of awe at the history or tradition being commemorated, a diminution of the human visitor's perspective and scale in comparison with the vast and seemingly limitless power or spiritual value being commemorated.

In an era in which newer forms of organized religion arise, and in which aspects of nonreligious popular culture creep into some religious sites as well (Beaumont and Baker 2011; Graham 2013), a number of sites (outside of those traditionally considered "religious" sites) also become invested with quasi-religious reverence. These sites share with traditional religious sites a certain functional purpose in the human psyche: they all mark locations where a force perceived as "spiritual," "enduring," and transcending human limitations is manifested to and makes a connection with a group of devotees. They also share certain structural and semiotic features which confirm and reinforce that spiritual aspect in the minds of visitors and perceivers.

The "Abode of the Gods": Language, Sign, and Ritual of the "Holy Ground"

The *locus classicus* of the reverenced landscape is the site identified as the "abode of the gods": some of the numerous examples include Mount Olympus in Greece, the Himalayan mountains in the north of India, Mount Kinabalu in East Malaysia, Uluru in Australia, the sacred rivers of India, and the sacred woods and trees of ancient Europe. What is instructive in these cases is that such sites are all natural spaces in many ways indistinguishable from other natural spaces – other mountains, other hills, and other rivers and forests. They are set apart as holy ground, not by space or geography as such, but by the narratives, rituals, semiotics, and structural processes that get attached to them. Thus, speaking of sacred mountains in the Sami religion, Myrvoll (2017: 107–112) notes that these were marked out by their names in the Sami language (which denoted a particular sacred significance or function), and by special markings such as a snow-marked outline on a mountain side that seemed to resemble a Sami shaman beating a drum. Likewise, in Malagasy traditional beliefs, the plethora of sacred sites were often denoted by place-names that denoted a spiritual site, or a site where a religious function or taboo takes effect; other markings of sacred sites take place through "miracles" associated with a site, and "oral traditions" which narrate the distinctive characteristics and recognizable features of the sacred sites (Radimilahy 1994: 85).

One key feature of holy ground is thus the aspect of separation, of being set apart from other (profane) space. This distinction is structured by some form of limitation of access (in the form of taboos, for example against women or children, those outside the "tribe," or those who do not perform certain rituals of purification or dedication). The corollary to this is that there must be some threat of punishment or retribution for improper access, which is framed as a violation of the sanctity of the sacred site. The threat of punishment, to be effective as a deterrent, has to include severe measures such as perpetual banishment from the tribe, the levying of a punitive regimen (incarceration, forced labor, slavery), and even physical violence or execution.

One of the most stringent and clearly documented examples of the separation of sacred and profane spaces is found in the Jewish Torah and the Christian Bible: the articulation of the rituals and prohibitions concerning the Tabernacle of God, which the ancient Israelites believed to host the presence of their God (Yahweh). This is signaled in a number of ways which reveal the essential semiotic features of the sacred site. In the first place, there is a narrative of a miraculous event, namely the ten plagues which Yahweh inflicted on the Egyptian masters in order to free the Israelites from slavery, and the parting of the Red Sea, and the provision of manna in the wilderness to facilitate their journey (told in Exodus chapters 7–16). The Israelites are specifically told to renarrate this account from generation to generation, the performance of specific religious rituals to be accompanied by a narration of God's miraculous works: "And it shall be when thy son asketh thee in time to come, saying, What *is* this? that thou shalt say unto him, By strength of hand the LORD brought us out from Egypt, from the house of bondage" (Exodus 13: 14, King James Version).

Secondly, the space devoted to the presence of God is clearly separated from profane spaces by a series of distinctions reinforced in the language of the Jewish Torah and the Christian Bible. While in the wilderness, the Israelites marked the presence of God in the "Tabernacle" that accompanied them in their journey; the tripartite form of the Tabernacle was later reflected in the permanent temple in Jerusalem built by King Solomon. This tripartite form – with the outer "courtyard," the inner "holy place," and the innermost "most holy place" or "holy of holies" – had a corresponding taboo structure. Only the priests descended from Levi (one of the sons of Jacob or Israel, the eponymous patriarch of the Israelites) are permitted to enter and serve in the Tabernacle, and that only with rituals of cleansing and atonement. There are other taboos, for example against any priestly descendant who has any physical deformity or has been emasculated:

No man that hath a blemish of the seed of Aaron the priest shall come nigh to offer the offerings of the LORD made by fire ... he shall not go in unto the vail, nor come nigh unto the altar, because he hath a blemish; that he profane not my sanctuaries: for I the LORD do sanctify them. (Leviticus 21: 21, 23)

As for the "most holy place" at the core of the Tabernacle, only Aaron (or his descendent designated as the "High Priest") was allowed to enter there, and only once a year, with the appropriate rituals of cleansing and sacrifice (Leviticus 16).

Although contemporary Christianity is considered a different religion from either ancient or contemporary Judaism, some of the common biblical bases remain in Christian practice, as reflected in the semiotic and linguistic regimes of certain (particularly older, Romanesque) churches. In such churches, the most holy part of the church is preserved as a raised platform at one end (called the "chancel"), occupied by and reserved for the priest, choir, and other officiating members. Part of the chancel furnishings would be the altar, an ornate table on which are placed items consecrated for the church service, such as the communion elements, a crucifix, candles, a display Bible, and so on. The chancel is marked as a separate and consecrated space not only by being raised, but (in some churches) by ornate screens or bannisters. Some churches also have panels behind the altar, or attached to it (called "reredos" or "retables," respectively), usually containing carved or painted biblical scenes, and thus again emphasizing the consecrated nature of the chancel and altar. In this example from the Wesley

Chapel in London (Figure 4.1), the pulpit area (where the preacher ascends to preach) is separate from the chancel proper (where the altar, bearing a cross, an open Bible, and candles, is located). Both use raised platforms to separate these inner sacred areas from the rest of the church interior and to signal that they are special consecrated areas. Both the chancel and pulpit area also have wooden barriers, while the pulpit is itself elevated from its platform, both features emphasizing their separation from the rest of the sanctuary space. Apart from these semiotic-spatial markers of separation and sanctification, the chancel also uses linguistic features, in the form of modified reredos behind the altar, each of the three panels headed by the word "HOLY," with the central panel inscribed with the "Apostle's Creed" (a commonly used affirmation of church belief), while the other two panels contain biblical verses (the words used by Christ as recounted in Matthew 22: 37 and 39).

   Similar prohibitions and taboos, with strict accompanying punishments for transgressions, pertained to the sacred places of other classical religions. In Hinduism, the maintenance of the sanctity of the temple and its idols was a "great responsibility":

Figure 4.1 Interior of Wesley Chapel in City Road, London, which shows the clear separation of the chancel by a combination of elevation, barriers, and linguistic demarcations

It was a crime to defile a temple or idol. For stealing idols of gods, destruction or damage of idols or temples, and for abuse of gods, severe punishments were prescribed by the law givers. (Das 1977: 46)

Specific groups, such as members of the lower castes, were prohibited from entering the temple, which was the preserve of the elite caste of Brahmins; these prohibitions were well publicized, including in poetry and song (Bharne and Krusche 2012: 8). Unlawful temple entry is met with "atrocities" and possibly even death (Sachidananda 1988: 29, 42). Similar prohibitions against unlawful entry to sacred sites were enforced by the Yoruba devotees of Oshun, in ancient Mesopotamian religions, among the Āma/Nyimaŋ of the Sudan, and in other religious traditions (Guichard and Marti 2013: 84; Kadouf 2013: 134; Tate 2006: 132). These sites were (in various ways, according to the belief systems of their respective religions) considered to be locations of spiritual or divine power or presence, so that their transgression by unlawful visitors was considered a desecration or defilement of the unique place of the spirit or deity. Punishment would take the form of human enforcement (usually led by priestly officers), or an imputed spiritual punishment in the form of a personal curse (taking the form, for example, of bad luck or illness) on the transgressor, or a collective blight (pestilence, natural disaster) for the entire community. In rituals from societies where the written word was less popularly accessible, the linguistic resources are often emplaced by oral narratives – the recitation of holy writ that marks out the space-time of the sacred. This is complemented by the visual signs (iconography, symbolic objects) and spatial separation that complete the semiotics of sacralization.

Genocide Memorials: Sites of Restive Spirits

Genocide memorials (hereafter GMs) – the preserved actual sites of genocidal atrocities such as Auschwitz (Oswiecim) in Poland, Dachau in Germany, and Choeung Ek in Cambodia – carry a particular resonance and atmosphere, one that has similarities with but is also distinct from the place of worship on the one hand and the cemetery or funeral site on the other. The cemetery in general requires attitudes and behavior that indicate respect, and, in the case of a specialist cemetery like the Arlington National Cemetery, also restricts those who can be interred there, and creates a specific affect which is shared by a special group (in this case, veterans and their families; Wee 2016: 111–113). Unlike places of worship, GMs do not restrict access to a special class or caste, and unlike specialist cemeteries they do not restrict who can be interred there (although GMs resemble general cemeteries in that both practice open access).

All three types of sites – GMs, places of worship, cemeteries – share an intended atmosphere of reverence which is constructed through various semiotic strategies, and this distinguishes them from sites outside of this class where reverence is not required or intended. The requirement for reverence is broadly attributable to a spiritual and even numinous dimension: while places of worship are more clearly believed to be sites of the irruption of the sacred, even GMs and cemeteries often rely on religious systems that support the notion of the perpetuation of spirits of the deceased. The semiotic mechanisms create a passive system of fostering reverence, which may be supplemented (to various degrees, depending on different sites) by an active system of policing behavior and suppressing transgression (through quiet admonition, reprimand, and, in more extreme cases, ejection from the site and even making a police complaint). GMs are thus interesting examples of reverenced landscapes, less obvious instances than places of worship, but nevertheless embodying many of the semiotic strategies of reverence that are employed in sites other than those of organized religions.

Although GMs are presented as open sites accessible by all groups (most do not even charge an admission fee), in effect there is one basic condition which governs access to these sites: a respect for the victims of the genocide, and a corresponding behavior which does not exhibit any emotions or actions inconsistent with that respect. While it is not possible for these sites to gauge the true inner state of visitors, they do police outward behavior for signs of discord with that attitude of respect; in this sense they are like primitive abodes of the gods, which likewise guard against external signs (the presence of visibly illicit persons, defiling contact with taboo objects, etc.) that would constitute desecration of the site.

At the most obvious level, a common way of fostering behavior consistent with attitudes of respect and reverence is to post prominent signs which forbid certain types of outward behavior. Thus, for example, a monument at the Old Jewish Cemetery in Frankfurt (part of a collective memorial site which includes a site marker of the old synagogue which was destroyed by the Nazis in 1938) bears a warning sign asking visitors to respect the monument (*bitte respektieren Sie die Gedenkstätte*) and explicitly forbidding (*verboten*) the consuming of alcohol, the presence of dogs, and littering (Figure 4.2). Other behavior for-bidden at GMs include touching or climbing up certain installations, crossing certain barriers or boundaries, talking loudly (including on cell phones), and taking photographs or videos of certain installations. Such signs regulating outward behavior are relatively straightforward, the violation of which are easy to detect by staff and other visitors, and will usually result in a warning, and in cases of persistent or flagrant violation, ejection from the GM.

Other signs, however, do not just forbid certain specific outward actions, but beyond also seem to aim at controlling inner emotional states. This is both problematic (to input a strict correlation between an outward display and an inner state) and overdetermined, allowing a broadly suppressive effect on emotional states and the atmosphere of the site. Thus, at the Tuol Sleng GM

Figure 4.2 Sign forbidding certain activities at the old Jewish cemetery/
synagogue site in Frankfurt, Germany

in Phnom Penh, Cambodia – a site in memory of the atrocities committed by the Khmer Rouge – a sign forbids the kind of facial expression represented by the iconic human figure (Figure 4.3). The accompanying caption is in Cambodian (despite the majority of the other memorial texts at Tuol Sleng being in English or having an English translation), which is of little or no use to the many non-Cambodian visitors to this GM. The effect, relying on the iconic resemblance of the human figure depicted rather than on verbal semantics, is to create a broad field of reference, forbidding any kind of facial expression that might be interpreted as resembling that of the proscribed figure depicted. Avoiding specificity, this sign might be interpreted not only as forbidding outright laughter, but also as silent laughter or the facial expression corresponding to laughter without the accompanying sound, facial expressions conveying merriment or pleasantry, smiling, the showing of teeth in a grimace, and other facial forms that might be interpreted as corresponding to these. This is a very different use of a figure than that discussed in Chapter 3, on *kawaii*. There, *kawaii* characters represent figures that are distinct from the reader/viewer of the sign. In contrast, the reader/viewer of the Tuol Sleng figure is expected to understand that it represents her rather than a distinct entity. In short, the Tuol Sleng figure is a normative representation of how the reader/viewer ought to behave while on the grounds of the site.

The Tuol Sleng sign is a version of a "blanket prohibition," which is a common semiotic strategy in reverenced landscapes. Making a broadly

Figure 4.3 Sign forbidding merriment at Tuol Sleng, Cambodia

inclusive and overdetermined reference (in our earlier example, *respektieren Sie die Gedenkstätte* or "respect the monument"), it fosters a general sense of guardedness among visitors, a continual self-scrutiny to avoid behavior which might possibly conform to that which is (vaguely) prohibited. In this way, reverenced sites nurture attitudes of wariness among visitors, an overdetermination of guardedness which is consistent with the atmosphere that is desired in such sites. A similar effect is created through what might be called (with Michel Foucault 1984: 206–208, following Jeremy Bentham) the "panoptic" signs at work in many reverenced sites: the presence of patrolling and vigilant uniformed guards, surveillance cameras (and prominent signs declaring a zone of camera surveillance), round-the-corner convex mirrors and other trappings which create a continual sense of watchfulness and a corresponding guarded behavior in visitors.

Like the religious rituals which (the more demanding or esoteric they are) ultimately distinguish religious believers from nonbelievers, GMs also rely on a number of what might be called "deterrent features": structured performances which curtail the visits of less interested visitors and create the desired attitude and behavior among the more engaged ones. In preserving or recreating many of the features of the original events or sites (internment, forced labor, torture, genocide) being memorialized, GMs also recreate some of their atmospherics. GMs like Auschwitz or Choeung Ek, which are preservations of the original camps with most of the original features intact, create a grim experience for visitors, with their barbed wire, hard concrete surfaces, pitted and stained walls, and lack of comforts such as proper furniture and (in some areas) heating or ventilation. With little that is visually exciting, entertaining, or uplifting, necessitating navigation of the exposed open spaces between buildings and the confined spaces within them, and surrounded by the austere and forbidding fittings of the original extermination camp, GMs structurally discourage visits by families, children, young people (with the exception of those on guided school visits), and those looking for an entertaining experience. This bears similarities with the way in which many (though not all) places of worship also structure their spaces and rituals so as to discourage children and casual visitors. This is done through such measures as the lack of comfortable furnishings, the required disciplines of standing or kneeling at specific times, the noise of chanting or religious music, the long duration of many religious ceremonies, and other means. "Deterrent features" ensure that those who do visit the site are strongly motivated enough to put up with the physical, emotional, or psychological discomfort entailed in the visit. Reverence may not be the only motivation, but it is the most common one, and deterrent features are a means to delimit visitors and control their demeanor in a way that at least simulates attitudes of reverence.

Ultimately, voluntary visitors to GMs (leaving aside those on enforced visits, for example school children) submit to the structural measures – the official instructions, the scrutiny of guards and cameras, deterrent physical features and rituals – in search of a clarifying experience that is in many ways similar to spiritual enlightenment. That clarity centers around genocide, and the fear and awe that such an atrocity could be committed by man on his fellow men. The ideological core of GMs is to educate and move people with the atrocities of the past, in the hope of transforming human society into a more tolerant, harmonious, and enlightened mold. The spiritual component of this project is usually implicitly structured into the semiotic-physical site of the GM, and at times emerges much more clearly: thus an installation artwork at Auschwitz consists of two stone tablets with large Roman numerals I to X inscribed on it (Figure 4.4). The artwork inevitably invokes the biblical Ten Commandments (stemming from the Jewish Torah), particularly given that the overwhelming majority of the Auschwitz victims were Jewish. Stained and cracked, the tablets perhaps evoke the moral and spiritual evil represented by Auschwitz, and could possibly serve to remind the viewer of the fragility of the moral foundation of

Figure 4.4 Artwork invoking the Ten Commandments at Auschwitz

human society and the consequences of the erosion of that foundation. Similarly, at Choeung Ek – the site of the infamous "Killing Fields" atrocities perpetrated by the Khmer Rouge – a tall stupa-like structure dominates the centerof the GM. A chilling and brutal memorial, the stupa displays skulls of Choeung Ek victims, piled up behind glass panels. This shocking reminder of the human cost of the Khmer Rouge atrocities is set off against the design of the stupa roof, which depicts both Garudas and Nagas, spiritual beings (resembling birds and serpents, respectively) from Buddhism (Figure 4.5). As the Choeung Ek audio tour narrative is intent to point out, Garudas and Nagas are traditional enemies, so to depict them both on the stupa roof is a spiritual emblem of peace and harmony – the desired spiritual goal of the Choeung Ek GM. This push toward a conclusion of (the importance of) peace and harmony is the more pressing and desired, in light of the constant reminders of atrocities and their victims that permeate the GMs, and the corresponding unease and restiveness in the visitor's spiritual state as a result.

GM narratives (including sequences of images) guide visitors along an arc of fear or wonder (at man's capability for large-scale cruelty to his fellow man, at the unspeakable atrocities of war and genocide), toward the conclusion of a moral-spiritual value, namely the affirmation of a common humanity and the

Figure 4.5 Roof of stupa-like memorial at Choeung Ek showing *nagas* and *garudas*

imperative to avoid a repetition of atrocity. This value is not couched in the terms of any specific religion, given the religious-cultural range represented by GM visitors overall, although where there are specific religious overtones, the logical frame of reference would be to the religion of the main victims; hence, the evocation of the Jewish law and the Ten Commandments in the Auschwitz art installation, and of the Buddhist figures of the Garuda and Naga in the Choeung Ek stupa roof. Even without explicit reference to any religion, the affect structured into GMs is akin to the spiritual affect of the "Holy Ground": an "irruption" (in the terms of Eliade 1959: 26) of the sacred imperative to respect human life, a fear (true to the etymological root of reverence, "vereri") of the awesome consequences of disobedience of that imperative.

Temples of Competition: Sports Arenas as Reverenced Sites

Another key example of reverenced sites are major sporting arenas, particularly for major teams in highly popular contact sports such as the soccer teams in England's Premier League, the US major league teams in football, basketball, and hockey (the NFL, NBA, and NHL), rugby league and rugby union teams in the United Kingdom, South Africa, Australia, and New Zealand, and so on. To these major professional sports teams can be added specialty sports (such as Australian rules football in Australia, or Muay Thai and its derivatives in Thailand and the wider India cultural sphere), which may not have a wide global following, but which inspire strong attachment from regional followers and a degree of competitiveness toward athletes and teams representing other regions. Reverence for great sporting figures is part of the reverence that attaches to the sporting arena, although (in team sports which form the majority of such competitions) there are other important factors at play such as the history of the arena, the history of the team associated with it, the relationship between the team and a particular city or region, the successes and achievements of the team, and related factors.

The relationship between sports and the sacred is a long one, from the ancient Olympic games which honored Zeus, to ritualistic competitive games to seek the favor of the gods in ancient Egypt and the Aztec empire, and among ancient Indian tribes in the Western Hemisphere (Baker 1988: 7–8; Swaddling 1999: 7). In many cases, the religious games were confined to one specific site (such as the grove of Altis where the ancient Olympic Games were commemorated), so that the site itself – significant to Zeus – conferred the dimension of the sacred to the games. In other instances, it was the other way around, where different sites could be used, but the games themselves, as religious rituals, conferred the dimension of the sacred to the site that was so used. Some of that latter relationship – the conferment of the sacred to a particular site by virtue of the ritualistic games conducted there – persists in present-day sports like Sumo, with its connection to Shinto beliefs and rituals (Light and Kinnaird 2002). Contemporary sports is arguably a sublimation of older religious needs and impulses, either culturally in the gradual merger of contact sports and "muscular Christianity" in the United Kingdom and United States from the late nineteenth century onward; or psychologically in the ways that belonging to a group of sports supporters may fulfil certain "needs and desires," the quest for the "infinite," that parallels religious impulses (Baker 2007: 3–4; Bain-Selbo and Sapp 2016).

Accepting the (cultural, psychological, and other) links and parallels between religion and sports still does not account for the fact that some sports and teams attract a more religious following than others, or that some sporting venues (even in an era of globalized competition and frequent "away" games) can become reverenced sites more than others. An analysis of the specific linguistic and semiotic features, through which sporting affect is created, furthers an understanding of the significance of space in the religious dimension of (certain) sports, and the creation of relative degrees of affect in different sports and different teams.

A number of well-known sporting arenas have grown a considerable reputation and affective component that arguably makes them sites of reverence in their own right, for supporters around the world. The importance of the arena is indicated by the fact that fans from far away travel to be part of the atmosphere and spirit of games played in the home stadium, and there are even guided tours of the stadium when games are not in session.

To take just one well-known example: the English football team Liverpool F.C.'s grounds at Anfield Road in Liverpool, has developed a unique culture and fan base that is in many ways separate from and parallel to the Liverpool team itself. Anfield (as the stadium is usually called) has been the home ground for Liverpool since 1892, accruing more than a century of history and developing its own unique culture and rituals. While the success of Liverpool F.C. (one of the most successful clubs in England's current football Premier League) and its host of legendary players over the years obviously have much to do with Anfield's popularity, the club's affect has developed and thrived even with the passing of great Liverpool teams and players, and periods of relegation to the lower division and dry spells without cup victories. In this as well as other ways, the parallels between a stadium like Anfield and a popular place of worship in an organized religion is pointed: if watching the great Liverpool teams and players is the spiritual experience, it is Anfield that shapes and structures that experience just as the built and cultural environment of a place of worship shapes the spiritual experience therein. While for true Liverpool supporters the experiences of watching their team and of being in the stadium are intertwined, it is possible for a visitor who is not a particular supporter of Liverpool to go to Anfield and be moved by the atmosphere, just as it is possible for a non-Hindu (for example) to go to a Hindu temple and appreciate the rituals and atmospheres without any corresponding belief in the Hindu gods. In this regard, it is clear that the kinds of affective regime found in sports arena include the interaction ritual chains that Collins (2004) identifies. As Collins (2004: 102) puts it, "Emotion is a central ingredient and outcome of IRs." According to Collins (2004: 44):

IR theory provides a theory of individual motivation from one situation to the next. Emotional energy is what individuals seek; situations are attractive or unattractive to them to the extent that the interaction ritual is successful in providing emotional energy. This gives us a dynamic microsociology, in which we trace situations and their pull or push for individuals who come into them.

Note the emphasis: the analytical starting point for Collins is the situation, and how it shapes individuals. Situations generate and regenerate the emotions and the symbolisms that charge up individuals and send them from one situation to another (2004: 107). The elements of a ritual, according to Collins (2004: 23; see also Turner and Stets 2005: 73), include individuals being physically co-present, having mutual awareness of each other (in this case as co-supporters of the same team and, hence, as being opposed to the other team and its own supporters), and coordinating their activities and behaviors so as to foster social solidarity. Thus, if Anfield is a site for the "irruption of the sacred" (Eliade 1959: 26) – as it may well be among fans who worship their Liverpool heroes, even bestowing on one of them, Robbie Fowler, the nickname "god" – this reverence is sustained in specific ways. The shared values and belief system of Liverpool supporters is marked by certain rituals: the uniform wearing of replica Liverpool jerseys and other official items (scarves, caps, and so on), the performance of certain mass actions (rising to the feet, pumping fists, choreographed waves, and stamping of feet) that reinforce intense communal bonds, the performance of ritual songs (of which the most important is the Liverpool anthem, "You'll Never Walk Alone"), chants, and cheers.

One popular chant, "Fields of Anfield Road," indicates the demarcation of the stadium itself as a special site of Liverpool "glory":

Outside the Shankly gates, I heard a Kopite calling, Shankly they have taken you away, But you left a great eleven, Before you went to heaven, Now it's glory round the Fields of Anfield Road.
Chorus: All round the Fields of Anfield Road,
Where once we watched the King Kenny play (and he could play), We had Heighway on the wing, We had dreams and songs to sing, Of the glory round the Fields of Anfield Road
Outside the Paisley Gates, I heard a Kopite calling Paisley they have taken you away. You led the great 11, Back in Rome in 77 And the red men they are still playing the same way . . . ("This is Anfield" website)

Since the lyrics for such songs and chants are not normally displayed on a screen or distributed in hardcopy during games, the knowledge of the lyrics and tune or rhythm is a way of distinguishing the old faithful from the newly arrived or non-Liverpool supporter. Even if the lyrics are disseminated to all visitors, they contain considerable insider knowledge which again serves to demarcate the Liverpool faithful from all others: only committed supporters would know that "Kopite" is an alternative name for faithful Liverpool supporters (a reference to one of the Anfield spectator stands, known as the "Kop"), and would recognize the revered names of Liverpool managers and players like "Shankly," "Paisley," and "King Kenny" and that "Rome in 77" refers to Liverpool's historical European Cup final win over German club Gladbach. The references to Christian terms like "heaven" and "glory," while semijocular, do also indicate the ways in which this chant and other rituals in the mind of Liverpool supporters are analogous to religious worship for Christians.

To return to the etymology of "reverence" – "vereri," to fear – it is of course true that for the diehard sports fans like the loyal Liverpool supporters, the fortunes and performance of their team are a secular displacement of older and more familiar religious impulses, so that the fear of misfortune coming to the team would be as real as a divinely ordained affliction (such as volcano eruption or drought) for the worshipper of Zeus or Oshun. Yet there is an even-more immediate source of fear or reverence associated with a site like Anfield: the very real awareness of violence emanating from perceived provocation of the Anfield faithful. If the Kopites are not the most feared and violent of the English football gangs or "firms," they have had their share of notoriety, and numerous riots have broken out at Anfield over the years. The biggest loss of life involving Liverpool fans admittedly took place outside of Anfield, at Hillsborough Stadium in Sheffield, in 1989, in a game between Liverpool and Nottingham Forest, where ninety-six people were killed and hundreds injured. It is also true that many games at Anfield and other stadia take place with no violence, and even courtesy and sportsmanship shown between the rival groups of fans; however, this is on condition that proper respect is shown, without incidents from one group that might be seen as taunting or provoking the other faction to violence. It thus remains true in general that sports fandom operates at a high level of intensity and with a constant potential for violence, thus engendering a suitable degree of caution, if not fear, on the part of visitors (except, of course, for football hooligans deliberately looking to start a fight).

Anfield is thus representative of a sports ground as reverenced site, with a long history of association with sporting performances and events (by the Liverpool players) which, for the faithful Kopites, are the equivalent of a miraculous or supernatural event, the connection with an infinite realm of quasi-superhuman ability or talent. There are other sporting arenas with a similar aura of reverence, accruing through long and rich histories of sporting "glory," complex rituals and practices of belonging and exclusion, passionate and volatile atmospheres with the constant potential of violence and commanding fear and respect, and other similar factors. Some examples include Camp Nou (the home ground for Barcelona football club in Spain), Notre Dame Stadium (of the University of Notre Dame's American football team), Eden Park (one of the principal home grounds of the New Zealand All Blacks rugby team, in Auckland, New Zealand), and Lumpinee Stadium (one of the principal Muay Thai arenas, in Bangkok, Thailand). If sports is a sublimation of human "needs and desires" such as those also fulfilled by religion (Baker 2007), then stadia are the temples of this form of religion, constructing affective regimes that intensify fan zeal and emotional investment in the game's moments of intensity. Mimesis and crowd behavior are heightened by the sharing of powerful emotions created (in addition to the athletes' performance) through tradition and narrative, dress and paraphernalia, songs and chants, ritual behavior, and other semiotic and performative means. The result is the creation of an atmosphere that commands reverence: for the team, but also for the fans and the stadium which is their temple and territory. As with much "religious" phenomena, reverence incorporates an element of fear and punishment: transgressing the rules of the sporting temple can lead to violent punishment, and (as has periodically happened) even to death.

Cults of Personality: Legacies, Burial Sites, and Monuments

The fundamental semiotics of reverence can also be seen in sites associated with persons popularly believed to be "great" or to have accomplished "greatness." The clearest examples, demonstrating the roots of this affect in organized religion, are the burial sites and monuments of religious figures like saints and holy men. The (reported or rumored) burial sites, or internment sites of relics such as bodily parts, of the holy men associated with Christianity, Hinduism, Islam, Buddhism, and other religions have very often become popular shrines attracting visitors from all over the world. Such holy men – founders or key leaders of religions such as the Buddha or the major prophets of Sunni and Shia Islam, exemplars of holy life particularly as manifested in remarkable deeds or miracles – inspire awe and reverence in believers for their perceived spiritual accomplishments. At the very least, the sites they are intimately associated with – sites of their birth, major events in their lives, their burial sites – can inspire believers to emulate something of their character and thus gain "spiritual inspiration" or a "transformative" experience, or both (Di Giovine and Picard 2016: 7–8). Beyond this, there is a sacred valence associated particularly with sites containing physical remnants, such as burial sites or relic monuments, which are often believed to contain and convey power, manifested especially in banishing evil spiritual influences ("exorcism") and the healing of ailments in penitents (Van Dam 1993: 6; Parrish 2005: 11). The reverse side is of course the power to curse if the site or relic, or the supernatural force or personage associated with them, is not given due reverence or otherwise desecrated (Loveridge 2013; Snoek 1995: 20–22).

Graves or relic sites of holy men – whether commemorated simply with a tablet or small shrine, or grandly with a temple or cathedral on the site – are thus hierophanic sites by a kind of metonymic logic, in which the shrine marks the physical remains of the relic, the relic stands for the saint, whose life and works stand for the supernatural power of the divine. They are governed by semiotics of reverence involving elements such as the demarcation of "sacred" (typically, a roped-off or bounded area) from profane spaces, the use of material (marble, stained glass, gold, or silver gilding) and scale/structure (elevation, visual centering, grand size of monument or tablet) to create a sense of grandeur, and rituals (processions, chants, prayers, petitions) to distinguish the serious believer from casual visitor. Narratives (e.g. of the miraculous or exemplary life of the holy person, or inspiring quotations from or about the holy person) and signs (commanding behavior which is taken as a proxy for inner attitudes of reverence) are also deployed to create the reverence affect. Also significant is the mimetic pressure from crowds of believers visiting the site, whose attitude of reverence – visibly marked in terms of somber expressions, quiet contemplation, without chatter or merriment or rushing – cues others to tend to adopt the same behavior. As with other reverenced sites such as holocaust memorials, this mass attitude is often structured in linguistic environments, for example with signs forbidding photography or cell phone usage and urging quiet or silence in the areas closest to the relics.

In many cases, the structured affect of the holy grave or relic is intertwined with that of the religious building in which the grave is located. One of the most striking examples is that of Thomas Becket, the twelfth-century archbishop of Canterbury who was murdered in the Canterbury cathedral by knights supposedly acting on the orders of Henry II. Canonized by the Catholic Church, his remains were destroyed in the reign of Henry VIII as part of the latter's anti-Catholic campaign, but bone fragments were salvaged and are now buried in a memorial site within Canterbury cathedral. Celebrated as a martyr, a saint, and a symbol of religious freedom, Becket's shrine has long been a draw for many Christian pilgrims, especially after miracles were associated with his name and his relics. The semiotics of reverence for Becket's remains are inextricably bound with the semiotics of Canterbury cathedral, one of the largest and grandest of England's old cathedrals. Today, the site where Becket's shrine once stood – still a draw for many visitors – is perpetually marked by a lit candle (Figure 4.6). Candles, of particular significance in the services and rituals of "High Church" Christian denominations like Catholicism and Anglicanism, signal to believers that something of spiritual significance and solemnity is actually occurring in this apparently empty space. The candle also has other connotations – enlightenment and truth, the passion associated with the flame, and (through the fact that a candle is perpetually lighted) an unquenchable spirit – that suggest eternal qualities valued and respected by man. The area is cordoned off by a chain, which sets it apart from the well-trodden public access areas; a nearby sign explains that this area is the site of the original shrine, also explaining that the shrine was "destroyed by order of King Henry VIII," thus enhancing Becket's status as a martyr, and the site as a set-apart space of tragedy and spiritual significance. The fact that Canterbury is a functioning cathedral – various signs all over remind visitors of church service activities and times, and of the respectful conduct expected of visitors to this religious space – also contributes to the general atmosphere of reverence surrounding the Becket site. The whole site of the former shrine is enhanced by the grand

Figure 4.6 Site of original shrine to Thomas Becket in Canterbury cathedral

scale and the soaring height of the surrounding cathedral, which dwarf the human scale and awe the visitor into a reminder of human insignificance. Becket's remains and memory, associated with the cathedral for centuries, transcend this human limitation and participate in the spiritual infinitude of which the cathedral and its atmosphere are a constant reminder.

In other words, for burial sites and monuments within (especially large and grand) places of worship, reverence for the holy one's memory and remains is inextricably bound with the reverence created by the semiotics of grandeur and solemnity created by the place of worship itself. The grand scale, solemnity, and great spiritual and historical capital of the cathedral reinforce a sense of the infinite (here associated with the Christian God), and this in turn reinforces Becket's enduring legacy – as a martyr representing the cause of religious freedom, a holy man and leader of the church, a canonized saint associated in the minds of believers with miracles and other supernatural deeds. A similar effect is found with holy relics and places of worship in other religions, for example the Buddha Tooth Relic Temple in Singapore or Gangaramaya Temple in Sri Lanka which house several Buddha relics. In these Buddhist temples, reverence for the Buddha relics is enhanced, not just with the grand scale of major cathedrals, but also with the intricate symbolism of Buddhist architecture in carvings and furnishings, and the profusion of gold which in Buddhism signifies spiritual worth and honor (Zorach and Phillips 2016).

It is worth remembering that the reverence affect is not co-terminous with religious zeal or the panoply of certain organized religious spaces and rituals. Rather, the religious sentiments seen in relics and the burial or martyrdom sites of holy persons can in semiotic terms be seen as a subset of a larger reverence affect, that can be mobilized in connection with any human experience that can be seen as hierophanic, as an encounter with the infinite. Thus, not all the burial sites of religious holy men inspire monuments reverenced by many visitors and believers; conversely, many such reverenced sites have nothing to do with organized religion, as we have seen with the examples of some sporting stadia and GMs. In addition to the divine principles recognized by organized religions, many of the customs and practices of contemporary societies also commemorate other forms of spiritual greatness which speak to man's "need and desires" to connect to an "infinite" (Baker 2007: 3–4; Bain-Selbo and Sapp 2016).

In the case of burial sites and monuments, the connection with the "infinite" consists in the inspirational example of the person commemorated – the sense that the transcendence of human limitations was achieved through the person's life, actions, and/or legacy. A saint or holy man within a particular organized religion, in this perspective, is someone whose life and legacy represent spiritual greatness as defined in that religion: whether Christian charity or obedience to God, or Buddha-likeness in terms of *satori* (enlightenment) or detachment from worldliness, or particular Hindu virtues like *ahimsa* (non-violence) or *seva* (charitable service). Thus, for both Catholics and Protestants in early modern Germany, the saints are examples which "strengthen the faith" of believers and point believers "towards God" (Heal 2007: 60). In regions or eras in which the values of organized religions exert a less-dominant hold on a society or culture, other notions of the "infinite" and man's connection with it come to the fore. These may include athletic or artistic greatness, great achievements of the intellect or wisdom, exceptional resilience or selflessness, and even great suffering (as with genocide victims or individuals who lived with remarkable disabilities). This desire to recognize and connect with (through visits, contemplation, rituals) individuals whose lives represent an exceptional breakthrough to a transcendent level of human experience explains the commemoration of places associated with great artists, humanitarians, thinkers, military men, and martyrs (including nonreligious ones).

The greatness associated with such individuals is thus enhanced by framing their lives with the great causes, events, and achievements for which they worked. Examples include the Martin Luther King Jr. tomb, located in Atlanta, Georgia, the Raj Ghat memorial marking the site of the cremation of Mahatma Gandhi in Delhi, or the John F. Kennedy grave at the Arlington National Cemetery. The King tomb is located within the King Center for Nonviolent Social Change, which is itself part of the larger Martin Luther King Jr. Historic Site maintained by the National Park Service. The tomb employs many of the structural, narrative, and semiotic features of reverenced sites: of imposing size and constructed of white marble, the tomb conveys a sense both of enduring solidity and purity of ideals. Unusual for the burial site of a great individual, the tomb also contains the remains of King's wife Coretta Scott King (her name and epitaph are beside King's, on the same marble tablet), perhaps suggesting the eternal nature of their union that persists even after death. Inscribed on the side of the tomb are two quotations: under King's name is the last line from his famous "I have a dream" speech: "Free at last, free at last, thank God Almighty, I'm free at last." Underneath Coretta King's name is a quotation from the Bible: "And now abide Faith, Hope, Love, these three; but the greatest of these is love, 1 Cor 13: 13." For Christian visitors, the quotations elevate King's words and achievements by juxtaposing them with the biblical verse. Even for non-Christian visitors, the inscriptions elevate King's life and achievements by suggesting that his contribution to civil rights is motivated by the kind of selfless love described in the Bible, and moreover has set "free at last" later generations of black Americans.

Placed on a little circular island surrounded by water – clearly visible and yet unapproachable and untouchable, the King tomb is literally set apart from visitors, emphasizing (as with the Becket shrine site) the exceptional nature of this site and the person interred therein. Like the Becket shrine, the King tomb draws on its surroundings to contextualize the magnitude of the great individual's achievements: the tomb, and the little island it is on, is placed within a long water feature and open mall, a space large enough for hundreds of people to gather. Although without the ornate architectural features of Canterbury cathedral, the King tomb is set in its own version of an outdoor cathedral, the space and the long mall suggestive of duration and continuity and emphasizing the comparative smallness of the individual visitor. As with the Becket shrine, there is a perpetual flame near the King tomb, conveying similar connotations of man's perpetual need and quest for truth and light, as represented by King's achievements.

The Raj Ghat memorial in Delhi contains similar semiotic features. It is a large black marble slab which commemorates the site of Gandhi's cremation (according to Hindu practice). The memorial itself is almost completely encompassed by four low concrete walls, leaving four points of access at the corners that are normally closed off with moveable rope barriers. As with the King tomb and the Becket shrine, this arrangement does not effectively prevent access by a determined vandal or desecrator; its goal is really symbolic, to mark out the space of the memorial as set apart from the common or profane space where visitors stand. Even to approach the memorial – to draw close to this sanctum enclosed by the low walls and strap barriers – visitors are required to remove their footwear, a practice familiar from places of worship in Asian and Middle-Eastern traditions such as Hindu temples and Muslim mosques. Again, a perpetual light – in a glass lantern built into the marble plinth itself – connotes a spiritual example whose impact is seen as enduring and unquenchable. Once again, the memorial is placed in a context which heightens Gandhi's achievements: near the Raj Ghat memorial is the National Gandhi museum, which contains exhibits and displays narrating the achievements of Gandhi in the context of the Indian independence movement. The importance of Gandhi's Raj Ghat memorial is also enhanced by the proximity of memorials to other Indian political greats, such as Indira Gandhi and Jawaharlal Nehru.

As with the King tomb, language plays a significant part in constructing the reverence affect. For visitors who are unfamiliar with Gandhi's life and works, the tomb is likely to inspire a feeling of somberness but not necessarily awe or reverence. Perhaps recognizing the limits of the merely spatial and symbolic elements of the reverence affect, the government has also placed a number of Gandhi quotations in the vicinity of the tomb. The intent is to inspire reverence for Gandhi (particularly among visitors not previously familiar with his life) by displaying the greatness of his thought and spirit (Gandhi's nickname "Mahatma" means "great soul") through his quotations. One of the most significant ones, prominently inscribed (in block capitals for emphasis) on marble near the entrance, reads:

I would like to see India free and strong so that she may offer herself as a willing and pure sacrifice for the betterment of the world. The individual, being pure, sacrifices himself for the family, the latter for the village, the village for the district, the district for the province, the province for the nation, the nation for all. I want Khudai Raj, which is the same thing as the kingdom of God on earth, the establishment of such a Rajya would not only mean welfare of the whole of the Indian people but of the whole world.

Like the verbal reminder of King's contributions to human freedom, the Gandhi quotation is intended to inspire visitors with a sense of this man's participation in an infinite and enduring idea, that of "sacrifice" for the larger "welfare" of all.

One final example, of the singer Elvis Presley, who attracted a huge cult-like following during his career and even after his death, demonstrates that the semiotics of reverence can be applied to figures outside of the more common religious or national significance. Elvis's remains are buried in his former home, Graceland, in Memphis, Tennessee. The whole of Graceland functions like the cathedral or museum both narrating Elvis's life and achievements as well as enhancing the stature and grandeur of the burial site. Displays of Elvis's elaborate costumes, his gold and platinum album awards, his collection of cars and airplanes, the size and grandeur of the mansion and grounds, reinforce in visitors the sense of Elvis's extraordinary success and impact. To the extent that Elvis's life and music transcend those of more common artistes and have left a lasting legacy on many more fans than usual, he is arguably an example of an artiste who connects man with the infinite, with something inexplicably enduring that transcends human limitations in terms of ability and impact.

Figure 4.7 Graves of Elvis Presley and family members at Graceland

Whether this view is subscribed to by non-Elvis fans, clearly the Graceland memorial and Elvis burial site borrow from reverence affect to attribute qualities of hierophany to Elvis. The burial site itself (Figure 4.7) clearly utilizes the semiotics of reverence familiar from the Becket, King, and Gandhi sites. The area of the tombstones (Elvis's and those of his parents and grandmother) is cordoned off with a low metal railing – again, not as an effective barrier against transgression, but as a symbolic marker of the reverenced ground from the profane area where visitors stand. Other symbolic elements are borrowed from grand Romanesque cathedrals like Canterbury: there are stained glass panels lining a nearby walkway, and the massive stone of the tombstone and aged patina of its brass inscription plate connote the massive stones and weathered stone and metal surfaces surrounding the Becket shrine site. A glass-encased eternal flame stands at the head of Elvis's tombstone, echoing the flames at the Becket, King, Kennedy, and Gandhi sites. To reinforce all the signs and narratives of Elvis's greatness and transcendent example, the inscription on his tombstone (attributed to his father Vernon) explicitly invokes God: Elvis is described as a "precious gift from God" with a "God-given talent that he shared with the world," becoming a "living legend" and "earning the respect and love of millions." The epitaph connects Elvis and his legacy with God, as a kind of divine gift that has touched and impacted "millions" and has thus transcended the realm of mortals (and more mundane artistes) to live on as a "living legend."

This final example nicely brings out a number of points that we emphasized in articulating our theoretical framework (Chapter 2). There is no sharp separation between the emotional and the cognitive. The epitaph is not merely informational but aims to encourage in visitors a particular way of thinking about Elvis, one that sees him as worthy of reverence. Moreover, in order to do this, language works in conjunction with various other semiotic modalities, such as the use of stained glass panels, stone and metal surfaces, and a glass-encased flame. And importantly, all these semiotic resources (linguistic and nonlinguistic) are not presented in a historical vacuum but are borrowed elements from other burial sites, thus providing visitors with signs that are also familiarly iconic rather than being purely symbolic (see our discussion of the inclusion rule in Chapter 2). In this way, the continued use of semiotic resources across different sites to signal that these are all burial sites worthy of reverence constitutes an affective economy of its own. This is a circulation of signs that are associated with the affective regime of reverence. This allows any particular site that wants to foster its own regime of reverence to partake of this already-extant-affective economy by deploying specific materializations and combinations of these icons of reverence.

Conclusion: "Spirit," Affect, and Sign

The discussion of reverenced sites shows (among other things) the wide range of psychological impulses, religious traditions, deep-rooted human needs and anxieties, and other possible factors which might be associated with "spiritual" sites. While this chapter has referred to terms like the "sacred," "hierophanic," and "infinite" (quoting from a variety of scholars), this is neither to insist on knowledge of one particular spiritual source or authority which is believed to govern the universe nor to confuse matters by insisting on a plurality of such spirits (including "great" human ones). This is where the discussion of affect as a semiotic phenomenon – as a human response structured by (the semiotic features of) an external object – is helpfully clarifying. Analyzing the reverence affect in a range of different sites allows us to see how this affect is fostered without having to insist on any particular numinous or psychological source of "spiritual" authority. While the reverence affect does posit some kind of force or entity to whom that reverence and fear is directed, it does not require any specific identification of that force or entity, nor any adjudication between different types of reverence (say, between different organized religions, or between religion and humanism, humanism and group behavior). Instead, the affective approach allows us to see how different reverenced behavior can be described in terms of a common language or semiotics of reverence. To return to our discussion of Peirce's semiotics in Chapter 2, we can say that reverence is most productively described as not caused by a spiritual force (as it were) "out there," but rather as an "interpretant," a semiosis that includes as one of its dimensions the human response to objects deemed worthy of reverence. Our approach thus allows a clarifying analysis of the (plural and potentially confusing) reverence regimes manifested in a wide range of human cultures and praxes.

5   Romancing the Landscape

Chapter 4 showed how reverence can be structured as an affect of place that operates on groups such as religious adherents, fans of a sporting team, followers of a "cult" figure – indeed, any entity which inspires attitudes of fear, solemn respect, and cognate attitudes that can be summed up as "reverence." We will now proceed to discuss a different kind of landscape affect, one whose semiotic terms make an appeal which is very much targeted at the individual rather than a group, and whose inducements are not fear and awe but rather self-realization, adventure, and personal growth. What we might call the "romance affect" underlies many touristic narratives, particularly those to do with sites that feature in popular culture as places of fantastical or uncommon journeys, the overcoming of special hardships or obstacles, and the attainment of a particular status attesting to personal growth or achievement. The romance affect is closely tied to the imaginative journey, but has very real socioeconomic and geophysical implications as seen in tourism, advertising, and spatial logic.

Bildung, Romanticism, and the Romance Affect

The significance of the romance affect in landscape is best understood in terms of the psychology of development or growth. For the psychologist Carl Jung, this idealistic phase of the individual was associated with youth:

And so it is with the ideals, convictions, guiding ideas, and attitudes which in the period of youth lead us out into life, for which we struggle, suffer, and win victories: they grow together with our own being, we apparently change into them, we seek to perpetuate them indefinitely and as a matter of course, just as the young person asserts his ego in spite of the world and often in spite of himself. (Jung 1971: 12)

The processes of accommodating to adulthood and human society, for Jung, necessitated a checking and suppressing of this youthful individual conviction and venturesomeness, a conformity with common values and behavior, a "social goal [that] is attained only at the cost of a diminution of personality" (Jung 1971: 12). However, the youthful impulse to strike out for oneself and on one's own is never fully eradicated, periodically asserting itself "in spite of the world and often in spite of [the individual] himself" (Jung 1971: 12).

This primal life phase can be expressed as a "myth" structured into language and symbolism, as archetypal theorist Northrop Frye shows. For Frye, the youthful phase of the "organic cycle of human life" was captured in a "dawn, spring, and birth phase" underlying certain types of narrative. The main features of this literary archetype were the following:

> Myths of the birth of the hero, of revival and resurrection, of creation and . . . the defeat of the powers of darkness, winter, and death. Subordinate characters: the father and the mother. The archetype of romance and of most dithyrambic and rhapsodic poetry. (Frye 1963: 16)

The flowering of this literature of youthful romance was seen in German literature of the latter half of the eighteenth century, associated particularly with writers like Rousseau, Schiller, and Goethe (Jeffers 2005: 2). What came to be known as the *"Bildungsroman"* – the novel of growth – popularized the figure of the young protagonist, not "ready-made" in terms of character and values, whose focus was inward on the emotional state of the self, and whose career involved the "nurturing of an individual's many-sided potential" (Jeffers 2005: 2–5). In many ways, the quintessential "Bildung" protagonist was the child, whose emotional and psychological development could be most clearly and dramatically seen as it grew in the course of the protagonist's experiences and struggles. The child-protagonist is seen most often in fantasy and speculative fiction versions of "Bildung" narratives (e.g. in Lewis Carroll's "Alice" novels, or J. K. Rowling's "Harry Potter" novels), but also in poetry and in more social realist novels (such as in many of William Wordsworth's poems, or Charles Dickens's *Great Expectations*).

The theme of "Bildung" or individual development, in early nineteenth-century England developed into the notion of the romantic self, typically isolated from human society and critical of its false values, hyper-aware of emotions, and pursuing the development of an artistic and spiritual ideal. Poets like William Wordsworth and Samuel Taylor Coleridge popularized the isolated romantic figure – aloof from society, introspective and highly sensitive, given to bouts of melancholy – that typically drew spiritual solace from nature rather than from human society. This "stereotype of the *poète maudit*," by personality an "outcast" from "the present competitive society" (Abrams 1953: 103), was reinforced in the overwrought isolated protagonists of gothic novels, and in the often gloomy landscape painting of the day. Brion (1967: 47) identifies as chief characteristics of romantic painting the "feeling for nature" – which took "the English landscape" as "an inexhaustible source of artistic interest and joy, a pure delight for the heart and the sense" – and "an inclination towards the supernatural, the irrational, fantasy, and the fantastic."

A particular version of romantic individualism arose and was popularized in America, with its sparsely populated frontier that confronted individuals with both sublime beauty and harsh physical challenges. In writers like Henry David Thoreau and Ralph Waldo Emerson, a love for nature combined with a resilient individualism that was also a rejection of materialist society. Others like James Fenimore Cooper, Bret Harte, Edward Ellis, and the "dime Western" writers romanticized both the American West and the often-quirky and hardy individuals that navigated it. In visual arts, Winslow Horner, Eastman Johnson, and Frederick Remington contributed to this romance of the American Frontier and its characters. While the American Western was a broad genre that encompassed many different themes and elements, it did propagate the figure of the hardy yet sensitive frontiersman whose struggle to survive in the wilds also contained a deep attachment to it and a rejection of the complicated sophistication and materialist ease of "Eastern" life.

The reason why romance and bildung narratives flourished from the end of the eighteenth through the nineteenth centuries onward may have to do with the rise of capitalist modernity. As Abrams's (1953: 103) summation of the characteristic pose of the Romantic poet observes, the "outcast" element in Romantic Bildung was predicated on a recoil from "the present competitive society" of a Western Europe reacting to the industrial revolution, the broadening reach of capitalism, the dominance of urban life, and other such features of modernity. These have of course intensified in the era of global capitalism, leading to a corresponding popularization of versions of the romantic outcast. In essence, the romance affect in landscape depends on landscapes that foster possibilities of individual development, in ways that are seen as inimical in the conventional spaces of modernity.

In the socioeconomic modernity which Europe encountered from the late eighteenth-century onward (and which has latterly influenced other parts of the world), a literary-artistic form (the Romantic Bildung genre) came to be interlaced with social practices that valorized rural, rugged, and picturesque spaces over urban ones. The work of writers like Walter Scott and William Wordsworth, and painters like J. M. W. Turner and Caspar David Friedrich, were the artistic expression (and often the inspiration) for the discovery of and travel to remote places like the Scottish Highlands and the Lake District as increasingly popular tourism sites (Ousby 2016; Yoshikawa 2016). Textual and physical spaces became increasingly intertwined in the public imagination, as tourists traveled specifically to see the types of landscape – if not the actual site – they consumed in viewing visual artworks, literary texts, and other cultural documents. At the same time, there was a similar convergence of landscape, journey, and identity, as leisure travel among the middle classes increasingly became a reflection of individual identity and choice in the face of fast-paced and crowded urban-industrial life. In the writings of William

Wordsworth, Mary Shelley, James Fenimore Cooper, Matthew Arnold, Robert Louis Stevenson, and others, the association of individual growth and fulfill-ment with solitude in nature – particularly rugged, mysterious, picturesque, and wild natural landscapes – was established.

In the mid-twentieth-century onward, the rise of mass media like TV and film coincided with an increasingly "filled" globe as many parts of Asia and Africa experienced decolonization and became independent nations. With the increasing knowledge and decreasing exoticism of hitherto-unknown regions, it became increasingly difficult to imagine mysterious and isolated realms. Special parts of earth – lost islands and continents, particularly inaccessible places like high mountain peaks, inhospitable deserts, or polar regions – hence came into focus, for example in David Lean's *Lawrence of Arabia*, or the island of Peter Jackson's *King Kong,* or the arctic in Philip Pullman's *The Golden Compass*. Other narratives go back in history to recreate the sense of individual isolation and development in (for example) nineteenth-century New Zealand (Jane Campion's *The Piano*), or the American West before wide-scale settle-ment (Larry McMurtry's *Lonesome Dove*). Speculative Fiction created other ways of imagining isolated landscapes, for example on other planets (Andy Weir's *The Martian*, James Cameron's *Avatar*), parallel worlds with different rules and parameters (Ian McDonald's *Brasyl* or the "Everness" series of novels), bodily transplants and the new experiences that come with them (Tarsem Singh's *Self/Less*, Hanif Kureishi's *The Body*), and other means of taking the protagonist out of the quotidian world and into new and challenging ones. In Fantasy, in particular, the use of strange imagined worlds was parti-cularly ubiquitous, for example in C. S. Lewis's "Narnia" series, J. K. Rowling's "Harry Potter" series, and J. R. R. Tolkein's "The Lord of the Rings" (LOTR) trilogy and *The Hobbit*, to name just the most well known in a highly popular genre.

With the rise of the internet and social media in the late twentieth and early twenty-first centuries, this conflation of landscape, journey, and identity was intensified. The internet facilitated the identification and growth of fandom based on particular cultural documents (the Harry Potter and LOTR phenom-ena are prominent examples) and allowed individual fans to share material, resources, and, ultimately also, aspirations with each other. The result was the increasing popularity not only of Cosplay and fan conventions, but also fan fiction, and fan-related travel and tours. The latter phenomenon, which will be discussed in greater detail below, constitutes a way in which fan identity intersects with Bildung journeys (imagined as part of the heroic journeys seen in films) and with landscapes associated with the films and the protago-nists therein. Image-based social media like Instagram facilitated the conflation of identity, travel, and landscape: the post of a popular Instagram "influencer" standing in a particular exotic location is not only an aspirational identity for his/her followers (i.e. to attain the same lifestyle), it is also an influence on travel and tourism (to get to the same location), and of course a promotion of the particular kind of landscapes depicted (whether isolated rugged terrain, or low-density exclusive luxury resort, etc.).

The popularity of the journey motif stems from the primal psychological symbolism of the journey, denoting renewal, the overcoming of challenges, and change and growth. For Jung, the journey archetype was essentially about "*individuation* – or the process of developing into a more complete individual" (Rawa 2005: 12). It is hardly surprising, then, that journey narratives should be ubiquitous in a modern society where the stage of historical development, the stresses, and the impersonal nature of late capitalist society have created considerable discontent, anxiety, and dissatisfaction in individuals (Bauman 1997; Bewes 1997; Jameson 1991). This is further intensified by the increasing sense of discontent, fragmentation, and inauthenticity that many individuals now feel, as exemplified in the values and attitudes of the American "Gen-X" and "millennial" generations (Henseler 2013: 7–8; Howe and Strauss 2000: 104–106). The fascination with bildung narratives, and thus also bildung landscapes, may have particular resonance with a "millennial" generation that rejects the conventional values of capitalist society (wealth, fame, career success) in favor of a personal fulfillment, a "heroism" found through "making a difference" in their own chosen, individualistic ways (Rainer and Rainer 2011: 16–17, 36–37; Winograd and Hais 2011: 4).

Examining some of the more popular landscapes depicted in media and culture, we can discern certain features of the romantic Bildung landscape. These are often wild and isolated, giving a sense of being difficult to reach. These wild landscapes thus also imply a particular kind of journey, a Bildung journey where the individual moves from ignorance to experience, helplessness to strength. The wild landscape and its Bildung journey have been popularized by a long literary tradition, in classic texts like Homer's *The Odyssey*, Biblical narratives like the "Book of Jonah," and the Hindu epic poem *The Ramayana*. In contemporary times, it can be seen in the HBO TV series *Game of Thrones* (based on George R. R. Martin's "Song of Fire and Ice" novels), Peter Jackson's "Lord of the Rings" and *The Hobbit* films, and the first trilogy of George Lucas's "Star Wars" cycle. Such hugely popular texts provide readers, viewers, and fans with several aspirations at once: in terms of identity, they offer protagonists who begin their journeys as young, naïve, and rather helpless individuals, which makes it easy for fans to identify with them. These protagonists (like Arya Stark and Jon Snow in *Game of Thrones*; Frodo in "Lord of the Rings"; Luke Skywalker in the first "Star Wars" trilogy) undergo a journey in which they navigate arduous journeys and overcome obstacles, in the process developing and affirming important personal qualities and values (courage, determination, honesty, loyalty, and the like) which again can form aspirational qualities for fans and followers. The landscapes which feature in these fictional journeys – wild and rugged, but often depicted with great cinematographic and framing (and, increasingly, digital) skill – also become aspirational destinations for fans, as they share online their information about filming locations, looka-like sites, and so on.

Variations on the romantic Bildung landscape and journey exist, but they have in common the linguistic-semiotic construction of individualism and personal growth achieved through an escape from modern society and into landscapes whose chief allure is that they offer a contrast to the crowded busy urban landscapes that typify the current age of global capitalism. One close variant is the insular landscape, seen in Daniel Defoe's novel *Robinson Crusoe* and its many film adaptations, although a similar use of landscape is seen in many other narratives like Joseph Conrad's *An Outcast of the Islands*, Michael Powell's film *The Age of Consent*, Robert Zemeckis's film *Castaway*, and Alex Garland's novel *The Beach* and the film based on the novel. The isolated nature of such landscapes usually involves a journey across a body of water that marks the individual's renunciation of the mainland and its society, and a need to make do with fewer resources that mark the individual's personal growth. The CBS TV series *Survivor*, in many seasons of which contestants were placed on islands (including Pulau Tiga in Malaysia, Nuku Hiva in French Polynesia, and the Pearl Islands of Panama) and competed against each other for resources like food and the ultimate cash prize, relies on the island affect of isolation from conventional society and the romance of rugged individualism and personal fulfillment. Of course, many uses of the island landscape in popular culture and social media do not feature survival, but instead revel in the luxury of island resorts in places like Fiji and the Caribbean (Thurlow and Jaworski 2010: 193–198). This "exotic" variation nevertheless relies on an overlapping semio-tic field with the romantic Bildung, in the idea of "getting away from it all" to an uncrowded and leisurely place where the individual can rediscover himself or herself, reconnect romantically with an accompanying partner, find romance with a new partner, undertake (admittedly guided and expensive) "adventures" such as snorkeling with whale sharks, and so on. However expensive and elitist they are, such luxurious resort trips are aspirational and desired precisely because of a common affective appeal of being away from everyday society and facilitating individual fulfillment or self-discovery.

Another popular version of the romantic Bildung journey involves what might be termed "liminal" landscapes, nebulous spaces often hidden in plain sight but only visible to or accessible by the specially gifted protagonist. Liminal landscapes (in contrast to rugged isolated landscapes) are often built-up areas, in cities or large buildings, but focusing on particular sites only accessible to the protagonist and a few rare others with special qualifications. Those qualifications may include magical ability, or rare technology, or a special aesthetic-spiritual sight, or a unique temperament determined to defy social conventions. The best-known example of this landscape is probably seen in J. K. Rowling's "Harry Potter" novels and the films based on them, where the young protagonist Harry's ability to see and access certain spaces in the nooks and crannies of the school for magic, Hogwarts, is growing proof of his special powers which separate him from the nonmagical conventional world of "muggles," and even from lesser wizards. The BBC TV series "Dr Who," with its "Time Lord" protagonist who possesses unique powers and a space-time machine, is both a part of the conventional world (the TARDIS looks like an English police box) and also apart from it (capable of traveling to strange realms and through time), and can be considered a version of the liminal landscape. So, too, can Neil Gaiman's novel *Neverwhere*, in which a protagonist encounters a shadowy magical realm of "London Below" overlapping with the quotidian world of "London Above." Another popular version of the liminal landscape can be seen in "hacker" romance novels, such as William Gibson's "Sprawl" novels, or Stieg Larsson's "Millennium" trilogy and the films based on those novels, or Neal Stephenson's novels *Reamde* or *The Diamond Age*. Here, it is the skills and knowledge of the hacker, usually accompanied by an idiosyncratic insouciance or rejection of conventional morality and way of life, that propel the protagonist out of social spaces and into liminal landscapes.

The general linguistic and imagistic regime, which governs much of the romantic consumption of landscapes in contemporary popular culture, can thus be seen as a complex one which governs the depiction of the individual, the journey, and the landscape in which the individual's journey takes place. While variations exist, the common affect of this popular phenomenon involves an aspiration of getting away from the pressures of everyday life, by going on a journey of self-discovery crucially involving a landscape which is at once isolated, possessing a degree of difficulty in reaching or traversing it, outside of the common realm of experience, and thus worthy of the individual's aspiration or attachment. This affect, although often originating in a fictional text and/or involving the digital manipulation of a physical landscape, is manifested in and has implications for a number of social practices impacting attitudes to and interactions with physical landscapes.

Tours and Tourism: Fantasy, Romance Affect, and Spatial Implications

In recent decades, there has been a rise in tours and tourism around outdoor film locations, with a focus not so much on the process of filmmaking per se, but on the journeys and development of fictional characters. The new phenomenon of film-related tourism has relied on immersion into the landscapes of fictional worlds, although, of course, elements of older film tourism – celebrity gossip, inside stories of filming problems and quirks – still play a role. As we will see, in film-related tourism, there are interesting attempts to create the appropriate affective regimes, which have to manage visitors who are simultaneously both tourists as well as fans. These visitors come with fairly detailed knowledge of the films that motivated their interests in the landscapes in the first place, and there is a need to ensure that the actual site visit accords with their filmic experiences and understandings.

Several factors decide whether or not a particular series or film – and thus a particular set of film locations – becomes popular among viewers and tourists. If the series or film is based on popular novels which have over time built up a strong readership base, it often translates into more anticipation and support when the TV series or film versions appear. Examples of these include Peter Jackson's "Lord of the Rings" and "Hobbit" films, based on the much-loved J. R. R. Tolkien novels that had built up a huge following for decades before the appearance of the films. Other examples include the HBO TV series *Game of Thrones*, based on George R. R. Martin's "Song of Fire and Ice" novels which had gathered a cult following, or the AMC TV series *The Walking Dead*, based on Robert Kirkman's popular comic book series. Star power does not seem to be a necessary condition, as many of the stars of bildung shows – Daniel Radcliffe as Harry Potter, Emilia Clarke or Maisie Williams on *Game of Thrones*, and Lauren Cohan and Steven Yeun on *Walking Dead*, to name just a few – were not well known until after these shows became hugely successful. Bildung films and TV shows, recounting the growth and development of (usually) young and undeveloped characters, often rely on casting young and relatively unknown actors in the roles of the protagonists. Obviously, the elements of good visual storytelling – the cinematography, production values, creation of suspense or tension, pacing, and action – all play a part in the success of bildung shows.

All this being said, it is clear that film locations play a very important part in the popularity of many bildung narratives. The identification that audiences feel with the young protagonists and the adventures and chal- lenges they go through in the course of their character growth also translate into a desire to seek out and interact with the locations associated with that growth. This is in some ways a familiar phenomenon, compar- able to the rise in tourism to England's Lake District in the late eighteenth- century onward, as a result of the writings of William Wordsworth and the romantic poets (Sharpley 2009: 143). With the rise of film, television, and their digital translations from the latter part of the twentieth-century onward, visual landscapes became an increasingly important part of the viewing experience, playing an increasingly important role in the popular- ity of certain films.

The most conclusive evidence of this is the rise, in recent years, of the phenomenon of film-related tourism. A number of highly popular films and TV shows have spawned a boom in tourism to countries used as film locations, and in tour companies creating tours around those shows. This is not just a secondary interest in the countries and regions because they were mentioned in – or known to be the sites of – popular shows. Rather, it is a tourism that is in many ways inseparable from fan interest in the shows, their characters and their development, the events, costumes, and other paraphernalia. There is in fact a kind of ontological blurring of boundaries, so that the real and reel sites merge in several ways, the tourist and the fan of the show are likewise indistinguishable, and the interest in the country or region is inseparable from the fan's interest in the scenes filmed in there. This ontological blurring is nicely captured in the title of a scholarly edition, *How We Became Middle-Earth* (Lam and Oryshchuk 2007). The essays in that collection, devoted to the impact on New Zealand by Peter Jackson's "Lord of the Rings" (LOTR) film trilogy, note the striking ways in which the popularity of those films did not just boost incidental tourism to New Zealand, but effectively conflated the nation with the fictional "middle-earth" of Tolkien's novels and Jackson's films. Fan-visitors to these film locations are not tourists in the conventional sense – their itineraries and agendas are much more focused on film-related sites and events, and less on the range of sites (restaurants, festivals, interesting urban neighborhoods, museums, and cultural sites) that tourists are usually interested in. Correspondingly, as the case of New Zealand shows, regional and national organizations also buy into the fan-based transformation of the landscape, reinforcing it in a number of ways such as superimposing film place-names, characters, and images onto signage, tourism material, and even the safety video for the national airline (Goh 2014). The New Zealand case thus presents an interesting twist to the affective economy. In the circulation of signs from the world of film to the physical settings in which the films were made, there are subtly significant shifts in how they are understood, giving rise to interpretants of higher indexical orders that blend both their film-based significations with the awareness that they are now being used (sometimes ironically) as marketing tools. For example, to celebrate the release of *The Hobbit*, a weather reporter even gave his forecast in Elvish (Pinchefsky 2012).

The combination of a well-structured bildung narrative and Jackson's beautiful evocation of New Zealand's striking landscape, in addition to the strong existing fan base created by Tolkien's novels, may explain why LOTR was the show that inaugurated a new phenomenon of massive film-based tourism. The impact of the films on New Zealand tourism has been well documented, including accounts of how the country reinforced the identification of the nation with the fictional "middle-earth," how some place-names were changed to names taken from the films, how film-related tours and tour sites mushroomed after the advent of the films, and so on (Barker and Mathijs 2007; Wong 2007). Within these tourism and marketing effects, and less well documented, is the phenomenon of landscape affect created by the films and consequent tourism and marketing strategies. According to Gregg Anderson, general manager for Tourism New Zealand (Pinchefsky 2012, italics added):

You'll be able to walk through the natural countryside and take in those scenic panoramas, that's really well kept as in the movie ... In New Zealand, a percentage of what you see on screen you can see in real life. We're not trying to sell the movie. *We're trying to say the sense of awe and grandeur that you get with the movie is very much what you'll get with the experience.*

What is worth noting here, then, is how the emphasis is on trying to assure visitors that the affective regime in the physical site is faithful to that in the movie.

The effectiveness of this regime is clear from LOTR visitors' comments, for example those on popular travel sites like TripAdvisor and Viator (on which many of these tours are marketed). Beyond the vaguely exuberant adjectives used (such as "awesome tour" or "fun"), many visitors register a personal identification or investment in the tour and sites. Indeed, some actually call the tour (which typically lasts several hours, although there are longer tours and even itineraries spanning several days) a "journey" as if they were the actual protagonists in the film. Again, this is part of the ontological blurring of real and reel life that is part of the affective regime of such tours. One feature of this blurring is onomastic, i.e. the ways in which New Zealand locations are not merely equated with, but effectively replaced by, their screen names. Thus, user Saiyan89, reviewing the LOTR Twizel tour (in Canterbury on the South Island), says, "It was an awesome Journey being on the Pelennor fields [the site in the films for which Twizel was used]" (TripAdvisor, Lord of the Rings Twizel Tour). Other terms and phrases used by visitors reinforce this process of identification and investment: Julswoody says, "I could quite easily live in this little village [actually just a film set in the middle of a field] with the hobbits!!", while Rich3393 says, "You feel like you're there ... when you recognize the mountains and the plains"; and Deirdre R says, "What a fantastic way to travel back to Pelennor Fields" (TripAdvisor, Lord of the Rings Twizel Tour). Onomastic substitutions are part of the linguistic resources which create the characteristic ontological force of romance film tours.

The tours capitalize on this process of identification, reinforcing the ways in which the tourists are imagined as protagonists in the films and, consequently, the ways in which physical sites become imaginatively identified with sites and scenes from the films. Common techniques include the narrative strategies of description, storytelling, and anecdotal recounting: tour guides are often people who had worked as extras or support staff on the films, and pepper their tours with anecdotes and insider stories of the filming process, in order to get tourists to begin the process of associating the physical site (devoid of any traces of the filming process) with film sites. The process of association is then intensified by several narrative strategies: showing short clips from the films (on a laptop or portable DVD player) featuring the physical site in question, narrating events in the films and matching them to the physical site, and asking the tourists to position themselves in specific sites and positions (supposedly) occupied by actors in the films. Some tours also offer physical artifacts which are meant to reinforce the tourist's identification with the film and its actors: these include items like copies of film scripts, actual plastic leaves from the "party tree" at the Hobbiton location, and replicas of weapons used in the films (Figure 5.1). Handling these artifacts is intended to intensify the tourist's identification with the films, its agents, and ultimately with the events and characters in the films. One tour strategy, in particular, concretizes the tourist's identification with the events in the film by positioning the tourist as an imagined participant in the film: tour guides often use movie stills of the landscape to help tourists identify the physical locations before them as actual mise-en-scènes in the film (Figure 5.2). Thus, while on the one hand conscious of being tourists on a tour of New Zealand, this strategy confers a dualistic vision in which they are at the same time looking at the landscape, and moving through it, as if they were characters seeing and moving through the film landscapes (Goh 2014).

If the films (as bildung narratives) invite viewers to engage imaginatively and sympathetically with the struggles and growth of the protagonists through their journeys, the tour companies explicitly use the landscape to foster the fan-tourist's identification with the films' protagonists. This is clear from the advertising language used by many of the tour companies, which frequently refer to their tours as "journeys," characterized by terms ("exciting," "adven-ture," the "fellowship" of other tourists) appropriate to the careers of Frodo and his companions in the films. Similarly, the physical sites visited are often referred to by their film names, as sites in "middle-earth" rather than as actual New Zealand locations. Sites are also specifically located in terms of events in the film that happen there, reinforcing their importance as key markers of the protagonists' careers and development. Thus, "Red Carpet Tours" – one of the most expensive and intense of the LOTR tours in New Zealand – markets itself by asking tourists to "take a once-in-a-lifetime journey to Middle-Earth, traveling from Auckland to Queenstown via many exciting LOTR filming locations, movie studios, and adventures" (Red Carpet Tours "14 Day Lord of the Rings Tour"). The prospective tourist is asked to imagine experiencing the journey "within a fellowship of like-minded travelers," with the word "fellowship" echoing the title of the second of the LOTR films ("The Fellowship of the Ring"). Some of the destinations are described exclusively in terms of their film significance, so that the traveler might not even know

Figure 5.1 Guide on the Southern Lakes Sightseeing company's "Trails of Middle Earth" tour exhibiting replicas of *Lord of the Rings* weapons and narrating details of their status and function in the films

where in New Zealand they actually are: thus, Day 10 of the itinerary says, "Head to the magnificent EDORAS! Survey the mountains and head to where the Golden Hall once stood," and Day 11 says, "Visit Pelennor Fields where King Theoden's battle speech roused men to battle and then to Laketown [a setting in the films]" (Red Carpet Tours "14 Day Lord of the Rings Tour").

Figure 5.2 Tour guide showing two film stills from *Lord of the Rings* at a location in the Twelve Mile Delta area west of Queenstown, South Island, New Zealand

Other linguistic features that foster ontological blurring include the use of imperative verbs that interpellate the prospective visitor into the "world" of LOTR. Thus, the Hobbiton movie set web page prominently declares: "Experience the magic of Hobbiton"; the teaser for the movie set tour begins thus, "Join us and experience the real Middle-earth" (Hobbiton Tours "Hobbiton Movie Set"). Red Carpet Tours' main page has a list of highlights with such imperatives combined with LOTR onomastics, such as "climb the magnificent Edoras," "explore Bilbo's shire," "experience breathtaking Mordor," and so on (Red Carpet Tours "14 Day Lord of the Rings Tour"). Also used prominently are experiential and immersive verbs, which again blur ontological boundaries by placing the prospective visitor (as it were) in the midst of activities and events "in" LOTR. Thus, for the Hobbiton movie set, visitors are promised that they will "find themselves engulfed in the sights, smells, sounds, and tastes of 'The Shire'" (Hobbiton Tours "Hobbiton Movie Set").

While LOTR, with its epic journey of growth and moral triumph of good over evil at the end (both in the internal development of the main characters, as well as at the level of overall plot and action in the films), is one of the most obvious examples of how a powerful bildung narrative has catalyzed a widespread landscape affect, it is far from the only example. In a similar fantasy genre is the HBO TV series "Game of Thrones," which like LOTR was able to build on a popular book series (George R. R. Martin's "Song of Fire and Ice" novels). "Game of Thrones" is different from LOTR in a number of ways, and owes its success to some factors not present in LOTR: a much more modern show, it has considerably more sex and violence, and has a dimension of political intrigue and family drama (including incest and parricide) more familiar from contemporary TV shows like "Dynasty" and "House of Cards." However, there is also much that is similar between "Game of Thrones" and LOTR: not only the familiar fantasy elements of magical creatures and evil beings (dragons and nightwalkers in the former, and the Ents or tree-beings and ringwraiths and orcs in the latter) and swordfights and battles, but also the fundamental bildung narratives centered on the Stark children, who must survive after their father, Ned, is murdered by the ruthless Lannister clan. The heir, Rob Stark, rises in rebellion and is defeated and killed, while eldest daughter, Sansa, makes her way through marriage and political compromise. Illegitimate son, Jon Snow, endures a harrowing time in the "Night Watch" that guards the northern frontier against wild tribes and (later) the zombie-like "nightwalkers," gradually growing in military prowess and stature to become the "King in the North" that leads the opposition to the Lannisters. The youngest daughter, Arya, takes a different bildung journey that leads her to the city of Braavos and an apprenticeship in a guild of assassins called the "Faceless Men," gradually becoming skilled enough to murder a number of her family's enemies. Fourth son, Bran, crippled as a child by the Lannisters, also takes an alternative bildung route, developing his supernatural powers as a "Warg," who is able to control animals. There is another brother, Rickon, who is murdered by one of the Lannister allies. The strongest bildung narratives – the trajectories that move from the lowest beginnings, and grow increasingly in prowess and stature – belong to Jon Snow, Arya, and Bran. Apart from these three Stark children, there are also strong bildung narratives around Daenerys Targaryen, who begins the show as a young girl cast off and defenseless after the death of her father, the former "Mad King," and who survives against the odds among the Dothraki horde, gradually growing in power as the commander of the Dothraki as well as the "unsullied" eunuch-mercenaries that she liberates, and the "mother" of three fire-breathing dragons who obey her commands. Yet another bildung narrative follows Tyrion Lannister, the dwarf youngest son who is rejected by most of his family members, who is on the run after killing his father (who condemns him to be executed), and who rises in fortunes to become the adviser ("Hand") to Daenerys.

"Game of Thrones" thus has a number of different bildung characters – principally the main protagonists and romantic interest Jon Snow and Daenerys, but also Arya, Tyrion, Bran, and other lesser characters – who are differentiated enough to appeal to different audience interests. Each bildung character, in addition to possessing different characteristics and bildung trajectories – from Jon's martial characteristics and trajectory, to Daenerys's nobility of character and her supernatural power over the dragons, to Arya's subterfuge and ruthlessness, to Tyrion's cunning and diplomacy – also pursues their respective bildung story in different landscapes, which become embodiments of their growth and development. Jon, for example, has to prove himself and redeem himself from the stigma of illegitimacy, by surviving the harsh winter environment at "The Wall" and north of it. In contrast, Daenerys' bildung journey from scared and defenseless young girl to the "Khaleesi" (leader of the Dothraki hordes) and "Mother of Dragons" is played out largely in the steppe-like landscape inhabited by the Dothraki, and then in coastal cities like Astapor, Yunkai, and Meereen as she grows in power and stature as a claimant to the throne of Westeros. Arya's journey is perhaps the most diverse in terms of landscapes, from her home in the cold northern fort of Winterfell to the large urban setting of King's Landing through the countryside and highlands, to the city of Braavos, where she learns to become an assassin, and subsequently back up north to Winterfell again. In each case, landscape becomes a symbol for the kind of process of maturation that each protagonist needs: for Jon Snow (perhaps as his name implies), his association with the frozen north (and the wild tribes and the social rejects of the Night Watch associated with it) is a process of finding himself from within, embracing his lot as rejected bastard and building up a role and power base from that isolated and rejected position. For Daenerys, in contrast, her bildung is characterized by wandering and accumulation, as the once-helpless young girl progressively accumulates resources (dragons, Dothraki hordes, the eunuch former mercenaries the "Unsullied," the mercenary band the "Second Sons," Tyrion, Jon Snow, and so on). Accordingly, she moves from hostile steppe, through wasteland, then through richer cities, and then to the island of Dragonstone just off the capital of King's Landing, a progression from emptiness to fullness, from the margins closer to the center of power. For the other main protagonists, their landscape journeys are equally colorful and symbolic, marking their dramatic growth in power and stature against key landscapes.

The significance of landscapes in "Game of Thrones" has not been missed by its fans; just as LOTR created a themed, dualistic tour phenomenon (where tourists saw the landscape as much as that of the films as that of the nation of

New Zealand), so has "Game of Thrones" done for filming locations in Northern Ireland, Iceland, Croatia, and elsewhere. Belfast in Northern Ireland, for example, experienced a pronounced boost in tourism when it marketed itself as the launchpad for coach tours to nearby filming sites. Currently, a large number of Belfast-based tour companies offer Game of Thrones tours. The format of the tours is fundamentally similar to that of LOTR tours in New Zealand: visits to filming sites outside Belfast (mostly in County Antrim and the coast), most of which bear no obvious resemblance to the places they represent in the TV show, but which are imaginatively contextualized by tour guides using verbal narratives of show scenes, linguistic interpellation, and ontological blurring, DVD clips and photo stills of corresponding scenes from the show, show artifacts and replicas, and so on. As with New Zealand (but to a lesser extent), local governments have also cooperated in this identification of the region with show sites, as in this place-sign from Ballintoy Harbor, which features a character from the show (Theon Greyjoy, played by actor Alfie Allen) and identifies this site as standing in for "Pyke Harbor" in the show (Figure 5.3).

Figure 5.3 Sign at Ballintoy Harbor in Northern Ireland. In lieu of the more expected information about the region, the sign merely declared that the site was used for Pyke Harbor in the HBO TV series "Game of Thrones," and featured actor Alfie Allen as Theon Greyjoy

The linguistic features of this affective regime cannot be overlooked. Onomastics feature prominently, with place-names from the TV show preceding or replacing real Irish place-names. One popular tour company even calls itself "Winterfell Tours," after the name of the castle that is the Stark family home in the show. The tour company advertises its tours by (among other things) inviting prospective clients to visit "Winterfell Castle & the tower Bran Stark 'fell' from, Robb's Camp, and Walder Frey's Twins & the savage Red Wedding" (Winterfell Tours "Home"). Again, the place-identification is often so complete that it is difficult for tourists to know where exactly in Ireland they are and what the real place-names are. To reinforce the place-identification, tourists are asked to imagine themselves in the place of the main bildung-protagonists as they undergo their journeys of development; here, imperative verbs, sensory experiences, and references to events and actions from the show predominate. Thus, Winterfell Tours invites clients to "Walk in the footsteps of Tyrion Lannister & Jon Snow" (Winterfell Tours "Home"). As far as possible (and without violating the expectations of truth in advertising), the use of language reinforces the ontological blurring or melding which interpellates visitors into the world of the show: thus, visitors are invited to "come and meet the actual Direwolf dogs from the Game of Thrones tour TV show" (Winterfell Tours "Home"). The Direwolves in the show are mythical creatures, wolves of immense size, and by calling them "Direwolf dogs" the tour company is clearly hedging in order to retain some semblance of truth; nevertheless, the invitation to meet the "actual" Direwolves practices the linguistic effect of ontological blurring that is a key feature of this romance landscape affect.

Other (Nonfantasy) Bildung Narratives and Their Affects

While LOTR and "Game of Thrones" show that the fantasy genre is one of the most compelling sources of bildung narratives and landscape affect in contemporary culture, it is worth noting that other genres can also spawn bildung narratives that lead to landscape affect and tour phenomena.

"Liminal Landscapes" can also be used in popular shows to dramatize a particular kind of bildung journey, with its own landscape affect and tour phenomena. One good example of this would be the Nordic urban landscape of Stieg Larsson's "Millennium" novels, featuring the central figure of Lisbeth Salander. Set largely in contemporary Stockholm, the novels portray the career and development of Lisbeth, a deeply troubled figure who has sociopathological features but is also a genius hacker. Lisbeth is clearly a bildung figure, a young and slightly built girl coming from a deeply dysfunctional background, whose father is a Soviet defector protected by members of a government agency, and who routinely beats Lisbeth's mother and despises the girl. After she sets her father on fire following a particularly brutal beating of her mother,

Lisbeth is committed to a mental institute where the chief psychologist (implicated in the plot to protect Lisbeth's father) abuses her and falsely declares her incompetent. Then assigned to an official guardian as a condition of her release, Lisbeth is brutally raped by the abusive guardian who sees the deeply scarred young girl as easy prey. The original trilogy written by Larsson (there are also to date two follow-up novels by David Lagercrantz) follows a bildung storyline in which Lisbeth struggles to escape the control of her father and his associates, is wrongly accused of the murder of two activists who are killed because their research points accusingly to the same group of people after Lisbeth, manages to kill her father and her psychopathic half-brother, is shot and nearly killed, and is finally exonerated. Along the way, she also uses her hacker skills and contacts to help her friend Mikael Blomkvist and his colleague Erika Berger (investigative reporters with the independent magazine *Millennium)*, and in the process also brings down a number of rich and powerful corporate figures who are guilty of various crimes and attack the *Millennium* crew in order to discredit them and protect themselves.

Deeply mistrustful of others (especially male authority figures), reclusive, and living at the fringes of conventional society (she dresses like a Goth, performs computer crimes, and is bisexual), Lisbeth starts out as a classic victim of a Swedish society seen as authoritarian, corrupt, and materialistic. Over the course of the novels, however, she acquires the resources not just to survive, but to exact revenge on her father and his associates, and by the end of the original trilogy she is exonerated, is extremely wealthy because of a cybertheft she performs in the first novel (committed on one of Blomkvist's enemies), and shows promise of growing in her relationship with at least two individuals, Blomkvist, and Lisbeth's occasional lover Miriam Wu. Lisbeth thus becomes a very attractive figure of contemporary bildung, and one that young single women in particular can identify with. Alienated, oppressed, and victimized (including sexually), she embodies the worst fears of single and vulnerable young women in a patriarchal society. The series also expresses a contemporary version of the bildung romance's indictment of modern society, depicting the trials of Lisbeth and her allies at the hands of a capitalist society characterized by large corporations seemingly untouchable by the law and sponsoring various forms of exploitation and violence. Her bildung trajectory is thus as much a vindication of the (female) underdog as it is a revenge story depicting the downfall of many of those powerful state and corporate oppressors.

So phenomenally successful were the Larsson novels that they inspired not one, but two series of films: one set of the full trilogy in Swedish (produced in collaboration by Yellow Bird and Nordisk Film), and (to date) one English-version film (of the first in the trilogy, *The Girl with the Dragon Tattoo*), a collaboration between Yellow Bird, Metro-Goldwyn-Mayer, and Columbia Pictures and starring Daniel Craig.

Both the novels and the (Swedish) films feature very specific Stockholm locations as the scenes of pivotal action and as the regular haunts of the protagonists. This combination has created a landscape affect among viewers who identify with either Lisbeth or Blomkvist, and who want to experience the Stockholm depicted in the films and novels. So popular is the "Millennium Walking Tour" of Stockholm that Lonely Planet once named it the best of the "Top 10 Literary Walking Tours of the World" (Richards 2014). The draw of this "atmospheric walk" is the opportunity to "relive the drama" and visit sites frequented by Lisbeth and Blomkvist (Richards 2014). The affective dimension of the tour is evident from some of the responses by fan-tourists on sites like TripAdvisor. As we have seen in the LOTR tours, fan-tourists value experiencing the landscape like the bildung protagonists, rather than simply as scenic or interesting sites. Representative of this view is reviewer "WanderfullExplorer," who commends the tour and says that the tour "will remind you of how much you hate Niels Bjurman [the court-appointed guardian who rapes and exploits Lisbeth]," while "JennyT" appreciated the fact that they "walked up and down the streets inhabited by Mikael Blomkvist and Lisbeth Salander" (TripAdvisor "Millennium Walking Tour Reviews"). The language typically used by enthusiastic tourists show the influence of this landscape affect, its ability to (at least temporarily and imaginatively) blur ontological boundaries and pull tourists into the landscape, characters, events, and experiences of the films.

The Stockholm of the Millennium novels and films, as a "liminal" urban landscape, differs in a number of ways from the "wild landscape" that is cultivated in LOTR and "Game of Thrones." "Liminal" landscape affect depends not on the exaggerated sense of scale, grandeur, isolation, and adventure associated with "wild" landscapes, but rather on the sense of a realm hidden within or beneath the everyday façade of a real landscape like Stockholm. Larsson's novels and the films emphasize the sense of a shadowy realm of corruption, patriarchal oppression, and authoritarianism underlying the seemingly peaceful and orderly façade of Swedish society. Lisbeth and Blomkvist are bildung characters who (as it were) descend into this realm (by virtue of being a social outcast-hacker and an investigative reporter, respectively) where they have to grow in strength and power in order to defeat their enemies and, thus, restore some degree of social/moral health to Stockholm and Sweden. While "wild" landscapes, heavily reliant on CGI transformations, are viewed through the dual perspective granted by juxtaposing movie stills on the landscape (Figure 5.2), for fans of "liminal" landscapes such as the Stockholm of the Millennium novels and films the dual perspective comes from imagining the fictional world within the real Stockholm sites that they are seeing: "Jenny T" in her review makes exactly such a dual-perspective juxtaposition when she says:

Spots included Mikael's apartment, Lisbeth's posh new digs, Kaffebar, and the Millennium offices. (Of course, the Millennium books are fiction, so the sites are, respectively, someone else's actual apartment at Bellmansgatan 1, someone else's apartment at Fiskargatan 9, Mellkvist Kaffebar, and third-floor apartments above the actual Greenpeace offices.) (TripAdvisor "Millennium Walking Tour Reviews")

Tourists also enjoy the sense of seeing a (as it were) hidden Stockholm, colored by the moral perspective of Larsson's fictional world. This is an aspect emphasized by the Millennium Tour guides as well, and several reviewers also expressed their pleasure in seeing (through the tour) the "social issues" and "social problems in Swedish society" that they would not otherwise have seen on Stockholm's surfaces (TripAdvisor "Millennium Walking Tour Reviews").

Another popular example of the "liminal" bildung landscape affect is that generated by the "Harry Potter" novels by J. K. Rowling, and the film versions. The "Harry Potter" phenomenon fits the bildung romance pattern in a number of ways: the main protagonist, Harry, is a young boy when the series begins, a social reject and underdog (an orphan, despised and bullied by his nonmagical relatives, the Dursleys). Over the course of the series, Harry discovers his innate magical ability and goes to a school for wizards (Hogwarts), acquiring both friends/allies as well as enemies, and gradually growing in power and stature even as he is opposed by a powerful evil wizard Voldemort and those who are in Voldemort's control. The films reinforced the bildung aspect of the novels by casting then-unknown young actors (Daniel Radcliffe, Emma Watson, Rupert Grint) as Harry and his two friends Hermione and Ron respectively, although a huge cast of older stars (including Maggie Smith, Richard Harris, and Alan Rickman) played supporting roles. The popularity of the novels and films is thus primarily due to the bildung pattern of young and helpless protagonists (played by young and unknown actors in the films) who overcome various obstacles and dangers to finally fulfill their individual destinies and overcome evil.

While the "Millennium" novels, with their darker urban settings and themes of sexual exploitation and abuse of authority, appeal to an adult audience, the "Harry Potter" series is targeted at older children and young adults, among whom it is hugely popular. While the school setting and the youthful protagonists facilitate young readers to insert themselves imaginatively into the series and identify with the protagonists, it is the compelling and complex bildungsroman aspect of the series – the "fuller development of [Harry's] character over a longer period," the parallel development of Ron and Hermione, the "range of issues" raised in this bildung – that helps explain the phenomenal success of Rowling's novels and their films, when compared to similar texts (Pinsent 2002: 50).

Although in some ways akin to LOTR in its use of the fantastical – including many CGI-created landscapes and settings – the "Harry Potter" series is a "liminal" landscape in that it is based on the premise of a magical realm hidden in plain sight within a normal reality that corresponds to our contemporary society. Perhaps the best example of this is the "Platform 9¾," supposedly at London's King's Cross station, which is the embarkation point for the train that takes students to the Hogwarts school of magic. Hidden from the eyes of and inaccessible to "muggles," who do not possess magic, the platform is accessed by Hogwarts students by walking through the brick wall between the station's platforms 9 and 10. Such was the popularity of the novels and films – and the landscape affect it generated – that King's Cross station installed a plaque marking the fictional platform, and later also installed the rear half of a luggage cart seeming to disappear into the wall. The site is now a popular destination for Harry Potter fans, and a Harry Potter-themed shop (also called "Platform 9¾") has opened in King's Cross station. Not surprisingly, the "Harry Potter" series has spawned a large number of tours to film locations and sites which inspired Rowling's novels: there are several competing tours in London and in other locations such as Oxford, Gloucester, Edinburgh, and the Scottish highlands.

The rugged and isolated, and the liminal, types of landscapes seem to generate the strongest landscape affects, as indicated by their widespread commodification in tour products. However, other kinds of landscapes are also employed in popular culture to generate affect. An example of an "exotic" landscape which has generated significant interest in its sites is that in Elizabeth Gilbert's 2006 memoir *Eat, Pray, Love*, and the 2010 film version starring Julia Roberts. A classic bildungsroman documenting Gilbert's journey of self-discovery after a divorce, it features but also caricatures the societies and cultures of Italy, India, and Indonesia (represented by Bali). It also led to considerable interest in those regions on the part of fans of the memoir and the film, and inevitably too the creation of "Eat, Pray, Love" tours and travel advisories to those three sites. Even the less-accessible sites, without many distinctive features, that are used in "isolated" bildung narratives, can generate a considerable landscape affect: the 2000 film *Cast Away*, starring Tom Hanks, turned the hitherto-obscure island of Monuriki in Fiji into a popular tourist destination, while the 2000 film *The Beach*, starring Leonardo DiCaprio, had a similar effect on Maya Bay, a beach on the small island of Koh Phi Phi Leh in Thailand.

The significance of certain media texts in creating massive interest in actual landscape sites cannot be underestimated, and the above examples can easily be multiplied. Not only do these texts spawn a host of competing tours to film locations, but also merchandise (replica costumes, props), themed amusement parts (such as Universal Parks and Resorts' "Wizarding World of Harry Potter," with several locations), Cosplay conventions, and social media sites which in turn generate more interest and momentum. Within this proliferation, two key questions arise: Why do some shows create massive spin-off industries while others do not; and what explains the landscape affect – the shared interest, almost a veneration, for particular landscape sites – that spurs so many fans to travel (often great distances, and at considerable expense) in order to satisfy a strong desire to visit a site associated in their minds with the show? An analysis of strong bildung narratives, and how these affect readers, viewers, and fans, gives us the critical leverage to answer these key questions.

Consuming the Romance Affect: The Nexus of Semiotics and Commodification

The romance affect discussed in this chapter can in many ways be seen as an instantiation of Willis's (1990) "grounded aesthetics," in that it is produced by everyday life, by the creative and imaginative participation of individuals, as opposed to being defined and curated as a "high art." The notion of a "grounded aesthetic" is also relevant in recognizing the key role played by media in disseminating and installing the icons of everyday popular culture. Yet, Willis's notion, based in particular on his work with youths and youth cultural expressions such as hip-hop, fashion, and graffiti, did not adequately emphasize the role of commodification within this process. Similarly, for film- and TV-related tours, complicit and significant in all this is the work of agents like tour companies, merchandisers, Cosplay organizers, and local authorities in translating the narrative impact into experiences for fans. This commodification of the landscape, its packaging as a thing to be consumed by fans eager to experience something (as it were) solid and tangible of their favorite shows, needs to be recognized as the ideological underpinning of the romance affect in landscape. We are reminded of the point made by Thurlow and Jaworski (2011) that tourism plays a crucial mediating role in the ideological consumption of the world and its cultures. What organizes and shapes the individual responses to popular shows into popular tours and highlighted destinations is undeniably a market mechanism which sees the profit potential in this fan demand. Tour agencies are thus the mediators between shows and their fans, creating a way for fans to experience (as it were directly, in the flesh) spatial aspects of their favorite shows, while also extending and propagating the popularity of those shows among existing and new fans. This consumerist mediation is part of the semiotics of the romance affect in landscape: it determines (among other things) the fans' approach to and experience of certain sites, selecting those most easily consumed within the usual tour format (while rejecting others), highlighting certain film scenes for their involvement in the film location (and again rejecting others without that commodifiable involvement), and creating a particular way of seeing the landscape-as-film (and thus also the film-as-landscape). This commodification of experience relates to what is known as the "experience economy" (Lazarus 2017, no page numbers):

The rise of the "experience economy" is currently one of the most important global trends in marketing. Now, more than ever, consumers desire unique, spontaneous, and immersive entertainment wherever they are. They want multisensory experiences, beyond sight and sound. However, they don't want to be restricted to specific venues or times for their entertainment, and crave experiences that say something unique about them, which they can share with their friends and followers.

Thus, Newman (2015), for example, argues:

Consumers seek – and often expect, whether we realize it or not – additional utility from the brands we patronize. We want to feel like they're listening. We don't just want the goods or services, but we want an experience to sweeten the deal.

The intersection between affect and the experience economy constitutes an interesting line of research, and we will say more about this in Chapter 9. For now, we return to our discussion of Ahmed's "affective economy" (see Chapter 2) to reinforce the notion that "emotions work as a form of capital" (2004b: 120) – in the case of the romance affect of certain popular shows, a "form of capital" based on fan desire to identify with and participate in the bildung experiences of their favorite characters. Our discussion nuances Ahmed's theory by extending "affective economy" beyond the emotion of hate and the mechanism of racial-cultural stereotypes. A full understanding of the capital of linguistic resources includes an understanding of how consumption and individual desire circulate, mediated by the profit-oriented agency of production houses, TV companies, tour agencies, and national tourism boards. Landscapes are powerful linguistic and semiotic fields for this form of affective economy, because they proffer an ontological conflation of identities, an imaginative immersion into the experiences, events, and characters of the tourist's favorite shows. While objects and symbols associated with the reel world are crucial to this affective regime, so too is the language of interpellation and belonging, which continually and repeatedly pull the reader/ tourist into the action and experience of the show.

The recognition of the role played by consumerism and commodification is important in any semiotic analysis of the romance landscape affect. We might say that this affect is the product of both "grounded" fan interest and marketing media which intensifies and channels that interest into profitable goods and services. While powerful bildung stories that resonate with contemporary viewers are the necessary foundation for the romance affect, shrewd marketing plays an important role in magnifying particular stories and their consequent impact on certain landscapes.

6   "Friendly Places"

Introduction

We have in the preceding chapters examined the affective regimes found in a number of different sites. Of course, to speak of different sites and their affiliated affective regimes presupposes that there are boundaries demarcating these sites (see Chapter 4). This is not to say that all such boundaries are necessarily established with affective regimes in mind, nor that these boundaries, once established, are hard and unchanging. For example, there are political and physical boundaries that serve to separate nation-states in order to establish their territorialities. These boundaries might then be treated as markers that also serve to distinguish affective regimes on the ideological assumption that each nation-state will have its own distinctive and essential national ethos (e.g. "Malaysia is less regulated and more fun to visit than Singapore"). But the very same boundaries might also then be ignored under yet other circumstances (e.g. "Malaysia and Singapore are both very strict about drugs").

The important thing is to acknowledge the "fictive" nature of boundaries (Beck, in Slater and Ritzer 2001: 266), that is, to appreciate that boundaries are always in the process of being drawn and redrawn using a variety of semiotic resources in order to serve different agendas and purposes. And precisely because the notion of affect is quite intangible, the boundaries of affective regimes are often reliant on other kinds of more tangibly established boundaries.

In this chapter, we therefore address the question of how the limits of affective regimes might be constituted. In other words, we ask the question of how the boundaries demarcating affective regimes might be established. As we have just noted, such boundaries may not have been established with affective regimes specifically in mind. Such boundaries might then be co-opted on the assumption that affective regimes are coterminous with the boundaries that have been established on other bases (as in our nation-state example above). However, there are also clearly attempts to establish particular affective regimes in their own right and such attempts then raise the issue of

how the contours of these intended affective regimes can be materially calibrated with other kinds of more tangible semiotic resources.

To address the abovementioned question, we begin this chapter with demar-
cations of "third places" (Oldenburg 1997, 2000), such as public libraries and
cafes, and how such places aim to cultivate a semiotics of conviviality. We
follow up with a consideration of the post modifier "friendly" and its use in
attempts to publicly signal that certain places are welcoming to particular kinds
of clientele or supportive of particular values (e.g. "pet friendly hotels").
The second half of our chapter then provides a detailed case study of an attempt
in Singapore to create a "dementia friendly" neighborhood. The discussion of
this case study helps brings together the various insights gleaned from our
discussion in the first half of the chapter.

"Third Places" and Affective Regimes of Conviviality

Oldenburg (1997) introduced the term "third place" to distinguish a social
setting that differs from that of the home and of the office. Whereas the
home (or "first place") is typically associated with family and the office (or
"second place") with work, Oldenburg considered as third places those
settings where members of the community might publicly gather so as to
socialize and converse. Because of this, for Oldenburg, third places are
important in fostering a sense of belonging and encouraging civic engage-
ment. Among the characteristics of a third place is that it is a "leveler"
(1997: 24, italics in original):

A place that is a leveler is, by its nature, an inclusive place. It is accessible to the general
public and does not set formal criteria of membership and exclusion. There is a tendency
for individuals to select their associates, friends, and intimates from among those closest
to them in social rank. Third places, however, serve to *expand* possibilities, whereas
formal associations tend to narrow and restrict them.

Examples of third places include libraries, cafes, parks, and community centers. In third places, face-to-face interactions are facilitated in an atmosphere
that can be situated somewhere between the more intimate and personal nature
of family interactions, on the one hand, and the more impersonal and formal
nature of work-based obligations and responsibilities, on the other. Oldenburg
(1997: 56–57, italics added) in fact likens interactions in third places to
encounters with "commended strangers":

Many among the regulars of a third place are like Emerson's "commended stranger"
who represents humanity anew, who offers a new mirror in which to view ourselves, and
who thus breathes life into our conversation. In the presence of the commended stranger,
wrote Emerson, "We talk better than we are wont. We have the nimblest fancy, a richer
memory, our dumb devil has taken leave for a time. For long hours, we can continue

a series of sincere, graceful, rich communications, drawn from the oldest, secretest experience, so that those who sit by, of our kinsfolk, and acquaintance, shall feel a lively surprise at our unusual power."

The magic of commended strangers fades as one comes to know them better. They are fallible. They have problems and weaknesses like everyone else and, as their luster fades, so does their ability to inspire our wit, memory, and imagination. *The third place, however, retards that fading process, and it does so by keeping the lives of most of its regulars disentangled. One individual may enjoy the company of others at a mutual haunt for years without ever having seen their spouses; never having visited their homes or the places where they work; never having seen them against the duller backdrop of their existence on the "outside."*

Third places, then, are places defined primarily in terms of affective regimes even though Oldenburg does not himself use the phrase. They are supposed to be places where there is a sufficient sense of being welcomed and accepted so as to be considered "commended strangers." This sense of welcome should not be so intimate that "commended strangers" come to acquire the kinds of familiarity that family members might assume with one another or the impersonal professionalism that workplace colleagues might share with one another[1].

Of course, the kinds of activities that are considered appropriate to libraries, cafes, and parks all differ. Consequently, interpretations about what it means to be a "commended stranger" have to be relativized and tailored to the expectations of appropriateness for these different places. For example, libraries are places where silence is generally expected and jogging or walking of dogs disallowed. The converse holds for parks. Nevertheless, these are all places that are, ideally, welcoming and comfortable, not expensive to patronize, and accessible to individuals from diverse social backgrounds (Oldenburg 1997: xviii, xxv) – which is what qualifies them all as third places.

A key concern in third places is to try to ensure that diversity is properly managed so that conflicts are minimized and, where possible, avoided. This makes it important to understand the ways in which conviviality is being theorized since such scholarly interventions do contribute to understandings

---

[1] Given the rise of social media, there is an interesting question as to whether third places can be virtual. Butler and Diaz (2016), for example, have suggested: "For young Americans, many third places are now virtual – from Facebook and chat rooms to group texts." Oldenburg (2015: 28), in contrast, has suggested they cannot:

Third places are face-to-face phenomena. The idea that electronic communication permits a virtual third place is misleading. "Virtual" means that something is like something else in both essence and effect, and that's not true in this instance. When you go to a third place you essentially open yourself up to whoever is there. And they may be very different from you. If you don't know your neighbors, you will be suspicious. And if you are suspicious, you will act accordingly. You don't get neighborly on that basis. If you spend time with people you're not going to hate them, it's just that simple.

We will address this question in Chapter 8.

of how public spaces can be made more accommodating to inhabitants coming from highly diverse backgrounds. As Nowicka and Vertovec (2014: 350) emphasize in their introduction to the special issue of the *European Journal of Cultural Studies*:

All in all, conviviality increasingly appears in the context of normative concerns with how to make spaces more positively interactive, or conversely how spaces might become more convivial through everyday practices and routines of people inhabiting them. However, conviviality offers more than just a descriptive category that captures the modes of peaceful and happy togetherness. The authors concerned with conviviality increasingly see the concept as a potential alternative to the notions that derive from the debates on community cohesion, inclusion, and integration (and their dichotomous "other": conflict, exclusion, dissolution); conviviality emerges here as a remedy to public and political discourse on multicultural societies and cosmopolitan world order.

Articulating what is meant by conviviality as a theoretical construct, especially if this is intended to serve as a "potential alternative" to other notions concerned with analyzing community relations, requires moving beyond "modes of peaceful and happy togetherness" (Nowicka and Vertovec 2014: 350). The results, however, are multiple and sometimes contested attempts at specifying how best to think of conviviality in order to take advantage of its theoretical potential. For example, Gilroy (2004, 2006) attempts to contrast conviviality with multiculturalism and to propose instead the notion of a multiculture. Gilroy's argument is that a problem with the concept of multiculturalism is that it takes as given racial, linguistic, religious, and other differences, and it further assumes that such differences represent boundaries that need to be negotiated, crossed, or accommodated. In Gilroy's view, this leads to the reification of what are in actuality highly changeable cultural constructs, and it lends these constructs unnecessary power to adversely influence community relations by foregrounding differences as potential flashpoints. Gilroy's suggestion is that if conviviality is to provide a constructive way of thinking about diversity, it cannot and should not begin with accepting unwarranted reifications. Instead, in contrast to multiculturalism (at least as this has been defined by Gilroy), the notion of conviviality should accept that "different metropolitan groups dwell in close proximity ... [but their differences] do not ... add up to discontinuities of experience or insuperable problems of communication" (Gilroy 2006: 27). Gilroy's (2004: xi) own preference is to think instead in terms of a "multiculture," and he makes the suggestion that conviviality should be understood as "the processes of cohabitation and interaction that have made multiculture an ordinary feature of urban life in Britain."

But the problem with Gilroy's position – even if he does not intend it – is that it goes too far in downplaying or disregarding the fact that recognizing and celebrating multiculturalism *qua* bounded cultural, ethnic, and linguistic differences can also contribute to a sense of inclusivity (Kymlicka 1995, 2007; Parekh 2000). That is, there are in fact times when multiculturalism of the kind where discontinuities and boundaries are highlighted may in fact be appropriate or even necessary. Just because boundaries are fictive does not mean that they are any less important. For example, as McDermott (2012: 187) points out in his discussion of Northern Ireland's two largest cities, Belfast and Derry/Londonderry, for linguistic and cultural minorities, community festivals and arts projects that highlight and celebrate their specific identities can be important ways in which "higher levels of inclusion and accessibility to urban spaces" are created for such communities. While acknowledging that such activities still remain contentious because opponents do claim that they "contribute to the creation of division, rather than the promotion of cohesion" (McDermott 2012: 193) – a point that Gilroy is rightly concerned about in his critical remarks about multiculturalism – McDermott (2012: 194–195) nevertheless notes that they have had beneficial effects in both fostering a greater sense of belonging among minorities and promoting a general interest in and appreciation of a city's social and cultural diversity:

One of the most prominent ways that migrant communities have established their visibility in city spaces is through open-air festival events and arts projects. These often celebrate a particular cultural or religious period of importance for migrant communities, or may simply be an attempt to showcase the community's culture, literature and language, music or dance. Festivals, therefore, provide an important alternative to the narrative which sees migrants "in terms of social problems – needing housing, education, language teaching, health provision, and so on." (Khan 2007: 4)

One example of a festival that has been supported includes the Belfast Mela, which has attracted over 60,000 visitors in its first four years of operation and which is organized by members of the Indian community. The aim has been to celebrate South-Asian identity and language but also to promote cross-cultural learning by "promoting a large number of cultures through the arts" (Belfast Mela 2011). Likewise, the Chinese community has benefitted from public funding for annual events like the dragon boat race held on the River Lagan in central Belfast and the Chinese New Year celebrations held in St George's Market, a well-known cultural space in the city which was renovated in the early years of the peace process.

As McDermott (2012: 195) emphasizes:

[F]estivals such as those described above are so important for linguistic minorities for their ability to make individuals feel comfortable to converse in their heritage language in a public place, which is not always possible. This is an important role considering that in some locations migrants feel uneasy when speaking their first language publicly and therefore is totally in keeping with the theme of shared and neutral space.

It is an exclusionary fallacy if conviviality has to be interpreted only in terms of multiculture and not multiculturalism. Conviviality has to be construed in broad enough terms so as to encompass the two. This is because when individuals from diverse backgrounds come together, there is a need to accept and understand the differences that give rise to the diversity in the first place while also being willing to change the boundaries that mark these differences where necessary.

For similar reasons, some scholars (Sengstock 2009; Suryadinata 2015; Yuval-Davis 1994, among others) insist on a hyphenated "multi-culturalism" as opposed to "multiculturalism," in order to call attention to the plurality that persists in such societies, and that must be deliberately overcome by convivial, intercultural actions and regimes. We will continue to use the term "multiculturalism," but acknowledge the relevance of the hyphenated "multi-culturalism" as a reminder of the inevitable seams and joins of a plural society that need to be actively negotiated and overcome. The point therefore is not to contrast conviviality with multiculturalism as though one precludes the other. Rather, it is to treat multiculturalism as but one of many possible ways of demonstrating conviviality. By drawing attention to the multicultural nature of a city's population and emphasizing that conscious and concerted efforts do need to be made in making minority communities feel welcome, urban spaces can indeed become more accommodating to diversity.

Unlike Gilroy, who works from a general conceptual level by critically evaluating the relationships between conviviality, multiculturalism, and multi-culture, Amin (2012) adopts an understanding of conviviality that draws specific attention to the ways in which urban spaces are designed, and which is therefore of especial relevance to the study of semiotic landscapes. As Nowicka and Vertovec (2014: 348) point out, "Amin distances himself from thinking of conviviality wholly in terms of social inclusion and cultural recognition, but he also diverges from Gilroy's understanding of conviviality as a virtue of everyday encounters with multicultural otherness."

Amin's (2012: 6) interest lies in recognizing "the bodies, objects, technologies, legacies, ideas, and imaginaries – tensely held together in relational space – that shape the affective proximities of humans to their worlds and with each other." For Amin (2012: 79–80),

Across these spaces, the task for a politics of togetherness is to make the connections and dependencies visible, to reveal the value of a shared and functioning commons, to show how life chances depend upon an urban infrastructure capable of accommodating new demands and new claimants, to argue the necessity of an open and dissenting urban public sphere, to show that to damage the commons is to damage the self and future possibility.

Unfortunately, in trying to argue that "affective proximities" can be shaped by urban infrastructure, Amin (2012: 73) comes dangerously close to treating city inhabitants as unsuspecting and manipulable actors[2]:

[2] In this regard, Ahmed (2004a: 44), too, seems to adopt the same view as Amin when she suggests, "What is repressed from consciousness is not the feeling as such, but the idea to which the feeling may have been first (but provisionally) connected."

Such resonances of situated multiplicity, always specific to a given ecology of urban co-presence, influence human behavior in quite profound ways by stimulating particular social reflexes of adaptation. The swirls of multiplicity, the rhythms of territorialization, the regulation of surprise, and the aesthetics of space all temper public feelings by working on the senses in a silent way. Awareness of this agency suggests the necessity of a different approach to public space as the ground of conviviality, one that must acknowledge the limits to human recognition in the city's streets, malls, libraries, parks, and buses. It points, for example, to interventions that attend to the resonances of multiplicity, its compliances and compromises, and its ominous tendencies (such as the uncontrolled crowd colonized by the powerful and menacing).

Certainly Amin is right that urban infrastructure is often designed with the aim of "tempering public feelings." However, it is his tendency to overplay the influence of the environment and, conversely, to underplay the agency and reflexive awareness of city inhabitants that Barnett (2012) objects to when he suggests that Amin

provides a general account of how social action is more often than not shaped by pre-conscious, embodied, subliminal dynamics rather than rational, deliberative ones. The uncritical reiteration of the dualisms that define contemporary affect theory allows Amin to develop a strong claim about the link between built and designed infrastructures and the enactment of social relations. Built environments, technologies, and media function to inculcate a "collective unconscious" that works on people's actions through subliminal factors and by triggering reflexes.

. . .

This understanding of affect and materiality informs a working concept of the political as a surface of manipulation, in which various "silent fixes" are embedded behind people's backs.

In Barnett's view, Amin assumes too strong a link between the design of infrastructure and the way in which social relations are realized, the former apparently exerting a subliminal effect on human behavior. Amin, like Gilroy, commits, or comes close to committing, an exclusionary fallacy. His focus on social action as the result of "pre-conscious, embodied, subliminal dynamics rather than rational, deliberative ones" ignores the many instances where highly conscious strategies are employed in order to foster conviviality (see the examples below). A more moderate position that emphasizes the importance of urban spaces while refraining from overestimating the ability of such spaces to manipulate or control patterns of social interaction is therefore needed. In this regard, it is worth noting that the artist and cultural critic Suely Rolnik, in a conversation with the artistic director of dOCUMENTA (13), Carolyn Christov-Bakargiev, prefers to define conviviality as the "human capacity to relate to the world" (Nowicka and Vertovec 2014: 347):

[C]onviviality is not about collaboration between people but about their capacity to be affected by the world which precedes them acting to transform what she terms "carto-graphy of togetherness."

... For Rolnik, conviviality is meaningful as it reminds us that it is not possible to prescribe ways of experiencing; Christov-Bakargiev, then, added that we ought not to forget that we may design spaces and expect particular effects, but we cannot control how togetherness happens.

Here, both Rolnik and Christov-Bakargiev are keen to emphasize that how spaces are designed can help facilitate a sense of togetherness, even as they caution us against trying to prescribe and control the specific forms that such togetherness might take. That is, while there is undoubtedly a normative dimension to conviviality (Nowicka and Vertovec 2014: 324), since the overall goal – despite the many ways in which the notion can be understood and manifested – is to instill a sense of peacefulness and social order in public spaces, whether or not such order emerges and what form it actually takes cannot be regulated, much less expected, to follow in a simple causal relation from design principles. Thus, the actual form that conviviality takes will vary according to circumstances and the roles of the participants. Space design is an important factor that cannot be ignored but whose influence must not be over-estimated. Being convivial to close friends and family members in an intimate setting is clearly different than being convivial to strangers in various public settings. Being convivial to tourists, migrants *qua* minority community, fellow citizens – these also involve different manifestations of conviviality.

Accepting this wide variance in manifestations of conviviality is therefore necessary. We need to recognize that, depending on the circumstances, what counts as conviviality can range from merriment to sociability to hospitality and even to what Goffman (1972: 385) describes as civil inattention, where strangers put on a show of intentional disregard in order to demonstrate respect for each other's privacy and autonomy. In fact, Cameron (2000) nicely shows that excessive attempts at being convivial can be disconcerting for the parties involved. In her discussion of how Walmart attempts to makes its customers feel welcome, Cameron (2000: 57) notes that employees are obligated by the company to smile, make eye contact, and utter a greeting "every time a customer comes within ten feet of me." This is an interactional routine that employees are expected to enact (bringing to mind Hochschild's display rules), and it is problematic for them because they are seen by customers as being unnecessarily friendly and the female employees, in particular, have to worry about inadvertently encouraging unwanted attention from male customers. It is also problematic for the customers, who oftentimes find it distracting to be greeted over and over again each time they encounter an employee. Having said this, it should be noted that regimes of conviviality will vary according to sociocultural and spatial contexts: something of the Walmart heartiness of greeting and closeness of attention would be less obtrusive and even expected in a Japanese restaurant, where diners expect to be greeted with a loud "*irasshaimase!*" when they enter, and where convivial dining often means sitting practically shoulder-to-shoulder with other diners at the counter or at tables. The point is that even in these varied manifestations of conviviality, each has an appropriate code of behavior that is structured and prescribed.

Given that conviviality is a phenomenon that many theorists agree ought to be fostered, what appears to be common across the various attempts at articulating conviviality is that it is construed as a form of affect, specifically a positive (as opposed to neutral or negative) orientation toward those others who happen to be sharing the same environment. Conviviality cannot, *qua* theoretical construct, therefore be reduced to the specific kinds of feeling and display rules that Hochschild (1979, 1983) refers to. That would be a serious conceptual mistake. This is because, even assuming that such rules could be specified without running the risk of unduly concretizing them, the rules would be both too numerous and varied so that we end up losing any hope of capturing any commonality. Instead, what appears to be common across the various attempts at articulating the notion of conviviality is a form of positive (as opposed to neutral or negative) orientation toward others sharing the same environment. This positive orientation applies regardless of whether it involves the highly conscious acknowledgment of diversity that comes under rubric of multiculturalism, the more "ordinary" kinds of interactions associated with multiculture, the right of hospitality that Benhabib argues ought to be extended to aliens, residents, and citizens, or the more mundane and day-to-day negotiations of urban multiplicities.

However, it is not sufficient to speak of conviviality as a specific kind of affect such as positive orientation. Especially if the goal is to understand conviviality's role in public space interaction, we then need to interrogate how the design and structuring of public space may be aimed at fostering this positive affect. This is the focus of the next section.

The Semiotics of Conviviality: "Friendly Places"

We have seen that the boundaries of affective regimes tend to be based on boundaries already established using physical and other spatial markers. Third places such as cafes, parks, or libraries are no exceptions since the physical boundaries of these places help to delimit the associated affective regimes. But let us now consider further how the affective regimes in such places might be sustained.

In this regard, we start with the simple observation that the design of urban spaces in order to foster conviviality includes the use of language in public signage. Many such signs are preemptive in nature, or, to be more precise, these signs aim to encourage social practices or behaviors that are intended to ensure that the inhabitants of shared public spaces do not end up antagonizing one another. By encouraging some behaviors and discouraging other behaviors, the goal is also to preempt the possibility of conflict in the shared public space. Consider the following examples, all taken from various locations within the same public library in Singapore:

(1) Feeling tired? Please refrain from sleeping in the library. Let's make this library delightful for all.

(2) Be considerate.
Everyone wants a quiet place to read.

(3) Be considerate.
Share the library materials and facilities. Sleep at home, not in the library.

(4) Be considerate.
Please do not reserve seats.

(5) This area is under CCTV surveillance.

Notice the constant refrain to "Be considerate" (in 2–4). While (1) does not use the word "considerate," it does request that patrons ensure that the library is "delightful for all." (2) provides a more specific rationale: that the library should be a place where reading can be done without distraction. (3) and (4) highlight specific social practices that are encouraged (sharing of materials and facilities) as well as discouraged (sleeping on the premises and reserving seats) in order to help realize this pleasantness. Finally, (5) is simply information that the library premises are monitored by closed-circuit television (CCTV), which therefore also serves as a warning that antisocial behavior could be recorded.

Needless to say, altercations sometimes occur – either between patrons or between patrons and staff – and this is where (5), with its warning of surveillance, becomes useful. The increasingly ubiquitous CCTV is a modern-day version of the Panopticon (Foucault 1984). As Elliot (2009: 73–74) points out, for Foucault, the Panopticon and its "element of surveillance of central control" represents a "structure of domination" that is "at work in more and more modern organizations, such as mental asylums, schools, hospitals, and the military and secret services ... power is imposed upon people through the bureaucratic surveillance of populations, the routine gathering of information, and the continual monitoring of daily life." The effectiveness of the Panopticon stems from the fact that individuals do not know when they are actually being monitored. This uncertainty encourages a particular kind of conduct (Foucault 1984), where individuals, it is assumed, are more likely than not to conform to the behavioral norms desired by the central monitoring organization or the individual in authority, especially if there are clear rewards for conformity and strong punitive measures for resistance. The surveillance here relies on and, indeed, makes use of the individuals' capacities as reflexive agents who can be expected to self-regulate (Foucault 1984: 221). As time goes by, this self-regulation may even result in individuals internalizing the externally imposed

Figure 6.1 Library sign requesting that patrons refrain from sleeping

norms so that the reliance on external controls becomes less critical. Here, then, in the location of the library, we have attempts to emplace a specific affective regime, one that aims to maximize everyone's enjoyment of the library and its facilities by consistently emphasizing the importance of being considerate. This affective regime is emplaced via a combination of resources, such as the use of public signs, surveillance cameras, and, where necessary, the physical intervention of library staff (who may, for example, ask misbehaving patrons to leave the library's premises).

Here is another example. According to Moss (2013):

Figure 6.2 Library sign emphasizing need for quiet

In 2010, the problem of dog excrement was one of America's biggest gripes, according to a survey by Consumer Reports. But despite posted signs, HOA regulations, and looks of disapproval from passersby, some dog owners just don't clean up after their pets.

Some of the signs that attempt to get Americans to pick up after their dogs are shown below:[3]

---

[3] Dog Poop Signs on Pinterest; www.pinterest.com/susantimko58/dog-poop-signs/; accessed February 22, 2015.

(6) Please be a good neighbor. Clean up after your dog.

(7) Please pick up after your dog.

The preemptive nature of these signs is especially clear from (6), where, similar to the appeal to being considerate in the library signs, the appeal here is to being a good neighbor. As Moss's statement above points out, there are often looks of disapproval from passersby. The hope then is that if dog owners conscientiously pick up after their pets, unhappiness from others who live in the vicinity won't boil over into actual arguments. (Of course, Moss also observes that some dog owners simply don't bother to cooperate.)

In both of these examples, specific social practices are being encouraged on the basis that these are behaviors that would be expected of individuals who are considerate or neighborly. Of course, it might be argued that the behaviors being encouraged do not always have a direct connection with conviviality. To this, we want to point out that the appeal to being considerate or neighborly makes the connection with conviviality very clear. The behaviors being encouraged are not arbitrary. They are selected on the specific basis that they are relevant to their respective sites and their contraventions can make the use of these publicly shared spaces unpleasant for other individuals. And conversely, observing the prescribed behavioral practices can help to preempt or at least minimize tensions or arguments. In this regard, it is assumed that if all users of the public spaces in question were to adopt the encouraged practices, this would help to create the conditions that might be described as convivial in the sense that strangers in public spaces such as libraries, or even neighbors sharing access to parks or sidewalks, can afford to engage in civil inattention (Goffman 1972) without tension or resentment.

Preemption works by signaling just what kinds of affective regimes are being emplaced in a particular site and, thus, what kinds of behaviors are expected or considered appropriate to the site in question. Visitors to the site are forewarned via such preemptive signaling and can be reasonably expected (at least from the perspective of the authorities managing the site) to either respect the emplaced affective regime or simply avoid the site altogether.

One interesting preemption signal is the use of "friendly" as a post-modifier, as shown in the examples below.

(8) "Bring Fido," www.bringfido.com/lodging/; accessed November 2, 2017: Top pet friendly hotels worldwide.

No matter where you're going, BringFido.com can help you find a pet friendly hotel for the trip. Our directory includes more than 25,000 hotels, bed & breakfasts, vacation rentals, campgrounds, and long-term apartments that welcome pets in more than 54 countries worldwide.

(9) "What to expect from a gay friendly hotel,' Hotels.com, www.hotels.com /articles/ar015478/gay-friendly-hotels-47110/; accessed November 2, 2017:

A good gay friendly hotel should be clean and have a relaxed and friendly attitude. There should be no expectations of you to have a certain style of dress and no problems with overnight visitors. The hotel should also be easy to find and not hide the fact that it is gay friendly. Also, the hotel should be a reasonable size with comfortable rooms with all the amenities you need, instead of being small and dingy. **Easy to make new friends** Another thing to look for in a gay friendly hotel is that it is easy to meet fellow guests from the LGBT community. This way if you come alone you won't have to look like you have no friends when you hit the bars and clubs.

(10) "TGV Cinemas," www.tgv.com.my/cinemas/halls/family-friendly.html; accessed November 2, 2017:

For the uninitiated, the TGV Cinemas Family Friendly sessions are our one-of-a-kind movie screening sessions in which we invite families with toddlers and the like to enjoy their favorite film whilst allowing their kids to run about and play to their hearts' content.

Such "friendly" places are a type of third place in that they are public places where individuals who do not necessarily know each other can gather on the basis of some shared interest or lifestyle values. The variable "X" in the "X friendly" construction (Fillmore, Kay, and O'Connor 1988; Goldberg 1995) signals the specific type of values or interests that the place happens to be supportive of. It is because of the presumption that there are shared interests/ lifestyles that the individuals are all "commended strangers" to one another. Thus, hotels that are "pet friendly," for example, are for pet owners who want to travel with their animal companions. The hotels welcome the pets, and guests of such hotels are expected to enjoy being around animals. Conversely, a guest who complains about the presence of a pet (notwithstanding cases where the animals are either badly behaved or cannot get along with one another) would be told to find a different hotel, one where pets are not welcome, that is, one that is *not* "pet friendly." And as an even more specific type of pet friendly, there are also cat cafes. These are cat-themed cafes where patrons can interact with cats while enjoying a cup of coffee or a slice of cake (Thoufeekh 2017).

The same considerations apply, *mutatis mutandis*, to (9) and (10). (9) specifies that hotels that are "gay friendly" should be "relaxed and friendly," neither impose particular dress codes nor have prohibition against visitors who want to stay overnight. Of course, such specifics may be disputed by other websites or other hotels that also claim to be "gay friendly." For example, there appears to be no contradiction in a hotel that states it is "gay friendly" while still insisting on particular dress codes. Varying interpretations of what it actually means to be "X friendly" are only to be expected given that indexical fields do shift. Finally, (10) is interesting because in addition to spatial boundaries being established (that of the physical confines of the cinema), the intended affective regimes also involve temporal boundaries, where the "Family Friendly" sessions occur only during the times that have been specifically set aside for such sessions. This is not particularly surprising since a given authority that is in charge of a particular site, such as a cinema or library, for that matter, may decide to divide the site into more specific zones where different affective regimes are emplaced. So, just as a cinema may have different times allotted to "Family Friendly" sessions, a library may also have some rooms and times allotted to activities that allow participants to speak without worrying about bothering others who may be present (e.g. a storytelling session for children and a guest author discussing her latest book). What is more interesting, however, is not so much the subdivisions within an already-demarcated site but, instead, what happens when a site attempts to expand its affective regime outside any established confines.

We will address this matter of the expansion of an affective regime below in our discussion of dementia-friendly neighborhoods. For now, though, we wish to point out that there is also a significant caveat that needs to be issued in treating such "friendly" places as third places. Such places are constructed specifically to cater to particular types of communities: parents with young kids ("Family Friendly"), members of the LGBTQ community ("gay friendly"), and pet owners and animal lovers ("pet friendly"). Consequently, as more such "X friendly" third places come to be constructed, the valuing of social diversity which inspired Oldenburg's original formulation of the third place is in danger of being lost. This is because patrons are expected to embrace or support the values signaled by "X as a pre-condition for entering the 'X friendly' place." Interestingly, Oldenburg (2015: 28) himself seems to not be too perturbed by such developments, if his recent comments are anything to go by:

The biggest surprise is that the business world picked up on them. Corporations used to believe that the longer they could keep each employee at the desk, the more productive they'd be. That's just been shot to pieces. Managers found out that if they let people work where they want and when they want, productivity went up. The marketplace is highly competitive and it's important to be first with new innovations. If you get people sitting together, talking together, innovation comes quicker. And I think that's going to be the thing for business and industry for a long time.

But if third places are being appropriated by corporations for the specific purpose of improving productivity and encouraging innovation, then Oldenburg's original notion of a third place as somewhere that is (i) distinct from family and work (especially the latter) and (ii) open to a socially diverse range of individuals is already being lost. Indeed, the notion of a third place has become something of a buzzword in the corporate world, and Starbucks apparently at one time even asked Oldenburg to endorse its cafes as "third places" – a request which he declined (Oldenburg 2015). This is an indexical shift (Silverstein 2003; see also Chapter 2) in the understanding of a third place, as the concept moves – via Giddens's (1987: 18) notion of a double hermeneutic, where social-scientific and humanities concepts get appropriated by the subjects of study themselves – from its scholarly origins to the public domain as a result of its popularization. In the course of this popularization, Oldenburg's third place has become something of a status symbol, something that organizations aspire toward having. But precisely because it is now a feature that organizations want to be able to boast having, it is now being employed to describe places that different organizations are creating so as to cater to their particular stakeholders, as evidenced by the various uses of the post-modifier "friendly." The corporations that encourage their employees to "work where they want and when they want" (Oldenburg, see above) are essentially appropriating the "third place" and subsuming it under the "second place" of work because the motive for these businesses, as even Oldenburg himself admits, is to improve productivity and to be more competitive. Likewise, the businesses that advertise themselves as "X friendly" are targeting particular kinds of clientele, which is in fact a branding strategy along the lines of "compassionate consumption" (Richey and Ponte 2011). These shifts in how third places are viewed mean that the concept is no longer interpreted in as inclusive or socially diverse a manner as Oldenburg originally envisioned. Increasingly, the notion of a third place is becoming commodified, if not actually fetishized, as a way of catering to a specific group of consumers. And it does this by explicitly asserting the specific and even specialized affective regime that it wants to be seen as supporting.

This commodification of third places also relates to a theme from Chapter 5, where we noted that digital technology cannot and should not be viewed as carving out a cyber landscape that is consistently and rigidly separate from physical reality. With third places becoming appropriated for work and with the widespread use of social media, communication is increasingly digitalized. The conveniences that are often touted as a major reason for adopting digital technology are motivated on the basis that they facilitate activities and interactions in physical reality. And this then brings us to the question of how the semiotics of affective regimes in third places might be impacted by digital technology, an issue that we elaborate on in Chapter 9.

Dementia-Friendly Neighborhoods: The Case of Yishun

As we have pointed out (see Chapter 2), the notion of an affective regime is amenable to analysis at multiple scales, at the level of the city as well as below and above. And in the examples that were discussed earlier in the present chapter, we have encountered affective regimes that are delimited to the confines of particular sites such as that of a library or a cinema, and even further delimited in smaller divisions within those sites such as a particular room or session. At the same time, we have also encountered affective regimes that emphasize conviviality and neighborliness that occur not only within delimited locations such as a public park but also extend beyond it to the general neighborhood (a vaguely defined notion with no clearly established boundaries). This is why it is theoretically more important to focus on affective regimes rather than feeling rules or cultural scripts when we are studying the semiotic landscape.

But as we also pointed out earlier, establishing subdivisions within the confines of a given site is less of an issue since the governing authority in charge of the site may easily decide to dedicate different subareas and times to different kinds of activities. More interesting, conceptually, is the question of how affective regimes emanating from different groups might come to be "stitched" together in order to expand their reach or scope. This is a point that we now develop in our discussion of dementia-friendly neighborhoods, giving especial focus to the Singapore neighborhood of Yishun.

In 2016, the Lien Foundation, a philanthropic organization, and Khoo Teck Puat Hospital (KTPH) started the Forget Us Not initiative, aimed at turning Yishun, a neighborhood located in the northeast region of Singapore, into a dementia-friendly estate. The following extract, from a document prepared by the Lien Foundation, outlines the rationale for this initiative as well as some of the ways in which the conversion is being carried.

The rise of persons with dementia (PWD) is a wave sweeping aging societies like Singapore. Today, it is estimated that one in ten people aged 60 years and above have dementia . . .

But with a supportive dementia friendly community, a significant number of PWDs will be able to avoid institutionalization and live in their own homes.

To this end, the Lien Foundation and Khoo Teck Puat Hospital (KTPH) are fostering in Yishun a community that understands, embraces, and supports PWDs and their carers. Their joint *Forget Us Not* initiative reaches out to people from all walks of life. It aims to de-stigmatize and improve awareness of dementia, improve acceptance of PWDs, and foster dementia-friendly communities where PWDs are valued and active contributors to society.

Urging Singaporeans to get dementia-friendly, CEO of Lien Foundation Mr Lee Poh Wah said, "Because of its prevalence and high cost to society, we need to make dementia friendly communities the "new normal" in Singapore, starting with Yishun – which has an elderly population and established network of support from KTPH." . . .

Fast-aging countries like the UK, Taiwan, Japan, and Australia have since developed "dementia friendly communities" to support PWDs and their families . . . These communities have public education drives on dementia, a strong physical network of supporters amongst individuals and across the civic, government, and private sectors, and supporting resources at hand for PWDs and their families. (Lien Foundation 2016: 1–2)

The extract makes clear that there is concern with how to provide help and a dignified lifestyle for individuals suffering from dementia, a concern that many aging societies are dealing with. The ultimate goal is for the entire country of Singapore to become as dementia friendly as possible. But the initiative is making a start by focusing its initial efforts on the community of Yishun because this is a community with a large elderly population but one that also already has institutionalized support from the local hospital.

The vision, then, is to create a dementia-friendly affective regime first in Yishun and to follow this, hopefully, with the establishment of similar affective regimes in other communities in Singapore so that at some point the entire country can be said to be dementia friendly. Whether such a goal will actually be realized is, of course, difficult to predict. But what is of interest here is that we are looking at attempts at expanding the coverage of an affective regime beyond the physical boundaries of locations that organizations like the Lien Foundation or KTPH themselves might have under their direct purview.

The point of a dementia-friendly community is to ensure, as far as is possible, that persons suffering from dementia are able to move freely and comfortably in public community spaces rather than being confined to their homes or to institutionalized care. To achieve this, the Forget Us Not initiative has mustered the support of more individuals and businesses in the Yishun area, inviting them to educational talks on dementia and training sessions conducted by KTPH:

Today, over 6,000 people and businesses have participated in educational talks on dementia and training sessions held by KTPH in the last six months. They come from Yishun and other parts of Singapore, and represent all walks of life and society, from local businesses to MNCs – like North Point Shopping Centre, Capitol Optical, and McDonald's; students from the National University of Singapore and Nanyang Polytechnic; and religious organizations like Evangel Family Church and Darul Makmur Mosque. Also to come on board are organizations such as Sheng Siong Supermarket, the National Library Board, and People's Association. ("Forget Us Not," Lien Foundation 2016: 2–3; accessed November 5, 2017)

Thus, some of the participating businesses include shopping malls, fast-food chains, educational institutions, libraries, and religious organizations. Also, the staff from the call center of KTPH and the Yishun Community Hospital, as well as their security personnel, have all undergone training in dementia. And the Yishun North Neighborhood Police Centre has also been involved: residents who are part of the Citizens-on-Patrol organization have been trained to detect, respond, and assist PWDs should they come across these individuals. According to Dr. Philip Yap, director of KTPH's Geriatric Centre ("Forget Us Not," Lien Foundation 2016: 3; accessed November 5, 2017):

Figure 6.3 Street shot of the Yishun community

With everyone chipping in, we hope Yishun will be a place where PWDs (persons with dementia) feel included, respected, and valued. Here, they can get around safely and continue to participate meaningfully in their usual routines because members of their community, be it a favorite neighbor, shopkeeper, or local police-man, can understand and assist them. Having such community support is a boost for PWDs and their families. It can help PWDs age in place and continue to stay plugged into society.

Fostering and sustaining a relatively new affective regime such as a dementia-friendly community requires ongoing efforts. As part of this, the Forget Us Not initiative is also relying on social media to build public support. Members of the public are asked to sign up as "Dementia Friends," where they will receive a handbook on dementia containing information on how to identify some of the common symptoms and what to do should one encounter a PWD. Dementia Friends are also encouraged to become "advocates for Singapore to become a dementia-friendly community" ("Forget Us Not," Lien Foundation 2016: 4). Thus, we see attempts being made to also expand the scope of the affective regime beyond Yishun. In this regard, some students from a local polytechnic have "planned to expand their outreach to Ang Mo Kio, and recruit more Dementia Friends" ("Forget Us Not," Lien Foundation 2016: 5).

To further expand the reach of a dementia-friendly neighborhood to cover as far as possible the entire country, the Agency for Integrated Care (which comes under the Ministry of Health) has pushed for a Dementia Friendly Singapore initiative ("Singapore Silver Pages"; accessed November 8, 2017):

Dementia Friendly Singapore seeks to build dementia friendly communities across the island. In these communities, residents, businesses and services, and the community at large are aware of dementia and understand how to better support seniors with dementia and their caregivers.
. . .
As such, there is a need to build communities to help seniors with dementia lead independent and meaningful lives. This can be achieved through Dementia Friendly Communities by creating support networks of residents, businesses and services, grassroots and volunteers, community partners, faith-based organizations, and the community at large.
Part of this network are Go-To-Points, which are part of the safe return system for seniors with dementia. Here, community partners form a network of four to five Go-To-Points, serving as safe return points for seniors who may not be able to find their way home. Members of the community can bring these seniors to the Go-To-Points, and leaders at these locations will offer general assistance to these seniors. They include identification and contacting of the senior's next-of-kin or family member to ensure that the seniors are reunited with their loved ones.

There are, then, loosely affiliated organizations (the Lien Foundation, KTPH, and the Agency for Integrated Care) that can be considered the prime movers in trying to establish and expand the scope of an affective regime concerned with being dementia friendly. And for this goal to succeed, these prime movers are hoping to get the cooperation of various other organizations (schools, businesses) and individuals.

As a result, the kinds of activities that go toward manifesting "dementia friendliness" can occur at various levels, from relatively ad hoc individual

Figure 6.4 A Go-To-Point in Yishun

activities to larger-scale events that require significant planning and organization. And perhaps of greatest relevance to the notion of stitching, the different
scopes of participation were largely collaborative in that they all act in affective
consonance. That is, while the main initiatives for the affective regime of being
dementia friendly are the three main organizations, the other parties and
individuals involved are also geared, if not actually coordinated, toward the

same show of support for PWDs. In this way, these affective regimes can all be said to be stitched together so as to constitute a larger unified affective regime, perhaps making it possible for Singapore to in time claim, with a highly degree of plausibility, that the country as a whole is indeed dementia friendly.[4] Given that the goal is to facilitate the movements of PWDs in public spaces, the involvement of these other organizations and individuals is crucial because, as, Roulstone, Soldatic, and Morgan (2014: 1) observe, "disablement is a spatial issue" in the following sense (ibid.):

Both policy and law embody constructions of "right" bodies and minds and thus frame current and future social possibilities for disabled people. Space, for example, being able to occupy freely certain public, private, or even "taboo" spaces, is heavily inscribed with disablist notions of just what is possible given disabled people's capability, capacity, and reason.

Making a similar point, Imre (2014: 13) points out:

A significant and persistent characteristic of society is disabling spaces that are rarely sensitized to the needs of disabled people ... More often than not, designed environments revolve around a spatial logic that separates people by virtue of their bodily differences and variations in cognitive and physiological capabilities. Such separations are tantamount to an infringement of disabled people's liberties, and curtail, potentially, their rights to occupy, and to inhabit and be present in, everyday places, the use of which is intrinsic to a person's realization of their well-being.

The spatial aspect of dementia-friendly neighborhoods thus complements the central feature of such a regime, namely the affective appeal to the community. The "Community" page of the Forget Us Not website makes this clear, by throwing the emphasis on the "community" mentality that is required to support PWDs, defining this community as one where "the public are patient and helpful when they encounter awkward behavior by PWD" (Forget Us Not "Dementia Friendly Community," http://forgetusnot .sg/dementia-friendly-community.html; accessed May 11, 2018). The ultimate affective appeal is to empathetic identification, via what has often been called the "Golden Rule": the website calls for "a community where we treat others the way we would want to be treated, should we ever encounter the condition." This linguistic regime thus nurtures convivial community behavior by emphasizing the common human bond between PWD and others, pointing out that one could oneself acquire the condition in the future, and encouraging an imaginative affective bridge to the treatment one would in such a case wish to receive.

---

[4] This nationwide ambition is already seen, for example, in the Dementia Friendly America project: www.dfamerica.org/; accessed May 11, 2018.

Conclusion

By way of closing, we want to point out that our discussion of how an affective regime might be stitched has some bearing on the study of social movements since the drive to create a neighborhood, if not an entire country, that is dementia friendly is certainly a social movement if nothing else. There has actually been a general tendency to underplay, if not completely ignore, the role of emotions in the analysis of social movements, often as a result of suspicion against emphasizing the role of culture. Thus, according to Calhoun (2001: 48, quoted in Buechler 2011: 194), "Emotions were banished from the study of social movements, to a very large extent, in reaction against a tradition of collective behavior analysis that ran from Le Bon through Turner and Killian and Neil Smelser . . . [w]ith the bathwater of some very serious biases, the baby of emotions was commonly thrown out." However, as Buechler (2011: 192) points out, movements have cultural dimensions in at least three significant ways:

First, movements often have important cultural roots alongside structural causes. This may occur through framing activities ... through newly expanded cultural opportunities, or through the identification of ideological and cultural contradictions in dominant belief systems.
. . .
Second, movements develop their own internal cultures that often become "worlds unto themselves that are characterized by distinctive ideologies, collective identities, behavioral routines, and material cultures" (McAdam 1994: 45–46).
. . .
Third, movements have cultural consequences for the larger society that often transcend their structural or political impacts. These may include new collective identities, alternative norms and values, or novel cultural artifacts.

It is therefore not possible to arrive at a proper understanding of social movements if their cultural dimensions are not given due recognition, and this cultural dimension of course includes the role of emotions. But it should by now not be surprising that any attention to culture still tends to assume that emotions and rationality do not go together, and this assumption has regrettably influenced the study of social movements (Eyermen 2006; Walgrave and Verhulst 2006). In critiquing this assumption, Walgrave and Verhulst (2006) examine what they call "new emotional movements," exemplified in their discussion by the Belgian White Movement, the Snowdrop Campaign in the United Kingdom, the Million Mom March in the United States, and the Movement against Senseless Violence in the Netherlands. The main characteristics of such movements are that they are triggered by violence, with the resulting outrage leading to mass mobilization. But these movements also tend to be short-lived because they lack organization. According to Walgrave and Verhulst (2006: 52, italics added)[5]:

A part of the type-like logic of "new emotional movements" is their consequential temporality. They are ephemeral phenomena. None of the movements under study is still active at present. They disbanded (UK), merged with a stronger existing movement organization (USA), or simple withered and disappeared from the societal scene although still mutely and marginally existing (Belgium and The Netherlands). The, for now, validated features all carry the seeds of the movement's destruction in them. Emotions tend to be short-lived and numbed. *Massive mobilizations function as emotional discharges but leave the movement short-breathed and devoid of stamina. The organizational deficit gets its revenge and, lacking basic organizational structures and procedures, the movement simply crumbles away ... Political support as well tends to be short-lived exactly because soon the movement appears to be not able to maintain pressure and to uphold high mobilization levels.*

This issue of "organizational deficit" is taken up by Eyermen (2006: 194), who begins with the position that movements are "often spurred into existence by cognitively framed emotions, anger, frustration, shame, guilt, which move individuals and groups to protest, to publicly express and display discontent." Eyermen's reference to "cognitively framed emotions" is clearly what we intend by "affect." Eyermen (2006: 195) also points out that movements may be sustained indefinitely by becoming objectified as cultural artifacts or as part of organizations and networks:

[T]his feeling of movement may move beyond the situational, becoming incorporated into individual biography as significant experience and memory, as well as objectified in representational form in cultural artifacts or more structurally in networks and organizations, "free spaces" (Polletta 1999), which can preserve and transmit this felling of "movement" between "protest events." One can be "moved," in other words, before, during, and after the fact, as one recalls a situation through hearing a piece of music or viewing a film or a photograph, which represents an event, as well as the movement itself becoming objectified in organizations and networks, which one may be "moved" to join or support. In this case, "movement" has moved from interactive experience to a narrative connected with individual and collective memory, from event to metaphor. (Amin 1995)

Emotions may provide the impetus for a movement to emerge. But for the movement to be sustained indefinitely, the emotional immediacy that might have spurred the founders has to be translated into or framed as forms that are emotionally available to and connectible with a wider group of social actors. That is, the emotions need to be cognitively framed as affect and objectified in ways that go beyond the initial experiences of the movement's founders. Only in this manner can the movement continue to attract and co-opt other social

---

[5] Page numbers are from the downloaded pdf article, which is paginated from 1–71.

actors instead of petering out once the initially strong emotions lose their intensity. However, this question of how movements can sustain themselves beyond the ephemerality of their emotions is a conundrum only because of a failure to broaden the scope of analysis to include affect. As our discussion of the push toward "dementia friendliness" in Singapore shows, a social movement starts and is sustained by emotions, but this is analytically less problematic once we focus on affect rather than specific emotions (see Chapter 1). It is the reliance on and appeal to affect that facilitates the gradual stitching together of various affective regimes and that also serves to draw in the continued involvement of participants from various aspects of community life.

7   The Affective Regime of Luxury and Exclusivity

There has been a considerable body of work on advertising signs in relation to luxury goods. The best-known work on "luxury" is probably that of sociologist Thorsten Veblen, who theorized the "specialized consumption of goods" in a display of the "pecuniary strength" as the ritualized "conspicuous consumption" practiced by the leisure class (Veblen 2000: 60–61). For Veblen, luxury was the sign of a conspicuous consumption that not only separated a leisure class from those in lower classes, but was also a phenomenon linked to the "traditional meritoriousness of wealth," the "good repute" that society attached to such consumption (Veblen 2000: 89–90). The "leisure class" displays and reinforces its superiority over "base" laborers through ritualistic behavior (chiefly characterized by "expensiveness" and "wastefulness") that proves its freedom from rational and productive economic behavior (Veblen 2000: 88). This luxurious manner of life becomes the basis of a "good repute" in society, and the target of an "emulative process" among others (Veblen 2000: 41, 90). From Veblen's theory we derive two points: that luxury is a position of superiority constructed by exclusion and that it also generates "emulative" desires in those excluded.

Veblen's emphasis was on the ritualistic aspects of luxurious consumption, in an era prior to that of "junk bond" and "subprime" crises and the "Occupy movement" of the 1980s and later. These later developments have admittedly taken some of the outright shine and "meritoriousness" that Veblen attached to luxury and conspicuous consumption (Cloutier 2015; Thomas 2007). The category of "luxury" is evanescent and shifting, with once-luxuries (e.g. water closets) one day becoming ubiquitous; it is also paradoxical, simultaneously relying on a sense of exclusivity while trying to increase desire and consumption (Berry 1994: 4–5). Despite this moral ambivalence attached to luxury, spending on luxury goods persists, and in fact has arguably become a mass phenomenon: as Twitchell (2002: 8) puts it, "entitlement to branded objects, or at least the wherewithal to buy such objects, is a given," at least in developed consumer societies.

Affect is of course central to concepts of both luxury and exclusivity, which are very much governed by emotional and psychological factors rather than economic rationality. Theorists of luxury brands recognize the emotional dimension involved in the successful marketing of such brands: buying a luxury item is not just a transactional purchase of the item itself, but "a complete parcel that comprises the product and a set of intangible benefits that appeal to the emotional, social, and psychological levels of [the buyer's] being" (Okonkwo 2007: 2). The systematic (and highly profitable) way in which consumers' notions of "luxury" are manipulated shows that this is not merely subjective emotion, but more properly what we have defined as affect, with a discernible object-orientation and a correlation of the subject's responses to that of his or her environment (here, including fellow consumers). The luxury affect manipulates common pragmatic human needs, which is why luxury goods (perhaps contrary to expectation) are not somehow extraneous to the basic categories of necessities – "sustenance," "shelter," "clothing," and "leisure," or rest – but created within (special bands of) these categories (Berry 1994: 5–6).

The root of the luxury affect can thus be said to be an appeal to a psychological or emotional state wherein these basic needs are so fulsomely addressed that no fear or anxiety attached to them can surface. It needs only a moment's consideration to realize that no individual can truly be in a state wherein she will never more be troubled by these basic needs: no matter how privileged an individual may be, uncontrollable circumstances – in the form of business failure, war, natural disaster, incurable illness, accident, and injury – can reintroduce straitened circumstances and an awareness of basic needs into that individual's life. Luxury is thus at best the effective illusion of a transcendence of basic needs. The luxury affect is an orientation toward an object (and its attendant field or peripherals) such that the perceiving subject has the feeling of transcending the normal or usual awareness of human needs. Exclusivity – the sense of being in such a rarefied state of privilege denied to the overwhelming majority of mankind – is accordingly an integral part of the luxury affect. This accords with the view of Thurlow and Jaworski (2010: 189), who see "elitism" as "something interactionally and semiotically realized," rather than "a function of . . . material wealth or political power."

In turn, the perception of emulation and envy on the part of others is confirmation of that exclusivity. Socioeconomic elites – those who own or can afford multiple luxury homes and the best of other goods like clothes and cars – are not the only ones upon whom the luxury affect operates. As Berry (1994: 5–6) points out, luxury is problematic and paradoxical as a category, since retailers do also want to maximize sales, and phenomena such as "mass luxury," "new luxury," and "massclusivity" (Roberts and Armitage 2016) indicate the emulative power and expansive concept of luxury. For those aspirant classes below the socioeconomic elites, another dimension thus enters into the affect of luxury and exclusivity – that of desire and emulation. We might consider this a derivative or secondary affect: it is not to possess and inhabit the exclusive world of the elites (and the sense of transcendence of human needs that comes with it), but rather to possess the sense of being in proximity to that world, of being (as it were) nearly exclusive and transcendent.

From this also follows a peculiarity of the "affective economy" (Ahmed 2004b) of luxury and exclusivity. While the affective economies of *kawaii*, reverenced, friendly, and romance landscapes (as discussed in the preceding chapters) work primarily on principles of attraction and participation, luxury works on a more complicated and dualistic economy where principles of attraction and repulsion are both at work. The affective economy of luxury might best be summed up with the phrase "many are called, but few are chosen": while most, if not all, individuals would want to be in an elite and privileged position of being far above basic human needs, the construction of the luxury affect relies on the active rejection or repulsion of the overwhelming majority of individuals. Yet, if everyone ceased to desire a particular luxury good altogether, then the luxury sign would also cease to circulate, transforming from affective commodity to bric-a-brac or relic. The peculiar attraction-repulsion, entry-denial dynamic of the luxury item does share some particular features with other affective economies: in its circulation and amplification through society, in its mediation through language and signs, and in its operation on and via multiple agents including both "grounded" players (Willis 1990) and powerful media producers. The luxury affect most closely resembles the reverence affect, which also contains dualistic elements of emotional attraction (of "faithful" and "reverent" visitors) as well as repulsion or at least containment (of potentially "irreverent" ones), although repulsion and rejection feature far more strongly in the luxury affect. The phenomenon of luxury is a useful reminder that affective economies are complex circulations, of different emotional responses to objects, and can even evoke contradictory emotions at the same time.

Exclusive Locales: Safety, Belonging, and Urban Fear

One's spatial surroundings and environment constitute perhaps the most significant and comprehensive need and source of anxiety. In many ways, individual space goes beyond "shelter" and encompasses many other aspects of the four categories of needs – "sustenance," "shelter," "clothing," and "leisure" – that Berry (1994: 5–6) postulates. Spatial safety also affects "sustenance" since one requires a safe space in order to consume, store, and enjoy sustenance. "Leisure" (or rest) is certainly dependent on the security and peace of mind afforded by one's spatial surroundings. "Clothing" is perhaps the category of needs least integrally connected to "shelter," as in some ways the two categories are alternates for each other: in a sufficiently safe and conducive environment one can walk around naked, as the shelter offers a protection that makes clothing redundant, and outside of a sheltered environment clothing can offer some of the benefits (warmth, protection, even indication of social status) of shelter. Yet there is also a corollary tendency between shelter and clothing, in that individuals tend to dress in ways that correspond to the perceived degree of safety or danger, prestige or abjectness, of their surroundings: an invitation to a mansion or palace will result in the best clothing and accessories, while, conversely, an unavoidable visit to a poor neighborhood will result in the use of one's shabbiest or most commonplace clothing. The semiotics and discourse of luxurious food will inevitably involve and depend on the ambience of the restaurant, that of leisure will usually feature the hotel (or other accommodation) and its environment, or the spacious and well-appointed business-class airplane seat or luxury liner cabin, and even that of clothing will involve a spatial setting characterized (in various ways) by luxury and exclusivity.

Anthropologists have posited a fundamental "territorial instinct" or "territorial imperative" which drives man to define and defend a space of one's own (Ardrey 2014; Taylor 1988). This territorial instinct, which governs human spatial attitudes from personal property to nation-states, is based on three basic psychological factors: "security, stimulation, and identity" (Ardrey, cited in Taylor 1988: 46). While security – the need to feel safe within one's own property – seems to be the central need, this is also intertwined with the "stimulation" of defining and defending the boundary, and the "identity" formation that goes on within the boundary (Taylor 1988: 46).

In modern urban and industrial society, the territorial instinct is evident in the phenomena of ghettosization, urban flight, and the formation of "gated communities" (whether in suburban housing or secured high-rise blocks in prime city neighborhoods). Frumkin et al. (2004: 26) describe how, as cities grew over the course of the nineteenth century onward, the rich tended to live in "fashionable and respectable addresses ... close to the center of town" (at the same time often also maintaining large country houses), while the edges of the city and the suburbs were occupied by "the lower classes," "prostitutes, ne'er-do-wells, and rascals." In American cities in the latter part of the nineteenth century onward, there came a radical shift as the pull of owning land and creating a private haven for the family, together with the increasing crowdedness and stresses of city life, led to the rise in popularity and prestige of suburban living. Even as major cities expanded in the face of increasing influxes of (intra-national and international) labor migration, and the newest arrivals were clustered together in the poorest housing areas of the inner city, the wealthier suburbs were able to resist annexation and became bastions of respectability (Frumkin et al. 2004: 34–35). Blakely and Snyder (1999: 1–3) show that from the 1980s onward, wealthier Americans increasingly chose to live in "gated communities" that present a "fortress mentality" and response to growing urban-social problems like crime, social change, and instability, and the "general degradation of the urban social order."

Fortress-like gated communities represent one (dramatic and highly visible) response to the fundamental need for exclusivity in housing. Although much of the scholarship on these communities focuses on the security aspects and their exclusionary treatment of common spaces (including roads and parks), this exclusivity is of course closely tied to the luxury of being able to afford a home in such a community, with the high purchase price and maintenance fees involved. Even where high-end residences do not employ such visible security deterrents as uniformed armed guards and high boundary walls, the fundamental impulse to define a luxurious community and exclude those who do not fit in is evident and executed through other (semiotic, spatial, policy, and cultural) means. As Blakely and Snyder (1999: 1–2) point out, gated communities are not merely about protection from crime and a desire for privacy: they also reflect "a search for sociospatial community," and a highly "active" attitude and response to personal and domestic security. As such, gated communities reflect the three basic psychological factors of "security, stimulation, and identity" that Ardrey (cited in Taylor 1988: 46) sees as the basic motives of the "territorial imperative." It follow that exclusive communities can be "gated" through a variety of means, without necessarily employing the more visible and forcible deterrents of the "fortress" communities.

Working alongside physical and spatial features (e.g. guards, fences, and cameras), linguistic-semiotic regimes play crucial roles in creating and maintaining the luxury affect of exclusive properties. These regimes can be described in terms of the following categories, which are all used (but to varying degrees, in varying properties) in exclusive properties: Security: the construction of the effect of being separate from the masses. While this is most obviously created by physical barriers and surveillance, in many ways it is the cultural and symbolic security which is the most psychologically interesting and significant. This is conducted not only through the language and semiotics of warning and deterrence, but also by discourses of elitism, the creation of acceptable and unacceptable types who (respectively) are welcome or rejected at the property.

Stimulation: this is the creation of particular activities that define and bond the community in contradistinction to those outside it. The most obvious spatial features that serve as stimulation are found in the golfing or yachting communities, where the golf course or marina serve as the central spatial hub as well as the uniting activity for those who choose to live there. However, stimulation is not merely a spatial or physical function, but has to be framed as a "higher" purpose or calling which separates the community from outsiders who do not possess the correct attitude or characteristics to subscribe to this purpose. This is where linguistic-semiotic factors are more important than the spatial facilities.

Identity: the most complex and highest-order parameter of exclusivity, in some ways it overlaps with and even subsumes some of the features of "security" and "stimulation." While the latter two aspects depend significantly on physical features of the property – facilities, location, environment, barriers, surveillance equipment, and so on – "identity" is largely independent of physical facilities or activities, relying instead on the inner qualities or attributes believed to inhere in owners of luxury properties. While this identity is both secure (having passed the entry qualifications) and stimulated (having subscribed to the community's characteristic activity or purpose), it is most characteristically associated with qualities inherent in an individual: the social standing, refinement, tastes, intellect, cosmopolitan outlook, that serve to badge the exclusive elite of society. These abstract qualities, harder to portray or manifest than aspects of security and stimulation, rely more heavily on linguistic resources to evoke and police.

Luxury Homes: The Semiotics of Exclusivity

The typical features of a gated community – perimeter walls or fences, uniformed guards, guardhouse checks on visitors, pass access for registered occupants (Blakely and Snyder 1999) –not only are a physical security barrier, but also form one kind of semiotics of exclusivity. Such features signal that the property is private and exclusionary, that bona fide visitors are only allowed on sufferance and at the cost of inconveniences and indignities such as checking in at the guardhouse, phone verifications with the host, being issued a temporary pass, parking at distant visitors' lots, and so on. They also signal that non-bona fide visitors – insurance agents and others soliciting for business, those seeking free use of facilities like swimming pools and golf courses, and of course those with criminal intent of various kinds – have no hope of passing through such stringent checks (although the unacknowledged reality is that some do still make it through).

Security in gated communities is a mind-set created via the use of language. The language of security signs, notices, and communiques serve to set a tone of high seriousness about security matters; the language is often dire, threatening penalties and prosecution for the violation of security protocols. Perhaps surprisingly, the threats are directed not only at outsiders and visitors, but also at residents and employees, striking a very discordant note with the idyllic and resort-like atmosphere that otherwise characterizes gated communities. In this sense, luxury residences create a quite different "linguascape" from the peaceful and exclusive silences that Thurlow and Jaworski (2010) identify in elite resorts, where (unlike everyday residences) such silences can be effected as a temporary contrast to everyday life.

The language of responsibility and accountability predominates in the notices and rules regarding gated community visitors. Typical of this is the language of the Tidewater Plantation Community Association, in Myrtle Beach, South Carolina. Item B of section VI (governing "Guests and Renters") declares:

Property owners are responsible for the actions of their renters/guests and can be fined for renter/guest violations of the Tidewater rules and Regulations. Owners are also liable to the TPCA for any damages to Tidewater amenities and/or common areas done by their guests or renters. (Tidewater Plantation "Rules and Regulations")

Renting has proven to be a major issue for gated communities, particularly in the light of new business models such as that of Air BnB. Even before Air BnB's challenge to the traditional definition of "renter," this notion has proven problematic for gated communities, which rely on as strong a definition of "resident" as possible. This is despite the fact that renters, unlike visitors, employees, and especially illegal intruders, are in many senses legitimate (albeit temporary) occupiers and thus members of the exclusive property. The language of gated communities has notably made a sharp distinction between owners – seen somehow as genuine, long-term members of the community – and short-term visitors, including (in some cases) renters of up to one year's tenure. If the language of responsibility and liability attaches to owners, then to "visitors" (broadly defined) is attached the language of limited and qualified access and privileges. Thus, Tidewater Plantation imposes the following conditions on renters:

Renters have access to only the Community pool/hot tub, Fitness Center, and Tennis Courts.
    Renters may not bring guests into Tidewater amenities.
    Renters may **not** have access to owner(s) Key Fob. If a Key Fob is used in violation of the Tidewater Rules and Regulations, the fob access to the Tidewater amenities can be deactivated and a fee charged for reactivation. (Tidewater Plantation "Rules and Regulations")

Likewise, Butterworth 8, an exclusive private community in Singapore, distinguishes between "resident passes" and "supplementary passes"; the latter may be issued to "resident's employees such as maids and chauffeurs," and "do not permit the holders to use the recreational facilities" (Butterworth 8 "House Rules and By-Laws"). Language which qualifies the privileges of renters, visitors, and employees, contributes to the creation of a privileged class – that of bona fide owners – even within the groups of people permitted to enter the gated community. By emphasizing the responsibilities and liabilities of owners to police and regulate the activities and access of nonowners, this use of language recruits owners as active agents within this disciplined and structured routine of class segregation.

Other spatial, semiotic, and linguistic features also reinforce security, but often in less direct ways which speak more to the sense of exclusivity and seclusion than to the privileges and liabilities of the owner class. Many exclusive properties use geographical features to create a sense of being cut off from the masses. Properties located on small islands – where the bulk of the island land mass is taken up with expensive properties, and with little or no amenities or spaces available for public use – project a clear sense of being separated from the mainland and, by implication, from the ordinary masses. In the case of small and highly developed residential islands close to major metropolitan areas, the insular geography contributes to the exclusivity by reinforcing the boundary between the community of inhabitants and those outside. Examples of this include Fisher Island off Miami, Florida, and Sentosa Island south of the main island of Singapore.

Fisher Island, "an exclusive paradise 3 miles from Miami," as *Forbes* magazine calls it, is under a square mile in total land area and has only 700 residential families, but is also "America's richest zip code" (Beyer 2015). It possesses some of the physical security features of gated communities, but with the added security of limited means of access to the island (which is by ferry, and by private boat, and helicopter, although docking and landing spaces for the latter two are limited). The small size of the island together with its desirable air of exclusivity means that "the island is approaching build-out," or maximum development capacity (Beyer 2015). This in turn stimulates demand among the ultrarich, for many of whom a home amid the limited available pool of housing on the island is a cachet. With this cachet and demand, property prices are well beyond the reach of the masses, with Sotheby's reporting 2017 listings averaging more than US$6.5 million for waterfront homes, and non-waterfront homes of more than US$1.5 million (Sotheby's International Realty "Fisher Island"). Sentosa Island is a resort island south of the main island of Singapore, and connected to the main island by a gated bridge, monorail service, and cable car; visitors are charged admission to visit the island's beaches, casino, amusement parks, and other attractions. The only residential zone on the island, Sentosa Cove, began sales in 2003. It offers a rare home concept in the context of Singapore, homes that could be "built right on the waterfront" (Sentosa Cove Real Estate). The waterfront houses and condominiums in Sentosa Cove are also unique in the Singapore context in a number of other respects: as the only residential developments permitted on Sentosa Island, supported by luxurious facilities like the adjacent ONE°15 Marina and W Hotel, and one of the rare private property developments in Singapore where foreign ownership of evenlanded homes has been encouraged in order to deliberately create a "highly cosmopolitan community" (Sentosa Cove Real Estate; Figure 7.1). The

Figure 7.1 Sentosa Cove condominiums with ONE°15 Marina in the
foreground. The condominiums project a proximity to the unique lifestyle of
the marina and trendy restaurants and bars and yet are subtly cut off from the
public by secured bridge-footpaths requiring a resident card for access

combination of lifestyle amenities, waterfront location, and limited supply
have resulted in property prices that are among the highest in Singapore, this
despite the fact that Sentosa Cove properties are all on 99-year leaseholds
(compared to many of the prime properties on the main island that are freehold
or on 999-year leases).

Small highly developed islands near metropolitan centers facilitate the
exclusivity affect by offering a concrete, physical corroboration of limited
supply of a community that is literally separated from the masses. Other
geographical features may also reinforce the exclusivity affect by projecting
a physical sense of limited supply and being separated from the masses. Hilltop
properties – again, in proximity to metropolitan centers, creating a sense of a
very limited supply relative to demand – confer a literal sense of being "above it
all," being close to but removed from, and looking down on the hustle and
bustle of urban life. One good example of this is Victoria Peak (also known as
"The Peak"), the highest point on Hong Kong Island. Historically, the residence
of choice for the top British colonial administrators of Hong Kong, The Peak is

Figure 7.2 Rare landed home on Hong Kong Island's The Peak
neighborhood, overlooking the condominium blocks of the Mid-Level
district and beyond that (not in picture) the high-rise downtown area. The
sloping topography, forest preserves, and parks that make up most of Victoria
Peak ensure that land for private residences is strictly limited

the most expensive residential neighborhood per square foot in Hong Kong, which also has some of the highest property prices in the world. The limited number of homes at The Peak are much in demand notwithstanding their price, and occupants include top civil servants like the Hong Kong chief judge as well as a string of "CEOs, expat professionals, high-net-worth entrepreneurs, and government officials" (House 2016). The topography of Victoria Peak, which is mostly hilly and preserved parks and forest together with several government and commercial developments, ensures that the supply of land for private residences will necessarily be strictly limited (Figure 7.2). Other examples of geography being used to create an air of exclusivity can be seen in prime beachfront housing with deeded private beaches or direct access to a public beach (e.g. Malibu Beach in California), or rare properties permitted in small numbers in national parks (e.g. the valuable so-called inholdings of private land within US national parks, or the few private houses available in Hampshire's New Forest, in the United Kingdom).

Not all islands project exclusivity simply by virtue of being islands: large islands with abundant supplies of zoned-residential land relative to demand, for example Vancouver Island in Canada, are not seen as exclusive properties. Nor are small undeveloped islands in rural and inaccessible areas, for example the many small islands in the Louisiana Bayous, or rural mountain areas with abundant land parcels. As these contrary examples indicate, geographical separation and containment are not sufficient factors to create an atmosphere of exclusivity. Ultimately, natural geographical features have to be enhanced and modified by cultural features – services, facilities, cultural and symbolic constructions, linguistic resources – in order to create exclusive and highly desired residential zones. Branding narratives, which create a distinctive character or atmosphere in a particular exclusive property, play a large role here. Highly desirable and exclusive neighborhoods propagate narratives and signs of a pedigree of ownership, founded on factors such as a famous founder, or the fame of former and current homeowners. Fisher Island, for example, derives a considerable part of its cachet from the fact that for a considerable part of its history the island was owned by the Vanderbilt family (Beyer 2015). For Hong Kong's Peak district, it is the historical association of that neighborhood with the colonial ruling elite, as much as the list of rich and important current residents, that creates the exclusive mystique. Existing owners in these areas derive distinction from being associated with these historical owners, while potential buyers require a certain socioeconomic distinction if they are to envision themselves as part of this distinguished community.

The terms used to describe the characteristics of the desired resident are usually idealistic but vague on particular details – deliberately so, in order to serve as a deterrent and to give regulatory bodies (such as co-op boards) the leeway to reject applicants who do not seem to meet the community's standards. The best-known example of this may be the co-op boards of New York's exclusive Upper East Side apartment buildings. The typology employed here is not simply wealth and the means to afford one of these expensive apartments, but a whole qualitative assessment that includes the sources and provenance of that wealth, its long-term sustainability, the occupation of the applicant, social circles, character and disposition, record of charitable work, and anything else that the co-op board may consider in deciding whether the applicant belongs to the co-op community. Thus, one of the more exclusive properties, 740 Park Avenue, has apartments owned by financial aristocracy (including John Rockefeller Jr), and a co-op board that has rejected TV personalities like Barbara Walters, Barbra Streisand, and Neil Sedaka (Hughes 2011). At another exclusive property, 2 East 67 Street, the co-op board ensures that prospective buyers are not only wealthy (and with wealth from similar sources to that of existing owners), but also have high "liquidity" to cover monthly maintenance costs without fear of economic downturns, a history of contributing to "philanthropic causes," and again is on the lookout for buyers "related to a prominent family" while rejecting buyers from certain backgrounds like TV celebrities (Hughes 2011). The qualitative bar is made even higher by the fact that the screening process, interview questions, and criteria are highly secretive at the most exclusive co-op buildings, and largely unknown to the public; the rules are "unwritten," and New York city co-op boards are not legally obliged to reveal reasons for rejection, all this creating the impression that a particular building "is sort of impossible to get in, not only for [ordinary people], but for rich people as well" (Hauseit 2017; Hughes 2011).

While the zealous work of exclusive Manhattan co-op boards are the best-known instances of intra-communal stimulation, similar processes also take place (in varying forms and to varying degrees) in other properties which are concerned with image protection and maintenance. A number of apartment buildings also require some degree of interview with a board or representative(s) before signing off on the purchase. They may not be looking for the same rarefied social elite as the most exclusive co-op boards, but they are still policing the character of applicants (by their own unwritten standards) to ensure that applicants "will add qualitative value to the community" (Hauseit 2018). This criterion of "qualitative value" – whose terms are generally unwritten, and whose definition and standards vary from property to property – becomes a socioeconomic and cultural yardstick whose exclusive properties (those which are able to exercise discretionary admission) are utilized as a form of security to protect existing owners. Effectively, this becomes a way of preserving the socioeconomic and cultural character of an exclusive property, by simply deterring buyers who do not conform to the board's image of "qualitative value."

Turning from "security" to "stimulation," we can see this as the extent to which an exclusive property has a visible and active community, whose activities directly or indirectly reinforce the exclusivity of the property. Stimulation can take intra-communal and extra-communal forms. Intra-communal stimulation involves the interactions between residents in the community, usually around social activities organized by the social committee of the Home Owners' Association (HOA). While social interaction can of course be an informal affair left to the wishes and initiatives of individual members of the community, what is evident is the conscious effort and encouragement that HOAs place on planned social activities. The very fact that most, if not all, HOAs have a social committee tasked with organizing a busy slate of social events is already indication of this. The language used by HOAs to describe the function of their social committees, and to foster the desired degree of internal stimulation, can be described as a discourse of emotional prescriptiveness that, while falling short of mandating participation by all community members, seeks to regulate members' social attitudes through events.

The function of social committees is generally described in terms of the goal of fostering a "strong sense of community" (Sanctuary Cove "Social Committee Charter"). For Sanctuary Cove, a waterfront community in Georgia, USA, the social committee's purpose is clearly spelt out in terms where the voluntary nature of social activities is framed within the language of social engineering and obligations:

Committee's Purpose: The Committee shall act to provide organized volunteer efforts within the Community's overall membership. The committee encourages owners parti-cipation by organizing holiday and social events and interesting community activities functions conducted within the community's amenity facilities. This committee has the responsibility to advise and support the Community by these activities include but are not limited to: An annual property owner's social event, a welcome meet and greet which, greets and shares community information with new residents, and a variety of social events designed to stimulate interest among neighbors in the Community. This will be accomplished by but not limited to the following actions: . . . (Sanctuary Cove, "Social Committee Charter")

Choice and inducement are conveyed through terms like "encourages owners [*sic*] participation," "stimulate interest," and "interesting community activities functions [*sic*]." Overarching the voluntary and social nature of such activities is the obligation that is embodied in the charter of the social committee itself, which "shall act" on and "has the responsibility" for its given mission, and whose actions "will be accomplished" via "designed" social events.

The reality is that in exclusive properties there is more at stake in social interaction than merely the individual social lives of residents. The property's work of protecting its security by regulating new owners is continued in the intra-communal stimulation which aims at an ideal social cohesion. The reg-ulatory nature underlying this social activity is not difficult to discern: thus, for Discovery Harbor Community in Hawaii, the general goal of the social com-mittee is "to foster a sense of community by organizing fun and interesting events where members can meet and socialize" (Discovery Harbor "Guidelines and Procedures of the Social Committee"). Sounding a different, regulatory note is another function of this committee, which is also "responsible for oversight of the Welcome (E Komo Mai) Wagon." Although the "Welcome Wagon" is a package that is "intended as a gift to new homeowners/residents welcoming them to the community," the first on the list of usual items in the package indicates the regulatory function of the gift: "Information regarding DHCA [Discovery Harbor Community Association] CC&Rs, Bylaws, Architectural procedures" (Discovery Harbor "Guidelines and Procedures of the Social Committee"). Internal stimulation in the form of social activities is essentially a way to project and protect a unified front in a community of owners, a function whose regulatory and engineered underpinnings are evident in its discourses. In addition to the regular internal communiques and packages conveying these goals and rules, many private communities (including Discovery Harbor Community and Sanctuary Cove) also use social media such as Facebook to project its social character (and reinforce its mission) via sharing of images, posts, and links which align with its regulatory mission.

This intra-communal stimulation also overlaps with an extra-communal dimension, which is the degree to which the community's residents actively project positive qualities outside of the community. This was explicit in the emphasis on "philanthropic causes" on the part of 2 East 67 Street's co-op board (Hughes 2011). However, this is not merely confined to a few high-end apartments with the kind of socioeconomic aristocracy for whom philanthropy is a given. Roitman (2006: 127) recounts a case of a gated community in Argentina which regularly undertook charitable work in the surrounding areas, partly (it is admitted) out of fear of being the target of looting and property crimes. However, it is clear that a number of gated communities and other privileged property groups also do this to project a positive image of their property and community to the larger society. Indeed, some high-end properties actually target high-net-worth individuals by advertising the community's charitable emphasis and projects, which at the same time nurtures "the loyalty of residents who feel deeply engaged with charitable programs" (McLaughlin 2017). The seemingly paradoxical reality is that while gated communities and exclusive properties rely on an image of transcending the socioeconomic lot of the common man, this distinction is at times stimulated precisely by a signature community charity that gives back to others in society. The paradox is explained by the fact that such projects – whether by a few famous philanthropists in exclusive Manhattan apartments or by a wider swathe of residents in higher-end gated communities – while seeming to engage with lower social classes (and, thus, potentially blur the line between the groups), really reinforce the gap between the groups by imposing a distinct hierarchy based on socioeconomic inequality, on the segregated roles of "giver" and "receiver."

While "security" sets the exclusive property apart from others by association with "aristocratic" individuals, and "stimulation" actively polices and reinforces the boundary between the exclusive inside and the outside, "identity" can be seen as the cultural image of the exclusive property (and its community) as a whole. It is the management of the image projected by the property and community, in order to perpetuate their distinction and separation from the common. The identity of an exclusive property is thus the cultural capital of the property as it is projected in the semiotics of associated spaces, activities, and objects.

As discussed above, the pedigree of past and present owners can reinforce the "security" of a property or neighborhood by associating them with a powerful and elite group that discourages those outside that group from attempting to enter. In the longer term – with repeated associations with elite individuals – pedigree contributes to a property's lasting identity, suggesting the durability of the property's special, exclusive nature, in contrast to other properties. Discourses of pedigree accordingly focus on rare achievements tested by time, such as the long-standing association of the Vanderbilt name with philanthropy and politics in the case of Fisher Island. Prominent American dynastic families like the Vanderbilts, Kennedys, Mellons, Rockefellers, and others, like their European counterparts the Rothschilds and Bettencourts, automatically lend an air of distinction and, thus, exclusivity to properties with which they are associated, and such associations are inevitably empha-sized in any stories or advertisements about those properties. In the case of these dynastic families, what confers the air of exclusivity is not only the extent of the family fortune, but the family pedigree and lineage, its prominence over many generations, and the name-recognition and influence that extends into multiple areas such as philanthropy (in named foundations, buildings, univer-sities, and professorships), culture and the arts, politics, and others.

These dynastic names are of course more recent versions of an older aristocratic tradition, which continues to convey exclusivity even in modern times, most obviously in the sale of chateaux and manor houses formerly owned by noble families, but also in boasts of the exclusivity of a neighborhood or village based on the fact that a noble family also owns one of the properties. Nobility, especially in the higher hereditary titles of older provenance, is the epitome of exclusivity in that it is confined to a few families and outside the purview of even the wealthiest individuals. The appeal to dynastic names is thus one of the most significant ways of enhancing luxury and exclusivity, and is always used in marketing properties with that pedigree. This can be seen, for example, in the 2015 marketing of the Rothschild's Rushbrooke Estate in Suffolk, England, as an estate "owned by one of Europe's most famous families since 1938," or the feature on New Lodge, Windsor, England, as a property "built to entertain the royal hunting parties" which "remained in royal hands until 1834" (Parry 2015; Passino 2013). However, even with properties which were not actually owned by nobility or industrial-capitalist dynasties, the semiotics and narratology of "aristocracy" is still very much at play to create a sense of exclusivity. We can see this in a 2004 sales campaign for homesites on Sea Island, Georgia, which market it as "a special place." This "special" identity is justified by an invocation of durable pedigree:

For four generations, this quiet paradise has won the praise of presidents, prime ministers, and the world's elite. Yet acclaim has never changed Sea Island; rather, those who love the place are changed, succumbing to her gentle spirit, her natural grace, and the timeless rhythms of the Georgia Coast that have always governed life here. And always will. (Sea Island Company 2004)

The eight-page section, in the pages of upscale design magazine *Architectural Digest*, is even printed on sepia-toned paper both to make the section stand out from the rest of the magazine and to convey a sense of weathering and age to resemble an important historical document. While "the world's elite" is a vague term, the appeal to "presidents" and "prime ministers" is a specific invocation of aristocratic provenance, since these, while not hereditary positions, represent the peak of political power and achievement such that only a limited number of such officeholders exist. That Sea Island has been so favored by political royalty for "four generations" establishes the "special" quality of the property.

Other forms of "aristocracy" frequently appealed to in property narratives can include the work of famous architects, particularly those who only built a limited number of properties and who are now deceased or near the end of their careers. Frank Lloyd Wright, touted as "the greatest American architect of all time" and known for his signature private dwellings, is perhaps the best example of this (Tardiff 2017). With both instant name- and design recognition, together with a fixed supply, there is a clear cachet in owning a Wright house, and a clear claim for such houses as being "a piece of architectural history" (Tardiff 2017). Other marquee-name architects either deceased (like Zaha Hadid) or near the end of their careers (like Frank Gehry or Norman Foster) confer a similar cachet of exclusivity to their properties. This kind of provenance is also likely to raise the price of the affected property relative to comparable properties in the area, which also reinforces the luxury affect. Well-known historical figures such as Charlie Chaplin, Elvis Presley, and Martin Luther King arguably have a similar effect on property, since there is instant name recognition and the number of homes they have owned is also fixed. Outside of the realm of "aristocracy" – the members of royalty or nobility, political heads of state, dynastic families with rare lasting power and influence, all of whose numbers are limited – there are other figures used to convey exclusivity, which might be loosely called "cultural luminaries." These include famous artistes, celebrities, civil rights luminaries, holders of other high official positions (senators and mayors), and so on.

Exclusive properties also project a special identity through associated spaces, the most common ones being the golf course and the marina or boat dock. These private spaces in exclusive properties are usually further distinguished from more common versions: in the case of golf courses, to boast of a "Jack Nicklaus-designed" course (built by the company founded by the former golf legend) is to elevate the golfing property high above ordinary membership golf clubs. In the case of boat docks, what distinguishes the exclusive property (whether a condominium or a single home) is the type of boats associated with the property. Properties which allow dockage for larger and more expensive vessels command a high premium, not only because of the relative scarcity of deepwater berths, but also because of the image of refinement and exclusivity created by neighboring luxury yachts (as opposed to the less-exclusive image of more commonplace boats).

Associated spaces serve to juxtapose the exclusive property with luxury objects – especially those that are rare and expensive, including irreplaceable antiques and bespoke items that are customized for a small clientele rather than mass produced. Properties that include rare antique fittings (such as staircases or fireplaces), or bespoke artistic fittings like customized art glass chandeliers, not only raise the value of the properties because of the rarity of these fittings, but also contribute to a distinct aesthetic sensibility as well (Californialuxury. com). Apartments with private car lifts or properties with built-in sophisticated wine cellars cater to elite buyers who own vintage collectible cars, Ferraris and Lamborghinis, rare premier cru Margaux and Yquem vintages, rather than more commonly owned expensive cars and wines. Certain objects thus play a significant role in the semiotics of luxury by associating their image of luxury, rarity, and refinement to the identity of the property. By extension, associated spaces and objects also imply certain activities: not just the leisure that Veblen (2000) sees as the distinguishing feature of the most wealthy class from all others, but a certain class of leisure activities that denote high social and cultural capital. These include connoisseur activities such as collecting art and antiques, specific skills activities (gourmet cooking, sailing, golf), broadly "environmental" activities (living near, appreciating, and interacting with parks, waterways, beaches), and high society activities (fund-raisers, galas, and balls). The association of a particular property with the collective identity of a community which is not only wealthy enough to enjoy leisure, but also highly refined enough to spend that leisure in activities which require high intellectual, aesthetic, social, and other forms of capital, results in a picture of a highly exclusive property.

One other dimension which is often invoked to reinforce an exclusive identity is "cosmopolitanism," or the association of a property with an elite international community. This should not be confused with the semiotics of (cultural, racial, or national) diversity, which is primarily about moral and political issues of inclusivity, and does not make the stipulations of high socioeconomic standing with which exclusivity is concerned. Cosmopolitanism in the semiotics of exclusivity is associated with a particular group of internationals, the elites who possess the capital to be highly mobile and who often own several homes in different locations. The association with an elite cosmopolitan community thus lifts an exclusive property above the limitations of its locality, by expressing its desirability and associated identity and capital in terms of the whole world's most highly qualified buyers. The discourse of cosmopolitanism is very much to the fore in the marketing of Singapore's Sentosa Cove, which from its inception had aimed to create "an exclusive cosmopolitan community," drawing on "the expertise of foreign consultants" for its design elements, and (unlike most of Singapore's real estate pool) permitting and encouraging ownership of stand-alone landed properties by non-Singaporeans (Sentosa Cove Real Estate). The appeal to cosmopolitanism is also writ large in the entire design and marketing of the "The World" archipelago of artificial islands in the UAE, in which a group of 300 islands approximating a map of the world was created and sold to ultra-high-net-worth international buyers and corporations – "the planet's wealthiest investors and real estate moguls" (Weller 2016). Some exclusive properties target the top echelon of international elites as a means not only of broadening the market but also of creating a community that implies cosmopolitan discernment and distinction.

The three parameters of "security," "stimulation," and "identity" are at play in various aspects of the semiotics of exclusivity, creating a whole image of the exclusive property as tightly limited to a particular elite community. Spatial elitism is a version of the "territorial imperative" (Ardrey 2014; Taylor 1988), in this case operating to create signs which circumscribe a highly select space and its community from the larger space of the general population. Here it is important to return to Berry's (1994: 5–6) observation that luxury is not qualitatively different from basic human needs such as sustenance, shelter, and protection, but rather exists at a special top band within these categories. Luxury is thus best understood in conjunction with exclusivity, which is the differentiation of luxury as being the proper domain of only an elite and select group, carefully contradistinguished from the common population. This work of constant separation and contradistinction persuades viewers (both those inside as well as outside the exclusive community) that the elite have nothing in common with commoners, that they so far transcend the realm of ordinary people that they are not prey or subject to common human needs. At the same time, exclusivity also relies on a contrary economy and narrative: the projection of the extreme desirability of the luxury property, even as it is held out of reach of the common man.

"Massclusivity": Affect, Aspiration, Desire

The power of exclusivity consists in the fact that it does not merely define an exclusive affect in a small number of socioeconomic elites, but exerts a pervasive influence in practically everyone else as well. In marketing terms, the recognition of a broader appeal of high-luxury brands can be seen in the broadening of such goods to more inclusive categories like "mass luxury," "massclusivity," "new luxury," and the like (Roberts and Armitage 2016). A similar impulse is evident in the so-called "diffusion lines" of fashion houses, where exclusive high-fashion names like Marc Jacobs and Prada offer slightly less pricey lines (called "Marc" and "Miu Miu," respectively) which have "a fashion presence of their own" (Robson 2006). Some car manufacturers (including Mercedes, BMW, Audi, and, to a certain extent, Porsche) also pursue a similar strategy, offering lower-end models priced at a fraction of the highest-end, high-specification ones. However, it should be noted that some brand names refuse to diffuse their high-luxury image, including fashion houses Chanel and Dior, and car manufacturers Ferrari, Aston Martin, and Lamborghini.

There is less of a clear "massclusivity" segment in terms of property and space, where (unlike entirely fabricated goods like clothing and cars) some of the key factors of exclusivity – such as prime location, aristocratic associations, even to a certain extent the signature work of hallmark architects and craftsmen – are unique and irreplaceable. Yet even in spatial terms, a massclusivity effect can be seen, where mass luxury properties borrow certain aspects of exclusive properties and spaces. One clear example of this is the way in which luxury hotel brands have also created niche diffusion lines, in some cases proliferating a large number of niche sub-brands catering to different consumer income brackets, interests, and backgrounds. The Marriott group of hotels, for example, consolidates its luxury image through the JW Marriott, Ritz Carlton, and St. Regis chains, while offering more affordable accommodations through chains like Courtyard by Marriott and Fairfield Inn by Marriott. Similarly, the Hilton group maintains a high-luxury segment in its Waldorf Astoria and Conrad hotels, and a more affordable segment in its DoubleTree and Embassy Suites brands. In the case of both groups, the more affordable brands still distinguish themselves from mass-market accommodations by leveraging on the luxury associated with the group names and their luxury segments.

There is a version of massclusivity in residential properties as well, where some select features of exclusive properties – those that can be isolated and reproduced elsewhere – are referenced in the next tier of properties in order to create some version of the semiotics of exclusivity. A good example of this is the private residences of Sembawang Greenvale estate in the north of Singapore. This site is very far removed from the prime residential areas of Sentosa Cove, or the downtown area, or the Bukit Timah prime residential enclave. However, it makes its own appeal to exclusivity by emphasizing its proximity to the sea, referencing Sentosa Cove in the process. One property writer describes the housing project thus: "A new waterfront housing enclave, with price tags a fraction of those at Sentosa Cove, is taking shape in a remote corner of Singapore" (Ong 2013). It would be foolhardy for the writer (or the developer or marketers) to deny the obviously "remote" nature of the Sembawang properties, their very un-cosmopolitan and un-resort-like nature, and their much lower price points, compared to Sentosa Cove. Yet it is true that one exclusive feature shared between the two properties is the proximity to the sea: while the Sembawang properties do not have the same private waterfront access of the Sentosa Cove ones, their proximity to the sea and immediate sea view are relatively limited in the context of Singapore property. The reference to Sentosa Cove not only points to this similarity, but with it also implicitly evokes something of the elite identity of the Sentosa Cove residences.

Massclusivity properties invoke some of the security, stimulation, and identity features of exclusive properties in order to assume some degree of exclusivity. While not all co-op boards have the same lofty standards as those of elite Upper East Side Manhattan buildings, it is nevertheless common for other co-ops to have a board interview for prospective buyers. Not all gated communities are located on exclusive islands or boast marinas or Nicklaus golf courses, but all use several of the common features (guarded gatehouses, private recreational spaces and facilities, community social bonding events) to foster an exclusive image separate from common society. If not all properties can boast of aristocratic past or present owners, many can implicitly or explicitly advertise ownership by a lower level of social elites such as prominent businessmen, professionals, minor celebrities and authors, and the like.

Other massclusivity features in private property include stylistic features that gesture toward aristocracy, for example turrets, crenellations, and other stylistic invocations of castles and manor houses (Figure 7.3). Forward technology can speak to "stimulation" or "security" (e.g. facial or fingerprint recognition for access to the condominium lobby or main gate of the property, or remote surveillance via smartphone). In place of grand full-scale recreational facilities, there can be substitute facilities (e.g. a small treadmill swimming pool on a plot that is too small for a regular swimming pool, a living room large-screen TV and sophisticated sound system in lieu of a proper home theater, and narrow nonload-bearing external planters in lieu of full balconies). In fact, many middle-class homes (whether single properties or apartments and condominiums) employ a variety of stylistic, spatial, and recreational features that are inspired by and gesture toward the features of exclusive homes. Singapore public housing, designed and built by the government agency the Housing Development Board (HDB) for a variety of dwellers (including the middle class), uses a variety of design features to gesture (with varying degrees of simplification or sophistication) to exclusive private property, as part of an ideology of socioeconomic "upgrading" that is essentially an aspirational, massclusivity project (Goh 2001).

Massclusivity semiotics is thus a version of the semiotics of exclusivity, and it is accordingly difficult to avoid the conclusion that all this is part of a slippery slope that extends all the way down to at least the second-lowest socioeconomic band: people with a roof over their heads, even if it leaks, will consider themselves superior to those unfortunate enough to be homeless. Even the owner of the humblest abode can feel pride in ownership, deep attachment to the home, an attitude of differentiation from others less fortunate in society, and a territorial desire to strongly assert the boundaries of that property against possible threats and encroachments.

Figure 7.3 Apartment building in Belfast with stylistic turret invoking grand manor houses or castles

Yet even as the phenomenon of massclusivity begs a slippery slope downward, it also strongly points upward to the power of images of exclusivity, the dominance of such images over all of society. Exclusivity is an aspirational and upward-oriented semiotics and affects most segments of society (apart, perhaps, from the few socioeconomic elites who comfortably inhabit it); the superiority that the owner of a humble abode may feel to those below him or her does not preclude (and, indeed, often accompanies) an envy of those above him or her, particularly those at the very top of the socioeconomic scale. For Melanie Klein and other psychological theorists inspired by Freud, envy is related to the "death instinct," man's fundamental fear of pain and loss that stems from the primal separation from the comforting oneness with the mother's breast (Ninivaggi 2010: 74–78). This may simply be another way of expressing the fundamental human need for the four basic categories of necessities – "sustenance," "shelter," "clothing," and "leisure," or rest – that Berry (1994: 5–6) speaks of. Aspiration is the relentless drive to accumulate more resources that staves off (or at least defers) the death instinct by seeming to satisfy those fundamental human needs. That drive inevitably directs individuals upward on the socioeconomic scale, aspiring to be in the position of those who possess more such resources and thus appear to be more secure and satisfied in terms of those needs.

Again, it is real estate – particularly an individual's residence, and its associated objects like cars and furnishings – that best embodies that socio-economic position, as the best indication of overall financial wealth, and as a close reflection of the individual's personality and identity. Housing design – broadly understood to include not just structural and stylistic elements but also the use of materials, facilities, associated spaces and objects, and other features that contribute to the overall character of the property – is thus governed by a set of basic semiotic codes, not just at the highest level of elite housing, but also for the levels below which invoke those codes wherever possible or feasible. The basic semiotic codes that project a level of security, stimulation, and identity above that of common people ultimately take priority over other housing considerations such as value for money, modesty, social integration with those outside the property, stylistic conformity with the surroundings, or ease of maintenance.

Conclusion: The Affective Economy and the Perpetuation of the Luxury Affect

Understanding luxury and exclusivity as expressions of fundamental human needs for territorial security, stimulation, and identity, goes some way toward explaining their perpetuation despite periodic (and often quite serious) move-ments of protest, anger, and even violence – in an age of "Occupy Wall Street" protests and other reactions against extreme wealth and socioeconomic inequal-ity, and of a "minimalist" reaction against clutter and possessions attributed to "millennial" demographics and values (Sernau 2014; Levitin 2015; Weinswig 2016). Even trends like minimalism may be nothing more than another mani-festation of wealth and privilege, a disguising of luxury under an appearance of simplicity and material renunciation (Chayka 2016; Fagan 2017).

Our discussion of luxury and exclusivity as affect contributes to the under-standing of the perpetuation of notions of exclusivity in society. While there are deep psychological bases of needs, anxieties, envy, and aspirations underlying the luxury affect, it is important to understand that luxury space is constructed and projected via semiotic and linguistic mechanisms. The role of real estate advertising, condo rules and regulations, community social activities policies, social media presences, co-op board profiling, the "pedigreed" stories of certain properties, and other ways in which language is used project the utter desir-ability of luxury properties in a comprehensive and pervasive system of mean-ings. These meanings, far from operating only on the socioeconomic elites, exert a powerful force on those seemingly rejected from the privileges and rights of ownership of such properties.

The peculiarity of the luxury affect is thus its circulation through contrary forces of attraction and repulsion. Like other affects discussed earlier – *kawaii*, reverence, niceness, romance, and others – the luxury affect generates sememes which circulate and gain currency through society. Unlike the other affective economies, however, that of luxury relies in large part on meanings of exclusion, denial, and rejection – the creation of security and identity boundaries that abject the mass, average person as being unworthy of belonging. Yet the duality of the luxury affect is that even as it defines an elite community for inclusion and cohesion, it can only do so by defining it in contradistinction to another (larger) community for exclusion. Luxury affect is thus by definition always also a discourse of the (non-elite) Other, who is caught up in this affective regime as the outsider looking in, and desiring what is described as unattainable. This visceral affect of exclusion circulates as effectively, if not more so, than the luxury and exclusivity which is the other side of its semiotic coin.

8   Affecting the Digital Landscape

Introduction

Technological developments in the semiotic landscape cannot be ignored. As we have pointed out (see Chapters 1 and 5), there is an increased interweaving of landscapes from both the filmic and nonfilmic worlds, so that, for example, tourism in the latter is boosted by audience experience of the former – despite the fact that a number of these filmic landscapes do not actually exist outside their cinematic reality, being the results of digital technologies that dramatically altered features of the landscapes so as to better suit the creative ambitions of film directors and producers. The consequence is that the experiences of visitors to these landscapes outside the filmic world are increasingly influenced and informed by their cinematic experiences of the "same" landscapes. This interweaving of the digital into our physical experience of landscapes is also resulting from the use of augmented reality (AR), which is increasingly being explored as a tool to aid in urban planning (Hürzeler and Frey 2017). And of course, social media is already a highly prominent aspect of urban living, its ubiquity often raising concerns about privacy (e.g. tracking of one's location or purchases through the use of smartphones), safety (e.g. texting while driving), and conviviality (e.g. sending messages or making calls in the movie theater). It therefore makes sense to understand the term "digital landscape" broadly, that is, to understand it as encompassing not just the worlds of cinema or cyberspace as *sui generis* but also the ever-greater interconnections that are being established between cinema, cyberspace, and the sorts of physical landscapes that have been more traditionally associated with urban studies.

Given the foregoing remarks, we begin our discussion in this chapter with a review of the R-word campaign (Wee 2015). This discussion allows us to analyze some of the techniques that are being used to mobilize affect on the Internet, and this is followed by a detailed analysis of cyberbullying, and attempts to combat it, such as the calls for a "safer, friendlier Internet." This discussion serves to highlight how there are attempts to foster specific affective regimes in cyberspace but also how these affective regimes cannot simply be understood as existing in a realm that is entirely separate from more physically located semiotic landscapes. It thus brings home the idea that the semiotic landscape is increasingly digital and, moreover, helps to illustrate some of the strategies that are used in helping to bring about this interweaving of the digital and the physical. Our discussion then moves on to explore the increased use of virtual and ARs, as possible ways of more effectively encouraging responsible online behavior by getting social media users to better appreciate the connectivities that can and do exist between the world online and the world offline.

The R-Word Campaign

The R-Word campaign was initiated in 2004 by the Special Olympics International Board of Directors to eliminate the use of the word "retarded" (and its morphological variants). While the original impetus for the campaign came from the request by Special Olympics athletes to "update the movement's terminology from 'mental retardation' to 'intellectual disabilities'," the campaign expanded its scope in 2008 from the Special Olympics community to include the general public when it decided to "combat the inappropriate use of the R-word in common usage."[1] The campaign's slogan is, "Spread the word to end the word." In discussing this campaign, we will pay specific attention to the divergence between illocutionary intent and perlocutionary effect, since a key feature of the campaign's argument is that the R-word is hurtful regardless of the speaker's intention.

The R-word campaign makes for an especially interesting case study of the intersection between affective regimes and digital technologies because its use of digital media, including the posting of small stories (Bamberg 2006; Georgakopoulou 2006), provides us with insight into how such media may be deployed for the mobilization of affect. This emerges with particular clarity when we compare the campaign's use of digital media with that of its detractors. This comparison helps to also highlight how it is that some discourse practices come to be authoritatively entextualized (Silverstein and Urban 1996) over others, particularly in an age when a significant amount of public discussion tends to take place in cyberspace. In this regard, the analysis of the R-word campaign allows us to bring together insights from studies of language ideological debates (Blommaert 1999) and verbal hygiene, particularly political correctness (Allan and Burridge 2006; Cameron 1995), to enrich our understanding of how digital technology impacts on attempts to influence the social circulation of semiotic resources (Stroud and Mpendukana 2009: 364) *within cyberspace as well as in the world outside.*

---

[1] Unless otherwise stated, all quotations are from the campaign's website, R-word.org. The different dates on which the site was accessed are indicated when specific examples are discussed.

To better appreciate the arguments employed by the R-word campaign, it is useful to situate them in relation to other debates over political correctness, such as attempts to reform language practices so as to combat sexism. Thus, Cameron (1995: 133) has observed that there were three distinct arguments employed in the push for "gender-free language." The accuracy argument (Cameron 1995: 135) asserts that "sexist language can (unintentionally) mislead ... and if speakers and writers do not want at least some people to misunderstand them they should not use generic masculine terms." The fairness argument (Cameron 1995: 136) appeals to the notion that "if you have two groups, they should receive identical or at least parallel treatment." The use of masculine terms to cover both genders when feminine terms lack the same wide scope is a clear violation of (linguistic) fairness. Finally, the civility argument (Cameron 1995: 134) suggests that sexist language may offend and alienate women, and calls for greater sensitivity on the part of men to the exclusionary effects of phrases such as "the man for the job."

There have, of course, been counterarguments. In response to the accuracy argument, the rejoinder has been that the elimination of gender distinctions actually "made the language *less* accurate by destroying a linguistic distinction" (Cameron 1995: 137, italics in original). The counter to the fairness argument asserts that some of the proposed guidelines for language use "in attempting to be fair to women, ended up being unfair to men" (Cameron 1995: 137). As regards the civility argument, the complaint has been that "the idea of civility, while intrinsically worthy, was being taken to absurd and self-defeating extremes ... [with] 'sensitivity' ... recast as *over*-sensitivity or even full-blown paranoia" (Cameron 1995: 137, italics in original).

Despite these counterarguments, Cameron (1995: 137) suggests that the accuracy, fairness, and civility arguments have been largely successful in gaining public support for the language reforms:

[F]irst, because they entail an analysis of gender relations that is relatively unthreatening – men and women are equally subject to prejudice and discrimination, and much of this is only a question of individual thoughtlessness – and second, because they resonate with ideas about the use of language, which many or most educated people hold dear – for instance, that it should be clear, unbiased, and sensitive to the feelings of the addressee.

Compared to the arguments for reforming sexist language, the R-word campaign gives much greater weight to the civility argument than to the accuracy or fairness arguments. But as Allan and Burridge (2006: 97) observe, "PC language" is about "public action ... there is more involved than simple politeness." Thus, as we now see, even "civility" appears to be too weak a term to describe the reasons given by the campaign for wanting to eliminate the R-word.

The overwhelming concern for the campaign's advocates is that the use of the R-word is deeply hurtful. To the extent that the accuracy argument is at all involved, this is implicit in the campaign's claim that the R-word's negative connotations serve to perpetuate a negative (and hence, inaccurate) stereotype about people with intellectual disabilities. Where the fairness argument is concerned, this comes to the fore in the campaign's assertion that everyone, intellectually disabled or otherwise, deserves to be treated with respect – which essentially brings us back to the civility argument. Thus, consider the following extracts from the campaign's website (bold in original, the shift between upper- and lowercase "R/r" is in the original as well):

(1) (Accessed August 8, 2011)
The R-word hurts because it is exclusive. It's offensive. It's derogatory. The R-word is hate speech.

(2)
When they were originally introduced, the terms "mental retardation" or "mentally retarded" were medical terms with a specifically clinical connotation; however the pejorative forms, "retard" and "retarded" have been used widely in today's society to degrade and insult people with intellectual disabilities.

(3)
Today the r-word has become a common word used by society as an insult for someone or something stupid. For example, you might hear someone say, "That is so retarded" or "Don't be such a retard." When used in this way, the r-word can apply to anyone or anything, and is not specific to someone with a disability. But, even when the r-word is not said to harm someone with a disability, it is hurtful.

In (1), we see the claim that the R-word "hurts." But perhaps even more significant is that (1) makes the very strong claim that the R-word is hate speech. Hate speech is generally understood as speech that is not only offensive; it is speech that is motivated by a speaker's irrational and extreme hatred for a social or ethnic group, and has the capacity to incite violence. In the United States, it has even been argued by the legal scholars known as the Critical Race theorists that because it is simply a form of assault, "hate speech can be made illegal without violating the constitutional protection of freedom of speech" (Hill 2008: 41). Thus, labeling something as "hate speech" attributes a particularly negative intention to the speaker, characterizes the impact on the hearer as especially intense and painful, and even casts it as a threat to a larger civil society. Precisely because of this, we have to be careful what we decide to actually categorize as "hate speech."
(2) provides a historically sensitive account of how the "R-word" has gone from being a specialist term to one that is widely used, and has, as a consequence, acquired a pejorative connotation[2]. Because this pejorative

---

[2] There seems to be an assumption here that the clinical use of the term is somehow innocent. Foucauldian-minded scholars might disagree on the grounds that such uses, even if not necessarily pejorative, represent a technology of subjection (Foucault 2000).

use of the R-word is often aimed at people with intellectual disabilities, this is why it needs to be eliminated. (3) describes the complement set of (2), that is, people who are not intellectually disabled (as well as things – to which the attribute is irrelevant in the first place). The claim here is that even such uses of the R-word are "hurtful," presumably because these help to continue the perpetuation of negative stereotypes about people with intellectual disabilities.

The focus on the emotional effects of the R-word motivates the campaign's "eradicationist" position (Hill 2008: 57; Kennedy 2002), where the goal is to "end the word." This eradicationist position seems to largely rule out the possibility that individuals who have been offended by the word might want to reclaim it as has happened with terms like *queer* and *nigger*, where these terms can now be used as in-group markers of solidarity and even pride (Cameron 1995: 148). This is not to suggest that reclamation is not a possible outcome, but simply to point out that any such attempts at reclamation will have to be in spite of, rather than because of, the campaign's activities.

The campaign's eradicationist position also suggests that there are almost no occasions on which the use of the R-word might be considered acceptable, appropriate, or even tolerable. Hence, the campaign's appeal to the circumlocution "R-word" is intended to reflexively minimize its own use of the word. Complete avoidance is understandably impossible since in order to explain just what the campaign is about, some mention of the R-word is necessary. (This raises the issue of whether the campaign makes a distinction between the use and the mention of the word, and I return to this later).

The Focus on Perlocutionary Effect

The campaign's arguments for eliminating the R-word appear to initially vacillate between a focus on the speaker's illocutionary intent and word's presumptive perlocutionary effect, but the pendulum ultimately swings in favor of the latter. While there is some reference to the fact that people do use the word to "degrade and insult" (2), the later assertion is that the word is simply "hurtful" (3), thus treating the hurtfulness of the word as an inextricable, if not intrinsic, part of its meaning.

Consequently, where the campaign is concerned, the use of the word is simply not acceptable, regardless of speaker intention and regardless of whether someone actually claims to have been hurt. The presumption here is that the very use of the word is hurtful. Thus, consider the following three examples, all taken from the campaign's website (accessed August 8, 2011). The first example is shown in (4), where the campaign's website celebrates the fact that on October 5, 2010, US president Barack Obama signed into federal law a bill known as Rosa's Law:

(4)
Rosa's Law, which takes its name and inspiration for [*sic*] 9-year-old Rosa Marcellino, removes the terms "mental retardation" and "mentally retarded" from federal health, education, and labor policy and replaces them with people first language "individual with an intellectual disability" and "intellectual disability." The signing of Rosa's Law is a significant milestone in establishing dignity, inclusion, and respect for all people with intellectual disabilities.

It seems obvious that the drafters of the various federal policies had no intention to insult or degrade when they used the R-word. And it is not really specified if anyone has found the experience of reading federal policies that contain the R-word to be hurtful. Nevertheless, because these policies do contain the R-word and because readers of the policies may feel insulted or degraded, the R-word, according to the campaign, must be removed.

The second example is shown in (5). Among the many links that the campaign's site provides under its "News" section is a link to a news article from *US Weekly* (2010); (5) is an extract from that article:

(5)
When Jennifer Aniston used the word "retard" in a *Live! With Regis and Kelly* interview in August, Peter Berns, CEO of The Arc (a nonprofit advocacy group for those with intellectual and developmental disabilities), told US Weekly her usage of the term was "extraordinarily offensive and inappropriate."

"Frankly, someone in her position ought to know better," Berns said of Aniston, 42. "She is using language that is offensive to a large segment of the population in this country . . . Even if [the word] wasn't intended to insult them, that is the effect of it."

Needless to say, Berns' assertion is consistent with the position of the R-word campaign, which is presumably why the campaign's website has a link to the article. Berns' statement makes clear that illocutionary intent is indeed irrelevant so that even calling Aniston's utterance a gaffe (Hill 2008: 88) is not enough excuse for her use of the R-word. The concern is specifically with the perlocutionary effect of insulting "a large segment of the population."

The third and final example comes from the fact, stated in the campaign's website (accessed August 8, 2011), that the Special Olympics along with a number of national disability organizations embarked on a campaign protesting against the Hollywood movie *Tropic Thunder*. According to the campaign, the movie, though "marketed as a satire about Hollywood actors and the movie industry in general, contains scenes promoting the idea that a 'retard' is funny."

In focusing on perlocutionary effect to the point where a speaker's illocutionary intent is disregarded, the campaign has adopted a position that is arguably stronger than its claim that the R-word is hate speech. The categorization of something as hate speech is still linked to a speaker's intent. So, while the use of racist terms in a movie may be accurate in portraying a movie character as racist, the actors and screenwriters themselves would not be leveled with charges of racism. In contrast, once the focus is shifted toward the presumption of perlocutionary effect, regardless of what happens onscreen, the actors and screenwriters themselves can be singled out for being thoughtless and offensive since they are effectively responsible for introducing the word in the movie and hence allowing it to circulate in the public domain.

This perlocutionist ideology contrasts significantly with the personalist ideology (Rosaldo 1981). Hill (2008: 38) points out that the latter holds that "the most important part of linguistic meaning comes from the beliefs and intentions of the speaker," and (2008: 111) observes that a problem with the personalist ideology is that it has sometimes been used to "insulate" speakers from accusations of racism, on the grounds that a speaker may have only been ignorant or insensitive. In this way, the personalist ideology sometimes errs on the side of being too lenient or kind, by allowing speakers to get away with racist remarks mainly because it is difficult to determine a speaker's actual intentions. In contrast, the perlocutionist ideology seems to go to the other extreme. Since speaker intention is no longer a consideration, no excuse is acceptable for using the R-word. In this way, the perlocutionist ideology errs on the side of being too strict, by breeding intolerance and perhaps more controversially, encouraging feelings of offense and indignation.

This final observation leads us to the question of just how the campaign goes about mobilizing affect in order to bring about its desired affective regime, an issue to which we now turn.

The Affective Economy of the R-Word Campaign: The Mobilization of Affect

The examples that we have had occasion to discuss in the preceding chapters dealt with the circulation of affect, and the R-word campaign is not an exception in this regard.[3] But what makes the R-word campaign interesting is that it is concerned with stopping the circulation of a family of related signs (i.e. the word "retarded" and its variants). This is the eradicationist position that we observed earlier. Thus, we have here an interesting variant on the affective economy, one where the goal is to discourage, if not altogether eliminate, the circulation of a sign or signs that the campaign considers to be hurtful.

And what the R-word campaign's perlocutionist ideology shows is that the campaign aims to achieve this goal of stopping the circulation of its targeted signs by imposing a particular interpretant. Specifically, the argument that the campaign presents is that the targeted signs are hurtful no matter what the

---

[3] All the examples discussed in this section are either taken directly from the R-word website or from other websites that are linked to it.

speaker may have intended. In this way, the indexical field of words like "retard" or "retarded" is being deliberately narrowed to exclude all other meanings except those where the words are understood as being derogatory or offensive. What we want to do in this section, then, is to examine in greater detail the specific strategies that are employed by the campaign as it tries to influence the affective economy of signs like "retarded" by suggesting that precisely because of the harm that they cause, these should have absolutely no currency.

We noted earlier that the campaign relies significantly on testimonies, endorsements, expressions of remorse, and pledges. Here are some examples. (6) is an appeal, quoted in Zara's Blog, from a Special Olympics athlete, Donny Knight, to the general public to stop using the R-word. Knight points out that "it hurts my feelings." (7) is from a site called "The Red Neck Mommy," where a mother is speaking on behalf of intellectually disabled individuals, including her children (italics in original):

(6)
When you say the "R" word it makes people feel bad and it hurts my feelings and I don't want to hear you guys say it. Instead, you can call me a leader, a hero, or a human being, but please don't call me the "R" word.

(7)
When you drop the 'tard bomb into casual conversation, you are demeaning disabled people and reinforcing the stereotype that mental disabilities are bad and that people who suffer these disabilities are lesser; to be excluded and ignored because they don't know any better. Heck, it's not like they even know what the word means right? Who are you hurting?

You are hurting *me*. You are hurting my *kids*. You are hurting *everyone* who loves someone who has been labeled a retard due to how they look, how they speak, or how they learn.

It's not okay to go on twitter and announce that your computer is retarded. Did you mean your computer's operating system is running slow? You might have meant to convey that your laptop is a piece of shit that doesn't work and you desperately covet a new one, but instead you just conveyed your ignorance and your lack of respect for the most marginalized, disparaged group of people in the world.

(8) is from the "The Diaper Diaries," which contains an expression of remorse from someone who, having realized how hurtful the R-word is, vows to "eliminate the r-word from my vocabulary":

(8)
And I will confess I use the word. Not to refer to people who are mentally challenged of course, but I don't think that earns me any sort of pat on the back. Words are meaningful. They matter and they have the power to lift up and the power to destroy. And I don't want mine to ever hurt someone. Especially someone who already has enough stacked against them.

So I am going to make every effort to eliminate the r-word from my vocabulary. Won't you join me?

(9) comes from the campaign's "Cheers" section, which provides news snippets where individuals and organizations have acted in support of the campaign. (There is also a "Jeers" section, providing snippets of individuals and organizations behaving "badly.") The list of celebrities/public figures and organizations speaks to the relatively wide support that the campaign has garnered. (10) is from the campaign's Pledge section, where visitors to the site are encouraged to sign up and pledge their commitment to the campaign's goal of eliminating the R-word.

(9)
Spread the Word to End the Word received amazing support from celebrities and influential organizations on March 2nd. These individuals/organizations took the pledge: Cat Cora, California Governor Gavin Newsom, Miami Heat, JaVale McGee (of the Washington Wizards), Sacramento Kings, Maria Shriver, Matt Barnes (of the LA Lakers), NBA, NBA Cares, NOH8 Campaign, Paula Deen, Al Roker, Dr. Oz, Vanessa Williams, and Nancy O'Dell.

(10)
I pledge and support the elimination of the derogatory use of the r-word from everyday speech and promote the acceptance and inclusion of people with intellectual disabilities.

With the exception of (9–10), (6–8) contain small stories (Bamberg 2006; Georgakopoulou 2006). Unlike the traditional focus on large-scale biographies that highlight temporal distance and self-reflection (Bamberg 2006: 146), the notion of small stories is instead "an umbrella-term that covers a gamut of under-represented narrative activities, such as tellings of ongoing events, future or hypothetical events, shared (known) events, but also allusions to tellings, deferrals of tellings, and refusals to tell" (Georgakopoulou 2006: 123). While the category is undoubtedly a heterogeneous one, small stories typically are shorter "snippets of talk" that have a more dynamic and immediate nature (Georgakopoulou 2006: 123, 126). Thus, they are not just smaller in length (i.e. shorter than biographies); they are also smaller in scope or ambition (i.e. less concerned with ruminating over the significance of a life story and what this says about the way the narrator remembers herself or wishes to be remembered, than with reworking "slices of life" (Georgakopoulou 2006: 126). That is, they are reinterpretations and representations of selected experiences as being of particular relevance or significance to ongoing activities or events.

With the foregoing in mind, we can see that the small stories in (6–8) are of a specific type: they highlight the personal experiences, in particular, the pain and hurt experienced by the narrators or their family and friends, as the result of exposure to the R-word. And these small stories are readily available for public consumption, since any visitor to the campaign's site can access them. Some of the stories are in the form of videos so that the emotional nuances of these stories are conveyed in more than just words. There are also an extensive number of links from the R-word site to other sites, which multiply the number of small stories exponentially, thus helping to attest to the widespread hurtful effects of the R-word. And of course, the R-word is also present on Facebook, Twitter, and YouTube.

Together with the (growing) list of celebrities and organizations in (9), the R-word campaign succeeds in giving the (probably not inaccurate) impression that it has strong public support. This impression is reinforced by the presence of a widget on the campaign's site that provides an update on the number of pledges accumulated. On September 21, 2011, there were 223, 413 online pledges. As of November 23, 2017, the number of such pledges had grown to 711, 273. In addition, the campaign's site also sells merchandise, such as bracelets, T-shirts, mugs, and banners. Visitors to the site can purchase these if they wish to publicly demonstrate their support for the campaign. There are also cards bearing the campaign logo that visitors can download; visitors can also opt to have the logo displayed on their own personal websites. These activities make effective use of digital media to cultivate the sense that the campaign and its supporters constitute a dynamic and highly active community – all sharing in the same affective regime that wants to stop seeing people hurt or offended by the continued use of the R-word.

This sense of community is further enhanced by the presence of yet another widget, the R-word counter. Users simply enter the URL of any site of their choosing, and they will receive a count of just how many times that particular site uses the R-word. According to the counter, as of September 21, 2011, "people on the World Wide Web have used the R-word 242, 022 times." More recently, ABC News (Australian Broadcasting Corporation) reported that the campaign's website contained the simple statement: "159, 204. The number of times the R word was used on Twitter in the last 7 days" (February 21, 2018, www.abc.net.au/news/2018–02-21/r-word-campaign-image/9470926; accessed March 14, 2018). Again, this is provision of a number without further contextualization beyond the number itself; its appearance on Twitter, and within a relatively short time frame, is intended to convey that the use of the R-word is rampant and thus needs to be checked. The specifics of who might be using the R-word and under what kinds of contexts are simply omitted and considered irrelevant.

This kind of count clearly does not distinguish between the use and the mention of the word, for example, and it is not clear if the count includes the campaign's own use of the word, since it is presumably possible to enter the campaign's own URL into the counter. Nevertheless, such a widget contributes to the sense that the battle to eliminate the R-word is an ongoing one that requires constant vigilance. It is also consistent with the campaign's eradica-tionist stance, since the very fact that the word continues to exist and to be used warrants the campaign. What the organizers of the R-word campaign have tried to do, therefore, is to submit the word "retarded" to a process of enregisterment, "whereby diverse behavioral signs (whether linguistic, non-linguistic, or both) are functionally reanalyzed as cultural models of action, as behaviors capable of indexing stereotypic characteristics of incumbents of particular interactional roles, and of relations among them" (Agha 2011: 55). In this case, those who continue using the R-word are portrayed as callous and insensitive to the hurtful effects it has on various individuals, their family, and friends. This enregisterment is carried out online by making available video and posted pleas from affected individuals to the general public to stop using the R-word. That is, once individuals are aware of how hurtful the word can be, there is no real excuse to continue using it. In this way, the campaign hopes to reduce, if not completely stop, the social circulation of the R-word. The affordances of digital technology also make it possible for the campaign's organizers to provide downloadable banners and slogans, as well as sell various merchandise, all in order to encourage members of the public to demonstrate their support. In particular, the replication of signs of support (i.e. banners and slogans) is in principle unlimited since it is not constrained by material production processes on the part of the organizers. Rather, it is up to each individual supporter to download and print out his/her own copy of the relevant banner or slogan.

The campaign's use of widgets is particularly interesting. A widget that counts the number of pledges gives a very public demonstration of the support that the campaign enjoys. And a widget that allows users to count the number of times that a particular site uses the R-word is essentially a technology of surveillance (Foucault 1977). Here, affect has clearly overtaken any objective quantifiable evidence: the point of the widget is not to show that usage of the R-word is high relative to the number of websites out there, or that it is objectively increasing, or even static. Rather, the number displayed on the counter operates affectively, to move the viewer with a sense of how prevalent the use of the R-word continues to be.

Since just about any site can be subjected to this form of surveillance, the use of this widget effectively means that the entire cyber landscape is open to being monitored by supporters of the R-word campaign. The cyber landscape is framed as a public space where individual sites are also fair game for monitoring since these are in principle accessible to just about any visitor, and, hence, any use of the R-word is potentially hurtful to a visitor who encounters the word. This is unlike the physical landscape, where it might be possible to treat each landscape as relatively autonomous by virtue of territorial boundary, e.g. Chinatown as a distinct landscape (Leeman and Modan 2009) or sites of necessity versus sites of luxury (Stroud and Mpendukana 2009). In contrast, the ability to create hyperlinks and the easy use of widgets mean that there is greater interconnectedness in the cyber landscape. As a consequence, struggles involving perceived hurts arising from language use, as in the case of the

R-word campaign, are arguably harder to resolve if the argument being presented is that what happens on one given site cannot be considered separate from what happens elsewhere in some other site. That is, the notion of "separatedness" is becoming harder to sustain as a consequence of interconnectedness in the cyber landscape.

There has, not surprisingly, been some opposition to the R-word campaign. But as we now see, what is interesting about these opposing arguments is the sense of resignation that accompanies them. That is, opponents to the campaign seem to feel that they are fighting a losing battle.

Opposing Arguments

Consider (11–12), from Jack Marshall, who expresses concern about the R-word campaign:

(11)
I can think of lots of other unsavory, mean words that begin with an "r." How about *"raghead," Ruskie," "redneck,"* and *"redskin"*? If "retarded" is banned (along with "retard"), can these be far behind? Then what … do we have to talk in terms of "r-word#1" and "r-word #2, 3, 4, and 5"? Do the Washington Redskins become the Washington R-word #5s?

(12)
Imagine how difficult it will be to discuss various historical and social issues when every group gets to condemn words they find demeaning … Women will ban the c-word, the b-word (too bad for dog breeders), and the d-word. Prostitutes will want to ban the w-word. Gays don't like the h-word or the q-word (unless they use it themselves, much as the n-word isn't the n-word if a black comedian uses it.)

(11) is aimed at the issue of accuracy, suggesting that the R-word campaign leads to a kind of Pandora's box, where other R-words too may need to be banned. The intentionally absurd scenario being painted is that the different R-words may need to be distinguished from each other via numerical markers. This accuracy argument is something of a nonstarter since the campaign is not simply aiming to eliminate the R-word, but rather to also replace it with an alternative that is supposed to be more "people first language" such as "individual with an intellectual disability" and "intellectual disability" (see [4] above).

(12) also paints a Pandora's box scenario, where it is envisioned that various groups will demand that words they find offensive be banned. Putting aside Marshall's sarcastic tone, (12) does raise an important issue, namely if the justification for eliminating a word is the offense it causes, then whose feelings are "important" enough to warrant such elimination? This raises the issue of fairness because it seems clear that not any individual or group that claims to have been offended by some language use should seek redress and have its

concerns taken seriously. There are probably no clear prima facie principles that we can appeal to in order to guide in addressing such concerns. Instead, what seems clear is that the individuals or groups are more likely to have their concerns taken seriously to the extent that they are already perceived as being relatively powerless, subject to discrimination, and worthy of sympathy. This last factor is particularly pertinent in the case of the intellectually disabled. Opponents to the R-word campaign who accuse the campaign (and hence by implication those that the campaign aims to protect and claims to be representing) of being overly sensitive or paranoid (Cameron 1995: 137) are likely to be accused of insensitivity or callousness.

Another important point in (12) is whether this need to avoid certain words might have a deleterious effect on the very ability to publicly discuss the social issues surrounding the discrimination of specific groups. This is a point echoed by Christopher Haxel, another critic of the campaign:

(13)
I fear the r-word movement discourages serious debate on the topic of mental disabilities. How many people avoid the discussion because they don't know the "proper" terminology or fear retribution from r-word apologists?

The R-word campaign could of course respond to critics like Marshall and Haxel by asserting that it is only possible to have a proper discussion about such issues if there is first a sense of mutual respect. And indeed, "PC language was often consciously devised to ease the difficulties that arise in this volatile area of interpersonal relations" (Allan and Burridge 2006: 111).

(14)
Just *stop*. **STOP!** Stop banning words and thoughts, ugly or otherwise. Teach people to be civil, to respect each other, and to treat fellow Americans with kindness and tolerance as long as they aren't hurting anybody or doing any harm. *And trying to control thoughts and speech by banning words, ideas, sentences, insults, poetry, jokes, opinions, stories, history, books, plays, and movies **is** causing harm,* and must not be [*sic*] tolerated.

Finally, in (14), Marshall attempts to address the civility argument by suggesting that uses of the R-word should be considered acceptable so long as no one is harmed. But as we have already observed, given the campaign's perlocutionist ideology, it is hard to see under what circumstances no one might be harmed by the R-word, since the potential for being hurt or offended is always there and thus in need of being preempted. Marshall also tries in (14) to counter the claim that the R-word is harmful with the assertion that banning the word is even more harmful, since it amounts to "thought control." However, the specter of thought control remains a relatively abstract and (for some) rather far-fetched scenario compared to the evidence that (at least some) individuals are actually hurt and offended by the R-word. This observation brings us nicely to the differences in how the R-word campaign and its detractors differ in their use of small stories and digital media.

The kinds of scenarios painted by opponents to the campaign are largely abstract, intellectual, and counterfactual. We see this, for example, in Marshall's questions in (11) ("Then what ... do we have to talk in terms of 'r-word #1' and 'r-word #2, 3, 4, and 5'?") and (12) ("Imagine how difficult it will be to discuss various historical and social issues when every group gets to condemn words they find demeaning"). We also see this in the question about the number of people who avoid discussing issues pertaining to mental disability (13). All these contrast with the highly personal and concrete stories of experiences presented by the campaign. The question in (13) makes reference to the number of people who might be unable to participate in discussions about mental disabilities ("How many people avoid the discussion because they don't know the 'proper' terminology or fear retribution from r-word apologists?"). But this also contrasts starkly with the campaign's widgets, which provide specific and updated counts of pledges and occurrences of the R-word on the web. The campaign therefore has much greater emotional impact, due to its use of small stories of hurt, its call for active support by making available various downloads and selling merchandise. The opponents, in contrast, rely mainly on blogs to post their concerns. They are trying to engage in arguments about whether the rationale for the campaign has any merits when the campaign has already moved into the mobilization of affect phase.

Hence, it is perhaps no surprise that opponents to the campaign seem largely resigned to the fact that they are probably fighting a losing battle. One event that perhaps symbolizes for them how the momentum of the campaign is against them comes from Marshall's (2010, underlining in original) description of what he sees as capitulation by Rahm Emanuel to pressure from the campaign:

(15)
White House Chief of Staff Rahm Emanuel, criticized for using the word "retarded" during a private meeting last summer, has told advocates for the mentally disabled that <u>he will join their campaign to help end the use of the word.</u>
I'm sure he will. Emanuel, like too many politicians, is willing to throw Freedom of Speech and thought under the bus if it gets him out of hot water with the politically correct.

Regardless of whether Emanuel was sincere in deciding to join the campaign, it is clear that the campaign's tactic amounts to a form of public shaming, where those who disagree with its goals are put on the defensive as possibly lacking compassion or respect for the intellectually disabled[4]. As Allan and

---

[4] In fact, in a similar incident, Harvard College recently asked each new student to sign a pledge, developed by the Freshman Dean's Office, which states that "each degree candidate stands ready

Burridge (2006: 102) point out, "A breach of PC protocol can quickly become an inquiry into a miscreant's character." And public figures and entities (such as politicians, celebrities, and organizations) have more to lose from going against the campaign than private individuals such as Marshall. Their reliance on public opinion makes them particularly vulnerable to such acts of shaming. Consequently, it is perhaps not surprising that public figures are quick to lend their support to the campaign, which, in turn, leads the campaign's opponents to feel that they represent a minority view.

Thus, in a supportive email to Marshall's blog, Glenn Logan (2010), another opponent to the campaign, makes the following statements:

(15)
I have ranted about this for years. It is futile. Nonetheless, it is welcome to see this sad trend rationally assailed again . . .
One can only pray that people will stop equating ethical speech with politically correct speech.
A hope, I fear, that is in vain.

Marshall, in turn, responds to Logan with the following (16):

Marshall:
(16)
Don't despair, Glenn. But it is disturbing to see the press so easily capitulate to totalitarian tactics just because the "good guys" are behind it.

Marshall's ironic characterization of the R-word campaign's organizers as the "good guys" indicates his belief that general public opinion is behind the campaign, and those individuals who oppose the campaign, such as him, risk being seen in contrast as the "bad guys."

It should be noted that the opponents to the R-word campaign are themselves mobilizing affect in some ways: (11) and (12) use a version of the *reductio ad absurdum* to garner indignation at what is seen as the inconsistencies and excesses of the campaign. (14) is much more overt, painting the campaign's policing of speech as "causing harm." However, it is clear that the R-word campaign is significantly wider (in appealing to all perlocutionary effects) as

---

to advance knowledge, to promote understanding, and to serve society" (Postrel 2011). While the goals of the pledge are laudable, the issue of concern here is that of coercion. As Postrel (2011) observes:

The original plan was to post the pledge in each dorm entryway, along with the names and signatures of the students living there. Although signing was supposed to be voluntary, any dissent would have been obvious.
    The posting constituted "an act of public shaming," Professor Harry R. Lewis, a computer science professor and former dean of Harvard College, wrote in a blog spot condemning the pledge. Some students signed because they felt they had to – a completely predictable, yet somehow unforeseen, result that Mr Tom Dingman, the dean of freshmen, says is "against the spirit of the pledge." The signatures will no longer be posted.

well as deeper (in its marshaling of personal anecdotes and stories, particularly of clearly marginalized and powerless figures like Paralympians) in its mobilization of affect. Also, it would of course have been entirely possible for opponents to the R-word campaign to also make use of widgets, create downloadable slogans, or post videos, to express their objections to the campaign. However, the desire to embark on these activities has apparently been pre-empted by the sense that to do so would be to fight a losing battle. In this sense, the R-word campaign has very effectively managed to mobilize affect to its side of the linguistic battle.

The Authoritative Entextualization of Political Correctness

We have seen that the R-word campaign can be considered relatively successful – in that it appears to be gathering broad public support, even if its goal of completely eradicating the word is yet to be achieved (and may perhaps never be achieved). A significant factor in the campaign's success clearly lies in how it has managed to keep the focus on the hurtful effects that the word has on various individuals. In the course of our discussion, we also had occasion to refer to the attempts to reform sexist language, which was also considered a success. In fact, as Allan and Burridge (2006: 101) observe, "[P]olitical correctness has been remarkably effective in getting people to change their linguistic habits, far more effective than other kinds of linguistic prescriptions and proscriptions."

This brings us to the issue of authoritative entextualization. Silverstein and Urban (1996: 11, quoted in Blommaert 1999: 9), point out that "[p]olitics can be seen ... as the struggle to entextualize authoritatively, and hence, in one relevant move, to fix certain metadiscursive perspectives on texts and discourse practices." And Blommaert (1999: 9, italics in original) goes on to observe that "[t]he struggle develops usually over *definitions* of social realities: various representations of reality which are pitted against each other – discursively – with the aim of gaining authority for one particular representation." In the case of political correctness, while it would certainly be an overgeneralization to suggest that efforts at introducing politically correct language are always successful, there are nevertheless reasons to believe that politically correct initiatives will tend to have the advantage in language ideological debates so that opponents to such initiatives will usually find themselves immediately on the defensive. In short, discourses promoting political correctness tend to get authoritatively entextualized over opposing discourses.

But why should this be so? Apart from the appeal to a wider sense of social justice – i.e. of fair play and righting a wrong – we suggest that the key point is because political correctness reforms tend to concern specific bits and pieces of language rather than entire varieties. In the case of sexist language, the focus was on lexical items (*chairman* vs. *chairperson*) or masculine pronouns used generically. In the case of the R-word campaign, the focus is on *retarded* and its variants. This focus on pieces of language leads to the assumption that the cost involved in modifying one's language use (including giving up the use of a particular word) is a relatively small one, compared to the possible social benefits (less people feeling hurt or offended, drawing attention to various kinds of discrimination). In other words, insofar as the affective economy requires the removal of a single sign or two, this is a small price to pay if the wider goal of not hurting the feelings of a significant number of individuals is achieved. In such cases, some attempt at language reform is the least that society at large can do to help combat social discrimination.

Thus, Cameron (1995: 133), in a discussion of the language guidelines proposed by the University of Strathclyde's Programme of Opportunities for Women Committee (POWC), observes:

No one was officially responsible for enforcing the rules, but anyone who noticed some lapse in a university document could legitimately draw the new guidelines to the attention of the perpetrator. Conversely, people who wanted to use non-sexist language in official communications no longer had to persuade their superiors that was not a silly or outlandish ambition; and to the extent that such people felt the need for concrete suggestions about non-sexist usage the leaflet provided guidance.

And, likewise, in a response to Marshall's critical remarks about the R-word campaign, someone named Julia writes:

(17)
I thought we lived in a society were [*sic*] we tried to remove negative labels that hurt people. I didn't realize so many people want to hold on to such demeaning and derogatory words.

In both these cases, the pressure appears to be on those who refuse to adopt the proposed language reforms to explain why they would insist on persisting with what is "clearly" unacceptable linguistic behavior. This is in contrast to cases where entire varieties are at stake. In such cases, the arguments tend to focus on the fact that the whole cultural heritage of a community of speakers (usually defined along ethnic or national lines) is being threatened, and, therefore, a tradition and a set of values and fundamentally formative identities are all under threat and, thus, in need of protection. The linguistic costs are not only too high but they also carry with them significant social costs without any apparent social benefits. These different assumptions about the relative linguistic costs incurred and the expected social benefits represent metadiscursive perspectives that inevitably influence the arguments and discourse practices that emerge from any language ideological debate.

In the case of the R-word campaign, the utilization of digital technology has enabled its organizers to mount a fairly aggressive attack on the use and users of the R-word. In this regard, it is important to bear in mind that the campaign's attempts to stop the circulation of the R-word are not just restricted to cleaning up the cyber landscape. Although, as an online campaign, much of the campaign's activities take place in cyberspace, the ability to post small stories, create video links, and links to news reports means that the campaign is also able to impact what goes on in the outside world as well (see [15]). And this brings us nicely to the issue of cyberbullying and attempts to, among others, create a "safer Internet."

Cyberbullying

The R-word campaign is just one example of a growing concern with how digital technology (particularly in the form of Internet access and social media) can leave its users vulnerable to being attacked, humiliated, or having their privacy invaded. And one particular phenomenon that has become a matter of concern of late is that of cyberbullying.

The widespread use of digital devices such as mobile phones, tablets, and computers means that cyberbullying can take place through the transmission of SMS, uploading of videos and photographs, and the various other ways in which content can be shared and distributed online. According to a US government website on cyberbullying ("Stopbullying .gov," www.stopbullying.gov/cyberbullying/what-is-it/index.html; accessed November 24, 2017):

Cyberbullying includes sending, posting, or sharing negative, harmful, false, or mean content about someone else. It can include sharing personal or private information about someone else causing embarrassment or humiliation. Some cyberbullying crosses the line into unlawful or criminal behavior.

The most common places where cyberbullying occurs are as follows:
• Social media, such as Facebook, Instagram, Snapchat, and Twitter
• Short message service (SMS), also known as text message sent through devices
• Instant message (via devices, email provider services, apps, and social media messaging features)
• Email

With the prevalence of social media and digital forums, comments, photos, posts, and content shared by individuals can often be viewed by strangers as well as acquaintances. The content an individual shares online – both their personal content and any negative, mean, or hurtful content – creates a kind of permanent public record of their views, activities, and behavior. This public record can be thought of as an online reputation, which may be accessible to schools, employers, colleges, clubs, and others who may be researching an individual now or in the future.

And this means that all users of digital technology have a responsibility to be more careful in what they post about others (to be considerate as to the effects on these others) as well as about themselves (to not allow themselves to be easy targets of cyberbullying). As the Media Literacy Council of Singapore points out (www.medialiteracycouncil.sg/campaign2017/index .html; accessed November 11, 2017):

> What we do online can spill over to the real world. Our actions can have far-reaching consequences as every comment or post we make online can be viewed instantaneously by people all around the world. By doing our part to think before we post and promote positive online behavior, we can help to make the Internet a better place for everyone!

The main issue in the case of cyberbullying, then, is the circulation of signs, not just within the cyber landscape but also their spilling over into the "real world." The reputational damage and psychological harm suffered by a victim of cyberbullying results from the circulation of signs that target her with the deliberate intention to cause her distress. Cyberbullying, then, differs from the R-word campaign in subtly interesting ways. Whereas the R-word campaign is concerned with the spread of a particular sign or set of signs, cyberbullying does not have that luxury. This is because what constitutes harmful information will vary depending on the identity, reputation, and circumstances of the targeted individual. Circulating nude photographs of a porn star is unlikely to have the effect as compared to circulating nude photographs of a housewife or politician. And whereas the R-word campaign wants to eradicate words like "retarded" *regardless* of the intention behind their use, cyberbullying is specifically concerned with intent. Accidental online sharing of someone else's private information for example, however harmful the consequences are, does not constitute cyberbullying. There needs to be a deliberate desire to cause the targeted individual pain and distress[5]. Thus, the challenges faced in tackling cyberbullying are much more difficult. It is not possible to simply target a particular signifier (such as the English word "retarded") because the kinds of signifiers involved are much more varied. And it is not possible to ignore intent because not all forms of online sharing are harmful to the individual in question; some may be shared in the spirit of lighthearted teasing and received in the same manner, and yet others may be shared thoughtlessly rather than with the specific goal of causing harm.

The forms that cyberbullying take are therefore both much more nebulous and heterogeneous than uses of the R-word. This means that any attempt to put in

---

[5] This means, of course, that the use of the R-word can constitute a specific case of cyberbullying where the continued use of words like "retarded" is known to and intended to cause hurt to the targeted individual.

place an affective regime, in this case one that aims to combat cyberbullying, has to employ somewhat different strategies. Rather than targeting specific words as a way of establishing an affective regime, the focus is directly on the affective regime itself—where, instead of cyberbullying, there is "cyber wellness" – and it is really up to users to decide for themselves just what kinds of behavior would help to bring about this desired affective regime. As with the R-word campaign and its opponents, it ultimately comes down to which affective regime is more efficacious in its mobilization of the more powerful response.

For example, as part of its support for Safer Internet Day, the Media Literacy Council of Singapore has initiated the Better Internet Campaign, which empha-sizes values such as empathy, respect, responsibility, and integrity (www .medialiteracycouncil.sg/campaign2017/index.html; accessed November 11, 2017, italics added):

Safer Internet Day (SID) is all about gathering like-minded people to create a safer, better Internet for everyone. Every year, on the second Tuesday of February, the whole world comes together to make the Internet a better place. SID kicked off in Europe in 2004, and is celebrated by over 100 countries globally[6]. The Media Literacy Council spearheaded Singapore's participation in 2013 and continues to celebrate SID each year through its Better Internet Campaign.

Based on our four core values of Empathy, Respect, Responsibility, and Integrity, the Better Internet Campaign raises awareness of cyber wellness issues that affect all of us, and encourages internet users to unite and play their part in creating a safer, better Internet for everyone.

However, an emerging challenge that needs to be addressed in trying to curb cyberbullying is the potential misuse of AR. Friedman and Kahn (2000: 163) point out that "augmented interactions have the potential to affect users' psy-chological and emotional states." These raise concerns about privacy and decep-tion because "the computation linked with an electronic tag can be designed to retain a record of the interaction between a person, the computation, and the physical object" and AR attempts to create "a system such that the user cannot tell the difference between the real world and the augmentation of it" (2000: 164). Basu (2016, no page numbers) summarizes some of the issues raised by Keith Miller, University of Missouri-St. Louis, and Bo Brinkman, Miami University in Ohio, computer scientists concerned about the implications of AR:

One of the most immediate problems both Brinkman and Miller see in augmented reality's future is that it empowers people to blur the lines between their fantasies and the realities of others.

. . .

---

[6] This is a form of stitching, where similar affective regimes are combined so as to widen their scope or coverage (see Chapter 6).

And that is frightening, given the morally questionable – yet perfectly legal – things you could do with augmented reality. You could tempt a diabetic or heart disease patient to purchase something they shouldn't. You could take cyberbullying to a whole new level by unleashing a phobia on a victim ... The point is this: You could use augmented reality to harm someone psychologically, perhaps physically, maybe even to the point of death – and you could walk away scot-free.

... Augmented reality has the capability to make our lives much better – more entertaining, more helpful, more interesting, less expected. In the interest of speeding mass adoption of a great new tool, Miller says it's incumbent on officials and experts to anticipate public concerns instead of waiting to troubleshoot until after the trouble starts, because by then, it'll be too late.

"I don't know of anyone doing anything to protect users from the future of augmented reality," Miller said. "And that's, frankly, not good."

The specific ways in which AR can be misused therefore remain highly speculative given that the public adoption and use of the technology remains still in an infant stage. But here is a simple example. Blippar is an app that "uses facial recognition software to recognize your image will be allowing users [*sic*] to 'claim their face' in the digital space. Blippar is a visual discovery app, using AR and machine learning to bring the physical world to life through smartphones" (Beat the Cyberbully "Blippar: augmented reality and facial recognition – potentially useful & dangerous all at once!" www.beatthecyberbully.ae/blippar-augmented-reality-and-facial-recognition-potentially-useful-dangerous-all-at-once/; accessed December 1, 2017). The app allows for information about an object to be accessed by simply scanning the object. This kind of technology is useful for museums, for example where scanning a display can bring up all sorts of information about it. And even Starbucks (Meyer 2017, italics in original) has begun using something similar in its Shanghai store:

The store will be in Shanghai, complete with an augmented-reality feature and an on-site bakery. The new Starbucks Reserve Roastery, part of the company's new line of upscale coffee venues, opens Wednesday ...

Augmented reality. AR, as it's known, becomes the new reality for Starbucks here. They point their mobile devices at various points around the store to get an AR tour about how coffee goes from bean to cup. There are also virtual badges to unlock and a Roastery filter to commemorate their visits.

But individuals, especially vulnerable young people, are also encouraged to upload their images and personal information so that they can be "recognized" by others. And, therefore, depending on how robust the privacy settings are on the app, strangers could scan someone (at a nightclub, perhaps) and immediately access otherwise personal information about that person, making the latter highly vulnerable to cyberbullying, cyberstalking, and even identity theft.

Conclusion

From an analytical perspective, what seems clear is that the use of AR will lead to transformations in signs in ways that could either be complimentary or defamatory to particular individuals. Signs are not merely the medium or means by which meanings are circulated; the signs are changed or transformed as they get reinterpreted in the course of being circulated.

Semiotic landscapes therefore have to be managed in ways that, as far as possible, protect potentially vulnerable individuals from the potentially harmful effects of AR as the technology becomes more and more embedded in everyday uses and encounters. This requires changing measures in how the landscapes are managed, in order to keep up with the ever-evolving ways in which AR comes to penetrate hitherto "purely" physical or nonvirtual landscapes.

Apart from the more obvious issues of misuse of personal data, what is interesting about AR (as with the other issues we have discussed in this chapter) is the ways in which affect can be mobilized to contest various AR applications. How will the language of "freedom" of data and access play out against the competing language of privacy and vulnerability? Which realm – the virtual, or the physical – will be seen as the more consequential in measuring positive and negative effects? The cultural politics of AR applications is not yet developed to the stage where trends in such contestations are obvious, but affect will no doubt be a crucial part of that cultural politics.

9 Conclusion

Introduction

Our argument in this book has been that affect is an inescapable aspect of the semiotic landscape, and unless careful and sustained attention is given to the study of affect, our understanding of the semiotic landscape remains seriously incomplete. To this end, we have presented a framework that draws upon the ideas of C. S. Peirce. And we have shown how this framework can provide the basis for analyzing the ways in which both linguistic and nonlinguistic signs work to help constitute affective regimes, and how signs of affect shift in their indexical meanings as they circulate in an affective economy.

While, in the preceding chapters, we have demonstrated the utility of this framework in relation to a variety of case studies, what we want to do in this concluding chapter is to discuss the wider issue of what it means to talk about a semiotic landscape, given the complexities observed and arguments presented in the preceding chapters. We identify three lines of research that we think are important for the study of semiotic landscapes: the impact of digitalization, especially on third places; the experience economy; and the dynamics of affective regimes. All three lines of research, it seems to us, will benefit from more critical dialogues between the field of sociolinguistics, on the one hand, and critical studies of emotions, on the other. We will say more about how the potential for such dialogues can be realized after elaborating on the three lines of research that we have identified.

The Digitalization of Third Places

One of the points that we made (see Chapter 6) was that third places are undergoing significant sociological and linguistic changes as a result of becoming commodified and the desire to cater to different kinds of clientele. Another point that we highlighted (Chapter 8) was that the cyber landscape is not a semiotic landscape *sui generis*. Rather, given the use of augmented reality (AR; a use that we can reasonably expect to increase in popularity), we need to be more aware of how digital technology allows for greater and novel ways of creating linkages between the cyber landscape and the physical landscape.

These two points, taken together, are related to an oft-debated question about whether cyberspace can or ought to be considered a third place in its own right (Oldenburg 1997, 2000). In one sense, this debate is a fairly trivial one as it boils down to definitions or criterial properties of what might be considered a third place, and such definitions can change depending on disciplinary perspectives or research agendas. In a less trivial sense, the debate also hinges on technological developments that might open up newer affordances (e.g. photos or videos that can more easily shared, real-time multiparty chats, newer emojis, or keyboard characters that could create a greater sense of inclusivity – though, even here, we are brought back to the debate of whether such inclusivity is "really" equivalent to the kinds of interactional opportunities originally observed by Oldenburg and hence to the issue of definitions). Consequently, we think instead that the more interesting question actually concerns the ways in which even traditionally recognized third places are being transformed by the use of digital technology and how this might affect the affective regimes in such places.

We highlight two lines of investigation that are worth pursuing further. We want to issue the caveat that these two lines are by no means unique to third places. However, given the sociological identification of third places as distinct from the first and second places of home and work, respectively, the two impacts that we highlight are in our view particularly consequential for the study of third places.

The first is that digital technology facilitates connectivity, and this creates not just the ability to be in constant communication but all too often the concomitant obligation to be communicatively available (Baron 2008). Zuboff (1988), for example, draws attention to how the development of communication technologies, particularly in the form of social media, has created a situation where more and more individuals feel compelled to "share" information about themselves – however trivial – and in so doing, submit themselves to social monitoring by peers as well as other members of the community. In this regard, the sentiment "If you're not on Facebook, you don't exist"[1] has become almost axiomatic. Smartphones, Instagrams, blogs, Facebook postings, and Twitter updates, among others, are, for many individuals, essential parts of how social life is normatively and routinely lived. Such media technologies allow individuals to keep their friends, family members and "followers" updated as to their whereabouts, activities, and viewpoints. And especially where having as many Facebook friends or Twitter followers as

---

[1] Post by tcooman, October 15, 2012, Social Networks Class Blog. http://courses.casmlab.org/sna fall2012/if-youre-not-on-facebook-you-dont-exist/; accessed June 24, 2014.

possible can constitute significant symbolic capital, it is not inaccurate to suggest that there is active, even eager, competition to be monitored by the many. This is certainly the case with social media "influencers" whose source of livelihood is in attracting large numbers of followers, and then deriving advertising and product-publicity income from their social media accounts. Examples of well-known social media influencers (among many) include Huda Kuttan (makeup and beauty), Zach King ("magic" and digital editing), Amanda Cerny (fitness and beauty), and others (CBS "Top Social Media Influencers of 2018"). This monetization of social media completely blurs the lines between "net" and "physical" identities and spheres, since these influencers arguably have little or no life and identity which is not translated into a social media presence. Where third places are concerned, this means that the boundaries that distinguish and separate first, second, and third places are increasingly not merely porous but in danger of being broken down. Cafes, for example, are no longer separate from work, but places where job interviews are in fact conducted, where insurance policies can be explained and sold, and where workplace meetings might be held. These activities are enabled by the use of mobile devices that allow for easy access to multiple sites so that information can be checked (if necessary), the portability of large files (that would be otherwise physically unwieldy), and the electronic signing of documents (so that a deal can be clinched on the spot).

The second is that Oldenburg's (1997) "commended stranger" (see our earlier discussion in Chapter 6) may not be that much of a stranger any longer. As the Blippar example (see Chapter 8) shows, digital technology makes it easier for an individual to share her personal information online and, conversely, also makes it easier for others to access that information. Absent sufficient control over this access (a perennial issue with digital information), encounters with others in third places may mean encountering someone who already knows more about you than you would like or be comfortable with. So, whereas Oldenburg is concerned about not *wanting* to know too much about an individual (so that this individual may remain both "commended" and a "stranger"), digital technology creates the danger that others may want to know too much about an individual and, moreover, may be able to satisfy that curiosity all too easily. From the perspective of the individual in question, then, the relationship of being "commended strangers" is no longer a symmetrical one. Oldenburg implicitly assumes that there is such social symmetry, that is, in the third space, we are all commended strangers to each other. But in those cases where a stranger knows more about you than you would expect or would want, there is no longer any such symmetry. The stranger may still be a stranger to you (though it is now an open question whether the label "commended" is appropriate) but you are clearly much less of a stranger to him or her.

We saw in Chapter 6 that the semiotics of conviviality typical of third places tends to emphasize the fact that these are shared public spaces. Thus, the main goal is to preempt the possibility of conflict by calling for an appreciation that resources are being shared and by also making clear (in the case of "friendly" places) the kinds of values or lifestyles that are being supported. Insufficient consideration, then, is given to the kinds of issues raised by the digitalization of third places. There are, of course, reminders in movie theaters for patrons to switch off their mobile phones and to not surreptitiously record the movie being shown. And some cafes do have notices reminding customers (especially students) to refrain from studying during peak hours out of consideration for other customers. But broadly speaking, such strategies stress the need to protect a public good such as the need for silence in the movie theater and the importance of sharing seats/tables in the café, or to protect a private good such as the movie's copyright. They are not specifically aimed at addressing the two points we have highlighted above. It seems to us, therefore, that there is a real possibility that the affective regime that makes third places distinct (at least in the way that these were originally characterized by Oldenburg) may become extinct.

Morrison (2017: 1) provides an initial attempt to grapple with this issue when he suggests that "the rise of new social environments is blurring the conventional separation between the first place (home) and the second place (work), and the third place, and this is" is leading to the emergence of a "fourth place," where elements of the first three are being combined. Morrison (2017: 5) describes *Station F* as an example of a fourth place:

The combination of the first place (home), second place (work), and the third place is the fourth place. Opened in 2017, *Station F* is a 34,000-square-meter innovation center that combines restaurants, bars, a post office, fablab, and 3,046 working desks for 1,100 startups (Dillet, 2017). In 2018, *Station F* will open *Home*, a 100 shared apartments residence for the entrepreneurs and knowledge workers working at *Station F.*

However, it is not clear to us that Morrison's idea of a fourth place actually captures the complex ways in which first and second places are being interwoven with traditional third places. It seems to us that a site that has bars, working desks, and shared apartments is primarily one with subdivisions (ostensibly) dedicated to first-, second-, and third-place activities. This strategy of subdividing a site so as to cater to different needs and even different affective regimes is not especially new (see the discussion in Chapter 6). Having these subdivisions within a single site is intended (again, ostensibly) to make it convenient to commute from one kind of place to another. We are certainly not claiming that the kind of example that Morrison describes is not interesting or worthy of analysis. Precisely because of their contiguity, it would not be surprising if the activities associated with one kind of place bleed into another, resulting in what Morrison (2017: 4) calls "coliving" and "coworking" spaces. Nevertheless, we think that of greater significance – perhaps because the effects are subtler and, one might even say, more insidious – are the ways in which third places are being transformed from within, as it were, by the infusion of digital technologies. The attractiveness of such technologies lies in being able to enrich the nature of third places (e.g. by facilitating the arranging of appointments and not requiring someone who wants to be in a third place to forego contacts/interactions with individuals in first and second places). But by the very same token, these technologies have the potential to undermine the activities that give third places their distinctive character.

The Experience Economy

About twenty years ago, Pine and Gilmore (1998, 1999) described what they then saw as the emerging experience economy. According to them (1998, no page numbers, italics in original):

Economists have typically lumped experiences in with services, but experiences are a distinct economic offering, as different from services as services are from goods. Today we can identify and describe this fourth economic offering because consumers unquestionably desire experiences, and more and more businesses are responding by explicitly designing and promoting them. As services, like goods before them, increasingly become commoditized – think of long-distance telephone services sold solely on price – experiences have emerged as the next step in what we call the *progression of economic value* ... From now on, leading-edge companies – whether they sell to consumers or businesses – will find that the next competitive battleground lies in staging experiences.

. . .

An entrepreneur in Israel has entered the experience economy with the opening of Cafe Ke'ilu, which roughly translates as "Cafe Make Believe." Manager Nir Caspi told a reporter that people come to cafés to be seen and to meet people, not for the food; Cafe Ke'ilu pursues that observation to its logical conclusion. The establishment serves its customers plates and mugs that are empty and charges guests $3 during the week and $6 on weekends for the social experience.

Though the above-mentioned example that Pine and Gilmore provide is somewhat extreme since it is not clear how sustainable a café is that only provides empty plates and mugs, there is little doubt that the phenomenon that they describe has become increasingly salient in the past decades. Companies are no longer merely focused on the sale and provision of goods or even services, they are increasingly aware that consumer experience is a key factor in staying competitive.

Our discussion in Chapter 5 concerning how landscapes are romanticized as a result of visitors' prior encounters with narratives, particularly filmic narratives wherein the landscapes are featured, highlights the experience economy at work. The increased interest in fan tourism to iconic sites, outdoor as well as urban settings, involves carefully ensuring that the actual visits are experiences that enhance rather than undermine the fans' dedication to the narratives that inspired the visits in the first place. There is an imperative to put in place the appropriate affective regimes such that the actual site visits evoke the filmic experiences and understandings of the visitors.

Arguably, too, social media influencers are peddlers of experiences – at least vicariously, for those of their followers who are not (yet) able to have those experiences themselves. Travel influencers, for example, excite their followers about a place, culture, or happening by posting pictures, videos, or texts which feature the influencer enjoying those things. There is an obvious monetization potential here, where travel agencies, credit card companies, travel wear brands, and others may associate their products with such influencers in order to boost sales. Some followers may actually replicate the influencer's visit and, in turn, post their own images or texts on social media. However, it is important to note that (even without product placement or physical visits by followers) these social media texts are themselves vicarious experiences, giving followers the sense of "being there" at a scenic or iconic spot, or at a colorful festival. There is a semiotics of interpellation or involvement, more or less obvious from the framing of the scene or event: one of the more overt examples of this is the well-known "follow me to" series of Instagram posts (dating back to 2011) by Russian photographer Murad Osmann. Osmann's series of posts, featuring his girlfriend in front of him, with her hand behind her and holding his, and leading him toward a series of scenic and iconic spots, has garnered him more than four million Instagram followers (Johnson 2016). Osmann's "follow me to" series epitomizes the way social media can interpellate followers into experiences: Osmann's own figure is never seen in these pictures, so it is easy for his followers to insert themselves imaginatively in his place, holding his girlfriend's hand and being led toward a series of stunning buildings or natural sites. The characteristic pose of Osmann and his girlfriend is the basis of an affective regime which is reinforced by captions which heighten the pleasurable quality of the visit: a picture of the Amer Fort in Jaipur is called an "amazing trip with our friends," the caption for a picture featuring the Taj Mahal says, "you will never forget the first time you see it ... it literally takes your breath away," and so on (Instagram "Muradosmann"). Osmann's millions of followers, most of whom will not ever visit these sites, consume his experience and the affective texture the pictures and captions provide.

However, it is obvious that the experience economy extends beyond fan tourism or social media experiences. For example, Brooks and Wee (2016) have noted that there are two models of consumption an appeasement model and an achievement model. The former is the more familiar model where the "customer is king," whereas the latter is "a more recent phenomenon that involves a different cultural positioning of the consumer. Here, the consumer is expected to labor as part of his or her consumption activity" (2016: 220). As Brooks and Wee (2016: 220) explain:

The idea of consumer labor is not in itself particularly new, of course. The need to cut labor costs and to increase productivity, and the availability of technologies that allow processes such as those associated with the point of sale to be off-loaded to the consumer, have made it possible for companies to encourage the consumer to take on some of the work traditionally performed by employees, usually in the name of increasing efficiency.

... What is different about consumer labor in the achievement cultural model is this: the appeal to efficiency and the offering of apologies are absent. The consumer's labor is celebrated but not on the grounds that it meets the consumer's wishes or that it improves efficiency; rather, it is foregrounded as being an integral part of the consumer experience – as that which makes the experience of consumption particularly memorable or worthwhile. Hence, there is a sense of pride and achievement on the part of the consumer when the act of consumption is finally consummated.

One example that Brooks and Wee (2016: 222) discuss is the purchase of Apple products such as new models of its iPhone:

Whenever the technology company Apple releases a new product, the enthusiasm with which this is met is manifested not only in healthy sales volumes but also in the desire among consumers to be the first to own the product. The formation of long queues, with individuals often lining up way before the actual sale commences, is now common enough to be considered normalized. It is no longer particularly remarkable or surprising when there are news reports of the endurance of consumers as they wait outside Apple stores under difficult conditions, of the competitive queuing that sometimes leads to bursts of anger and frustration, and of the triumphant displays from the individual who successfully becomes the "first" to own the product.

And this success in being the first is oftentimes reported in the media so that this act of consumer is publicly lauded even, as the following two news extracts (Sky News, 2013c: "Gallery: iPhones Snapped Up Around World." September 21, quoted in Brooks and Wee 2016: 223) exemplify:

(1)
Jimmy Gunawan holds up his new iPhones after being allowed in first to Apple's flagship store in Sydney.

(2)
The first man in the queue for the iPhone 5S poses for photos at the Apple Store in the Ginza District of Tokyo.

The important point to note, as regards affect, is that the more recent achievement model involves curating the effortful labor of consumers. This has to be done carefully in ways so that the labor is perceived as achievement and, hence, something that the consumer can take pride in rather than as onerous work that the consumer might resent having to perform. The specific strategies that service providers adopt so as to put in place affective regimes that foster pride as opposed to resentment, then, constitute another direction of study that we think is worth paying attention to.

Relatedly, service providers also face the question of how to sustain the experience (which is hopefully a positive one) beyond the site visit itself and conversely, how to minimize the spread of negative experiences. This is important given that social media, word of mouth, online postings of reviews from consumers, and Uber ratings are all parts of the affective economy, where the circulation of opinions can easily spread and serve to either benefit or work against the affective regime that a given service provider has tried to foster. Here, we return once again to the work of Collins (2004), where it is suggested that emotional energy could be treated as a form of cultural capital. As von Scheve (2013: 10) puts it:

His [Collins's] theory is based essentially on the exchange of resources, namely "emotional energy" and "cultural capital." The basic assumption is that actors are disposed to constantly strive to maintain or increase emotional energy, which can be understood as a form of gratification (Collins 2004). Consequently, actors tend to prefer those interactions that they expect to increase their emotional energy and to avoid those that are likely to produce losses. As a result, emotions become a resource and part of actors' preferences.

In this way, the spread of reviews and opinions from earlier cohorts of consumers feeds into the decisions of subsequent cohorts of potential consumers on whether or not to partake of the experience that a given service provider provides. Specifically, for potential consumers, the issue (at least where Collins is concerned) becomes one of whether their emotional energies are likely to increase or not.

Increasingly sophisticated technology that heightens online experiences – 360° "virtual tours" of properties and other sites, AR interactive experiences, eventually even taste, touch, and smell sensations – will make the experience economy increasingly significant, not as an adjunct or collateral to a physical commodity that is seen as "primary," but in its own right as a commodity. This is certainly not the end of the physical commodity, since online technology can in many cases serve to market and increase interest in the physical object being sold. However, with the rise of an experience economy in which digital experiences are themselves the commodity, a rethinking of the traditional notion of the commodity is required. In this, affect becomes increasingly important, not just as a marketing device, but as an integral part of the digital experience itself. Emotional capital – whether in the form of curated labor (like archiving the queuing up for the latest iPhone), or exciting and attracting millions of followers on social media – is nothing more or less than the affective economy in operation.

The Dynamics of Affective Regimes

We noted earlier that affective regimes can be stitched together so as to expand their coverage. This stitching requires of course that the affective regimes be largely compatible with one another. In the case that we discussed (Chapter 6), different communities and organizations in the Singaporean neighborhood of Yishun were consciously trying their best to support the activities of individuals suffering from dementia.

But it is also important to be mindful of cases where affective regimes may be in conflict, as exemplified by the public reactions to the death of the former British prime minister, Margaret Thatcher. Margaret Thatcher, one of Britain's most influential and controversial prime ministers, passed away on April 8, 2013, at the age of 87, after suffering a stroke. Views of her legacy were highly polarized given her involvement in the Falkland Islands, and her strong neoliberal views that influenced her economic reforms and her policies regarding trades union law. While some politicians, such as her successor, John Major, felt that she deserved a lot of credit for turning Britain around, others, such as Leanne Wood, leader of Plaid Cymru, were highly critical of her polices that had devastating effects on Wales. The Associated Press even quoted a number of coal miners from Orgreave, South Yorkshire, as saying "good riddance" in response to news of her death.

In order to mark her passing, the Union Flag was flown at half-mast at key institutions, such as Downing Street, Buckingham Palace, and Parliament. Flowers were also laid outside her home. Thatcher herself had vetoed a state funeral and instead agreed on a ceremonial funeral. Nevertheless, the scale of the ceremony, where she was accorded military honors as well, ultimately amounted to that of a state funeral (Oborne 2013). Flags along Whitehall were flown at half mast, Big Ben was silenced for the duration of the funeral itself, and a gun was fired every minute at the Tower of London. Thatcher's coffin was carried into St. Paul's Cathedral for a service where the Bishop of London gave an address. At the end of the service, the coffin was brought to Mortlake Crematorium for a private service attended by family members.

With four thousand police officers on duty in central London, the BBC reported that of the £3.6 million spent, £3.1 went to paying for police operations, most of which were aimed at anticipating demonstrations and protests.[2] Particularly noteworthy were the street parties that greeted the news of Thatcher's death in London and Glasgow. According to Neild (2013):

---

[2] BBC News April 25, 2013. "No 10: Baroness Thatcher's funeral cost taxpayer £3.6m."; accessed May 7, 2015.

Several hundred people gathered in south London on Monday evening to celebrate Margaret Thatcher's death with cans of beer, pints of mil, and an impromptu street disco playing the soundtrack to her years in power.

Young and old descended on Brixton, a suburb which weathered two outbreaks of rioting during the Thatcher years. Many expressed jubilation that the leader they loved to hate was no more; others spoke of frustration that her legacy lived on.

To cheers of "Maggie Maggie Maggie, dead dead dead," posters of Thatcher were held aloft as reggae basslines pounded.

. . .

In Glasgow, more than 300 people gathered in the city center for an impromptu party, organized on Twitter.

Members of organizations included the Anti-Bedroom Tax Federation, the Communist party, the Socialist party, the Socialist Workers party, and the International Socialist Group, were joined by members of the public in George Square.

A chorus of "so long, the witch is dead" erupted, along with chants of "Maggie Maggie, dead dead dead," from the gathering as champagne bottles were popped.

Thus, in contrast to the official affective regime that mourned her passing, there were also expressions of joy at her death at the more informal group levels. As we have pointed out, groups legitimize individual emotions by assuring individuals that these emotions are shared with others. In this way, group-based activities provide the participating individuals with the sense that their emotions are morally acceptable (Collins 2004). So, while it would have been odd to treat individual expressions of emotions as an affective regime, when individuals come together as they did with the street parties celebrating Thatcher's death, these parties then constituted affective regimes that countered the more official affective regime of respectful mourning.

Then there is the question of why some affective regimes gather traction and have a broad impact, while others remain muted or die a quiet death. Put another way, some affective regimes enjoy a vibrant economy and circulation (the economic analogy is apt, since this is often monetized as well), while others are underconsumed and uncirculated. The Thatcher example shows that there can be different social spheres ("markets") for different affective regimes: the "mourning Thatcher" affect for official and government-linked circles associated with London, and the "rejoicing" affect for left-leaning public elements in regions far from the capital. There are also other factors such as the prevailing ethos (explaining, for example, why LGBT-linked affects were largely uncirculated in the 1970s and 1980s, but are generally widely circulated today), media factors (widely used vs. less-effective media), governance, and legal issues (which may tip the balance one way or another). However, the point running through our earlier chapters must not be overlooked, which is that affective economies depend on linguistic-semiotic regimes. All other things being equal (and sometimes even when they are unequal), the social phenomenon with the more linguistically effective affect will have the greater social impact. Hillary Clinton's 2016 US presidential election campaign is an interesting example, where a candidate with prima facie advantages (a woman, a mother, an experienced politician, a democrat, taking a considerably more inclusive platform than her opponent) loses the election. This has been partly attributed (including by Clinton herself) to the "charisma gap" between the media presences of the two candidates, the way Clinton's media coverage failed to show voters what they "should be excited about," whereas Trump was able to manipulate media affect much more successfully (Stein 2017; Sullivan 2017).

And in addition to affective regimes being stitched together, being in conflict, or having quite different circulatory effects, it seems that affective regimes can also be erased altogether. Consider as a possible example the Tiananmen Square Massacre. The Tiananmen Square Massacre took place in 1989, starting with student demonstrations in mid-April. The students had gathered in Tiananmen Square in central Beijing to protest against widespread corruption and to call for a more open political system. It climaxed on 4 June with a brutal crackdown by the authorities when tanks were used, leading to several hundred, if not several thousand, protestors being killed.

To this day, Beijing forbids any attempt at commemorating the Tiananmen Square Massacre, perhaps because it is a reminder of an unnecessarily violent official response that could only be excused on the grounds of poor internal communications, lack of control over its own troops, or the intentional desire to make an example of the protestors by being deliberately brutal. Whatever the actual reason, Beijing's decision not to allow any Tiananmen-related observance means that it has to actively work against any perceived attempts at organizing such observances. This is almost impossible to achieve, of course, but we are not concerned in this discussion with the actual effectiveness of erasure, merely the steps taken in trying to achieve it. For example, in contrast to Beijing, commemoration of the Tiananmen Square Massacre does take place in Hong Kong. Organized by the Hong Kong Alliance in Support of Patriotic Democratic Movements in China, there has been an annual memorial since 1990. Wan and Denyer (2014) describe the 2014 memorial as follows:

In stark contrast to the silence in Beijing, tens of thousands in Hong Kong converged Wednesday night on Victoria Park for a candlelight vigil. Organizers said more than 180,000 people participated. The territory, a former British colony that returned to Chinese rule in 1997 but has a separate political system and greater liberties, has been a focal point of Tiananmen commemorations.

Under Hong Kong's looming skyscrapers, rally organizers read out the names of those who died in the protests 25 years ago, including a 9-year-old girl. A wreath was laid beside replicas of the Monument to the People's Heroes at Tiananmen Square and the Goddess of Democracy statue erected by protestors in 1989.

Speaking to the crowd, Teng Biao, a prominent human rights lawyer from the mainland, said that despite the many killed in Tiananmen, more have stood up for their rights in China. "You can't kill us all," he said.

Holding up candles, the crowd at one point repeated two chants: "Pass on this spirit from generation to generation" and "Fight to the end."

The materialization of emotions in the Hong Kong commemoration takes relatively conventional forms. The gathering of a large crowd, the candlelight vigil, the remembering of the victims (in this case, by reading out their names), and the laying of a wreath – these are all fairly common ways in which past tragedies are observed, although the chants are admittedly less about the past than an expression of defiance since the very things that the Tiananmen protestors fought for have yet to be realized.

But it is this very materialization that the Chinese authorities have to contend with in their attempts at erasure. So, it is no surprise that a key erasure strategy is to prevent the formation of a crowd in the first place. Thus, large gatherings are banned in and around the Square in the days leading up to 4 June of each year, with security stepped up on the day itself. Likewise, visitors are warned not to lay wreaths, unfurl banners, light candles, or engage in any behavior that could be construed as showing sympathy for the Tiananmen protestors. Individuals who attempt to violate these rules are arrested, or taken away for questioning. And in what can only be described as preemptive moves, prominent individuals who had participated in the Tiananmen Square Massacre or who are known activists may also be put under house arrest or forced to leave Beijing for a "vacation" (Wan and Denyer 2014):

Human rights activist Hu Jia, 40, who participated in the 1989 protest, said by phone that he had been placed under arrest the past three months . . .

Among dozens of activists detained by authorities ahead of the anniversary was Yan Zhengxue, a painter featured in a Washington Post report Sunday about artists trying to keep alive the public memory of Tiananmen. Before he was spirited away by authorities, he recounted being repeatedly forced by state security to leave Beijing on "vacations" ahead of sensitive dates such as Tiananmen anniversaries.

He described awkward trips with his wife to rural areas accompanied by police, who he said were perpetually at the couple's side to prevent them from talking to others or participating in events.

The possibility of materializing an affective regime of mourning and remembrance in a key locale such as Tiananmen Square itself is therefore subject to particularly strong preventive measures from the authorities. But as the Hong Kong example shows, similar materializations elsewhere are much more difficult to prevent. The same difficulty applies to the Internet. The Hong Kong Alliance in Support of Patriotic Democratic Movements in China also has a website where sympathizers can sign a "Condolence Book for the victims of Tiananmen." In this regard, the Chinese authorities have also tried to block internet searches by making search engines and international news websites inaccessible in the days leading up to 4 June. According to Kaphle (2014), "The country has gone as far as to call June 4 'Internet maintenance day,' in which Web sites might be down for fixes, a move that clouds which sites have been restricted."

All these efforts at erasure have been relatively successful because many Chinese today, at least publicly, claim to have no knowledge of the massacre (Wan and Denyer 2014). Even those who do know about the massacre often question the rationale behind the protests, considering the actions of the protestors to be ill-advised and holding them responsible for their own deaths. According to Wan and Denyer (2014), "Many former protestors, who witnessed those deaths, blame such reactions on the government's propaganda, with classes and textbooks casting the 1989 protests as counterrevolutionary riots that threatened the country." This final point is significant because it demonstrates that to erase an affective regime, especially one that is observed regularly in order to commemorate an original trigger event, it is necessary to not only eradicate (where possible) recurrent attempts to materialize the regime, it is also useful to control the historical narrative such that current and future recollections of the trigger event are themselves reshaped. It is because of the latter strategy that subsequent generations might come to have a very different understanding of the trigger event and they could then even begin to question the appropriateness of even wanting to organize regular commemorations.

We have identified three possible ways in which the dynamic relationships between affective regimes might be understood and analyzed. Whether these possibilities need to be expanded or perhaps reduced constitutes, in our view, a fruitful line of future inquiry.

Concluding Thoughts: Affect, Dis-affection, Mediation

In this volume, we have focused on an aspect of our social environments which, because ubiquitous, is often unnoticed or unremarked upon: namely, the role that linguistic-semiotic regimes play in maintaining landscapes. To bring this point home, at the conclusion of our volume, we ask: What is the impact of the absence of affect? Can we speak of landscapes and spaces where affect is absent – of "un-affected" landscape?

The cases examined in this volume suggest that there is, in fact, no landscape which is "un-affected" or entirely untouched by the representational systems which shape its appearance to viewers and regulate the interactions of visitors with it. Even seemingly "natural" landscapes, such as the New Zealand countryside or unsettled "frontier" territory, have already been inflected by discourses of "romance" or "bildung," as we showed in

Chapter 5. Landscapes – whether physical, virtual, or some combination of the two (as with AR) – come already mediated with attitudes, responses, and ideologies constructed through sociolinguistic structures.

However, as we have been at pains to show through a variety of cases, "affect" is not necessarily a positive valence, and should not be confused with the marketing or advocacy of a site through "feel good" campaigns. Indeed, some of our cases – such as the use of "*kawaii*" in merchandising, the "R-word" campaign, the touristic impact of blockbuster films, the creation of luxury spaces, and others – have some qualities of "spin" or advertising campaigns to create positive associations in the name of social or commercial capital. However, these cases involve not merely selling or creating positive affects, but also other affective functions such as regulating public behavior, territorial protection and exclusion, contesting other narratives, and so on. In other cases we have referred to – such as the Arlington National Cemetery or Genocide Memorials – elements of "spin" or advertising campaigns are largely absent, the affects in play here being those of reverence, somberness, and respect. Affective economies are complex phenomena, in some instances intersecting with and behaving like consumer goods, but in other respects functioning like regulatory, governance, socializing, and public sphere phenomena.

If we agree with the term "affective economies" (Ahmed 2004a, 2004b), this is not to privilege consumerist ideologies in our treatment of affect, but only to capture its circulatory quality, the way in which affect depends on processes of social exchange such as "sharing," "re-tweeting," "liking," citing, and other acts of *homo loquens*. Or, to conceptualize Ahmed's understanding in another way, we could say that consumer goods themselves function like affective signs, and are the product of "circulation between objects and signs," as well as between signs and other signs (Ahmed 2004b: 121; Deely 1990: 23; see also our discussion in Chapter 2). The effectiveness of an affective regime, then, consists in its circulation and social influence; while this may be mobilized toward other (secondary) goals such as increased sales and revenue of luxury goods, or the passing of particular regulations and policies, it would not do to confuse these pragmatic ends with the affective means that are deployed.

If this is so, then we also need to be able to describe a landscape affect that circulates, but does so (as it were) badly or dysfunctionally. In this chapter, we have described competing affective economies and those with opposing circu-latory effects, such as the competing discourses of the Tiananmen episode and Margaret Thatcher's death, or the different media campaigns of Hillary Clinton and Donald Trump. In this sense, it might be meaningful to speak of "dis-affective" regimes and economies. "Dis-affect" is not the absence of affect, nor even the creation of less "feel good" and more somber affects. Rather, it is a "losing" affect, one which circulates poorly and ineffectually and, conse-quently, loses ground to a contesting and more powerful affect. In the intense media-tion of contemporary society, the causes and factors that underlie affect and dis-affect become crucial in creating influential and circulatory regimes versus uninfluential and poorly circulating ones.

The consequences go far beyond the emotional responses and management of landscapes, monuments, and sites, although this is significant enough. While this volume has focused on landscape as the site of affective play, it should be clear that affective regimes are also operative in a number of other aspects of everyday life. Crucially, the affective processes we analyze could be fruitfully studied with regard to charisma studies, the "nation" or "community" as abstract constructs, institutions such as MNCs or religious organizations, and the like.

References

Abrams, M. H. (1953). *The Mirror and the Lamp: Romantic Theory and the Critical Tradition*. Oxford: Oxford University Press.

Agha, A. (2011). Commodity registers. In *Journal of Linguistic Anthropology*, 21(1), 22–53.

Ahmed, S. (2004a). *The Cultural Politics of Emotion*. New York: Routledge.

Ahmed, S. (2004b). Affective economies. In *Social Text*, 22(2), 117–39.

Allan, K. and K. Burridge. (2006). *Forbidden Words*. Cambridge: Cambridge University Press.

Allison, A. (2006). Cuteness as Japan's millennial product. In J. Tobin (ed.), *Pikachu's Global Adventure: The Rise and Fall of Pokémon*, 34–49. Durham, NC: Duke University Press.

Amin, S. (1995). *Event, Metaphor, Memory*. Berkeley, CA: University of California Press.

Amin, A. (2012). *Land of Strangers*. Cambridge: Polity Press.

Amit, R. (2012). On the structure of contemporary Japanese aesthetics. In *Philosophy East and West*, 62(2), 174–85.

Anderton, K. (November 14, 2016). Augmented reality, the future, and Pokémon Go. In *Forbes*. Retrieved March 13, 2017, from www.forbes.com/sites/kevinanderton/2016/11/14/augmented-reality-the-future-and-pokemon-go-infographic/#51ab92357e98.

Anthon, Charles. (1871). *A New Classical Dictionary of Greek and Roman Biography, Mythology and Geography*. New York: Harper and Brothers.

Ardrey, Robert. (2014). *The Territorial Imperative: A Personal Investigation into the Animal Origins of Property and Nations*. USA: Storydesign Limited.

Atkin, A. (2013). Peirce's theory of signs. In E. N. Zalta (ed.), *The Stanford Encyclopedia of Philosophy*, Summer 2013 edn. Retrieved February 11, 2018, from https://plato.stanford.edu/archives/sum2013/entries/peirce-semiotics.

Backhaus, P. (2007). *Linguistic Landscapes: A Comparative Study of Urban Multilingualism in Tokyo*. Clevedon: Multilingual Matters.

Bain-Selbo, Eric and D. Gregory Sapp. (2016). *Understanding Sport as a Religious Phenomenon: An Introduction*. London: Bloomsbury Academic.

Baker, William J. (1988). *Sports in the Western World*. Rev. ed. Urbana and Chicago, IL: University of Illinois Press.

Baker, William J. (2007). *Playing with God: Religion and Modern Sport*. Cambridge: Harvard University Press.

Bamberg, M. G. W. (1997). *Narrative Development: Six Approaches*. New York and Oxon: Routledge.

Bamberg, M. (2006). Stories: Big or small. Why do we care? In *Narrative Inquiry*, 16(1), 139–47.

Barbalet, J. M. (1998). *Emotion, Social Theory, and Social Structure: A Macrosociological Approach*. Cambridge: Cambridge University Press.

Barker, Martin and Ernest Mathijs. (2007). Seeing the promised land from afar: The perception of New Zealand by overseas *The Lord of the Rings* audiences. In Adam Lam and Nataliya Oryshchuk (eds.), *How We Became Middle-Earth: A Collection of Essays on* The Lord of the Rings, 107–28. Zollikofen: Walking Tree.

Barnett, C. (September 18, 2012). Review of land of strangers by Ash Amin. In *LSE Review of Books*. Retrieved February 1, 2015 from http://blogs.lse.ac.uk/lsereviewof books/2012/09/18/book-review-land-of-strangers-ash-amin/.

Baron, N. (2008). *Always On*. Oxford: Oxford University Press.

Barrow, B. (May 2, 2013). "Thinking outside the box" and "going forward": The management phrases which irritate us the most in the office. In *Daily Mail*. Retrieved June 3, 2014, from www.dailymail.co.uk/news/article-2318029/Thinking-outside-box-going-forward-Most-irritating-office-management-phrases.html.

Basu, T. (October 6, 2016). How to get lost in augmented reality. In *Inverse Science*. Retrieved November 11, 2017, from www.inverse.com/article/21706-augmented-reality-technology-ethics-advertising.

Bataille, Georges. (1992). *Theory of Religion* (Robert Hurley, Trans.). New York: Zone Books.

Bauman, Zygmunt. (1997). *Postmodernity and its Discontents*. Cambridge: Polity Press.

Beaumont, J. and C. Baker. (2011). Introduction: The rise of the postsecular city. In J. Beaumont and C. Baker (eds.), *Postsecular Cities: Space, Theory and Practice*, 1–14. London: Continuum.

Beck, U. (1992). *Risk Society: Towards a New Modernity* (M. Ritter, Trans.). London: Sage.

Beck, U. (2000). Risk society revisited. In B. Adam, U. Beck, and J. Van Loon (eds.), *The Risk Society and Beyond*, 221–9. London: Sage.

Beck, U. (2006). Living in a risk society. In *Economy and Society*, 35(3), 329–45.

Belfast Mela. (2011). Belfast Mela: Website. http://2011.belfastmela. org.uk/about/mela

Bell, Catherine. (1992). *Ritual Theory, Ritual Practice*. New York: Oxford University Press.

Benhabib, S. (2004). *The Rights of Others: Aliens, Residents, and Citizens*. Cambridge: Cambridge University Press.

Benjamin, A. (1997). Building philosophy: Towards architectural theory. In *AA Files*, 37, 44–51.

Ben-Rafael, E., E. Shohamy, M. H. Amara, and N. Trumper-Hecht. (2006). Linguistic landscape as symbolic construction of the public space: The case of Israel. In D. Gorter (ed.), *Linguistic Landscape: A New Approach*, 7–30. Clevedon: Multilingual Matters.

Berlant, L. (2011). *Cruel Optimism*. Durham, NC: Duke University Press.

Berry, Christopher J. (1994). *The Idea of Luxury: A Conceptual and Historical Investigation*. Cambridge: Cambridge University Press.

Besnier, N. (1990). Language and affect. In *Annual Review of Anthropology*, 19, 419–51.

Bewes, Timothy. (1997). *Cynicism and Postmodernity*. London: Verso.

Beyer, Scott. (2015). Fisher Island: An exclusive paradise 3 miles from Miami. *Forbes* November 3. Online at: www.forbes.com/sites/scottbeyer/2015/11/03/fisher-island-an-exclusive-paradise-3-miles-from-miami/#1d4a115d5dfc

Bharne, Vinayak and Krupali Krusche. (2012). *Rediscovering the Hindu Temple: The Sacred Architecture and Urbanism of India.* Newcastle Upon Tyne: Cambridge Scholars Publishing.

Blakely, Edward J. and Mary Gail Snyder. (1999). *Fortress America: Gated Communities in the United States.* Washington, DC: Brookings Institution Press.

Blommaert, J. (1999). The debate is open. In J. Blommaert (ed.) *Language Ideological Debates,* 3038. Berlin: Mouton.

Blommaert, J. (2013). *Ethnography, Superdiversity, and Linguistic Landscapes.* Clevedon: Multilingual Matters.

Blommaert, J. and B. Rampton. (2016). Language and superdiversity. In K. Arnaut, J. Blommaert, B. Rampton, and M. Spotti (eds.), *Language and Superdiversity,* 21–48. London: Routledge.

Bois, J. (May 10, 2011). LeBron James apologizes for saying "That's retarded." In *SBNation.* Retrieved from www.sbnation.com/nba/2011/5/10/2163542/lebron-james -apologizes-retarded-r-word.

Brasor, P. (2008). The obsession over those dumbed down cute mascots. In *The Japan Times.* Retrieved July 26, 2017, from www.japantimes.co.jp/news/2008/08/03/natio nal/media-national/the-obsession-over-those-dumbed-down-cute-mascots.

Bremner, B. (June 24, 2002). In Japan, cute conquers all. In *Bloomberg.* Retrieved January 13, 2015, from www.bloomberg.com/bw/stories/2002–06-24/in-japan-cute-conquers-all.

Brennan, T. (2004). *The Transmission of Affect.* Ithaca, NY: Cornell University Press.

Brion, Marcel. (1967). *Art of the Romantic Era: Romanticism, Classicism, Realism.* New York: Frederick A. Praeger.

Brooks, A. and L. Wee. (2016). The cultural production of consumption as achievement. In *Cultural Politics,* 12(2), 217–32.

Brown, P. and S. Levinson. (1987). *Politeness: Some Universals in Language Use.* Cambridge: Cambridge University Press.

Buechler, S. (2011). *Understanding Social Movements.* Boulder, CO: Paradigm Publishers.

Burdelski, M. and K. Mitsuhashi. (2010). "She thinks you're *kawaii*": Socializing affect, gender, and relationships in a Japanese preschool. In *Language in Society,* 39, 65–93.

Butler, S. and C. Diaz.(September 14, 2016). "Third places" as community builders. In *Up Front, Brookings.* Retrieved November 2, 2017, from www.brookings.edu/blog/ up-front/2016/09/14/third-places-as-community-builders/.

Butterworth 8. House Rules and By-laws. Retrieved March 15, 2018, from http://butter worth8.sg/houserules.

Calhoun, C. (2001). Putting emotions in their place. In J. Goodwin, J. Jasper and F. Polletta (eds.), *Passionate Politics,* 45–57. Chicago, IL: University of Chicago Press.

Californialuxury.com. Art glass chandeliers in the Beverly Hills real estate market. Retrieved February 3, 2018, from http://californialuxury.com/art-glass-chandeliers-in-the-beverly-hills-real-estate-market/

Cameron, D. (1995). *Verbal Hygiene*. London: Routledge.

Cameron, D. (2000). *Good to Talk? Living and Working in a Communication Culture*. London: Sage.

Campbell-Kibler, K. (2007). Accent, (ING) and the social logic of listener perceptions. In *American Speech*, 82, 32–64.

Carslaw, Yolanda. (2014). Buy a five-star hotel apartment as your luxury home. *The Telegraph* May 4. Online at: www.telegraph.co.uk/finance/property/luxury-homes/10772182/buy-five-star-hotel-luxury-home.html

CBS. "Top social media influencers of 2018". Online at: www.cbsnews.com/pictures/social-media-influencers-influential-2018/2/

Celebrities take the pledge. In Cheers section, *R-word*. Retrieved September 18, 2011, from www.r-word.org/r-word-cheers.aspx.

Chayka, Kyle. (2016). The Oppressive Gospel of "Minimalism." *New York Times* July 26. Online at: www.nytimes.com/2016/07/31/magazine/the-oppressive-gospel-of-minimalism.html

Chuang, Y. C. (2011). *Kawaii* in Taiwan politics. In *International Journal of Asia Pacific Studies*, 7(3), 1–17.

Clough, P. T. (2007). Introduction. In P. T. Clough and J. Halley (eds.), *The Affective Turn: Theorizing the Social*, 1–33. Durham, NC: Duke University Press.

Cloutier, David. (2015). *The Vice of Luxury: Economic Excess in a Consumer Age*. Washington, DC: Georgetown University Press.

Collins, R. (1987). Interaction ritual chains. In J. C. Alexander, B. Giesen, R. Munch, and N. J. Smelser (eds.), *The Micro-macro Link*, 181–92. Berkeley, CA: University of California Press.

Collins, R. (2001). Social movements and the focus of emotional attention. In J. Goodwin, J. M. Jasper, and F. Polletta (eds.), *Passionate Politics: Emotions and Social Movements*, 27–44. Chicago, IL: University of Chicago Press.

Collins, R. (2004). *Interaction Ritual Chains*. Princeton, NJ: Princeton University Press.

Coluzzi, P. (2009). The Italian linguistic landscape: The cases of Milan and Udine. In *International Journal of Multilingualism*, 6, 298–312.

Crang, M. (1996). Envisioning urban histories: Bristol as palimpsest, postcards and snapshots. In *Environment and Planning A*, 28(3), 429–52.

Das, Sukla. (1977). *Crime and Punishment in Ancient India*. New Delhi: Abhinav Publications.

De Saussure, F. (1983). *Course in General Linguistics* (R. Harris, Trans.). London: Duckworth.

Deely. J. N. (1990). *Basics of Semiotics*. Bloomington, IN: Indiana University Press.

Di Giovine, Michael A. and David Picard. (2016). Pilgrimage and seduction in the Abrahamic tradition. In Michael A. Di Giovine and David Picard (eds.), *The Seductions of Pilgrimage: Sacred Journeys Afar and Astray in the Western Religious Tradition*, 1–52. London: Routledge.

Dillet, R. (2017). A walk around Station F with Emmanuel Macron. In *TechCrunch*. Retrieved from https://techcrunch.com/2017/07/01/a-walk-around-station-f-with-emmanuel-macron/. (Cited in Morrison 2017).

Discovery Harbour. Guidelines and procedures of the social committee. Retrieved March 31, 2018 from http://discoveryharbour.net/wp-content/uploads/2014/03/Social-Committee-Procedures.pdf

Doll, J. (2013). Why drag it out?: An investigation into what inspires so many people to toss extra letters into their text message. In *The Atlantic*. Retrieved February 5, 2017, from www.theatlantic.com/magazine/archive/2013/03/dragging-it-out/309220/.

Dosse, F. (1997). *History of Structuralism*. Vols 1 and 2. (D. Glassman, Trans.). Minneapolis, MN: University of Minnesota Press.

Du Gay, P. (1996). *Consumption and Identity at Work*. London: Sage.

Duncan, J. S. (1990). *The City as Text: The Politics of Landscape Interpretation in the Kandyan Kingdom*. Cambridge: Cambridge University Press.

Eastman, C. and R. Stein. (1993). Language display: Authenticating claims to social identity. In *Journal of Multilingual and Multicultural Development*, 14(3), 187–202.

Eckert, P. (2008). Variation and the indexical field. In *Journal of Sociolinguistics*, 12, 453–76.

Eckert, P. (2012). Three waves of variation study: The emergence of meaning in the study of sociolinguistic variation. In *Annual Review of Anthropology*, 41, 87–100.

Eliade, Mircea. (1959). *The Sacred and the Profane: The Nature of Religion* (Willard R. Trask, Trans.). Orlando: Harcourt, Inc.

Elliot, Anthony. (2009). *Contemporary Social Theory*. London: Routledge.

Eyerman, R. (2006). Performing opposition or, how social movements move. In J. C. Alexander, B. Giesen, and J. L. Mast (eds.), *Social Performance: Symbolic Action, Cultural Pragmatics, and Ritual*, 193–217. Cambridge: Cambridge University Press.

Fagan, Chelsea. (2017). Minimalism: Another boring product wealthy people can buy. *The Guardian* March 4. Online at: www.theguardian.com/lifeandstyle/2017/mar/04/minimalism-conspicuous-consumption-class

Fairclough, N. (2001). *Language and Power*, 2nd edn. Essex: Longman.

Fauconnier, G. (1994). *Mental Spaces: Aspects of Meaning Construction in Natural Language*. Cambridge: Cambridge University Press.

Figueroa, R. M. and G. Waitt. (2011). The moral terrains of ecotourism and the ethics of consumption. In T. Lewis and E. Potter (eds.), *Ethical Consumption: A Critical Introduction*, 260–74. London: Routledge.

Fillmore, C. J., P. Kay, and M. C. O'Connor. (1988). Regularity and idiomaticity in grammatical constructions. In *Language*, 64, 501–38.

Foucault, M. (1977). Discipline and Punish (A. Sheridan, Trans.) New York: Pantheon.

Foucault, Michel. (1984). Panopticism. In Paul Rabinow (ed.), *The Foucault Reader*, 206–13. New York: Pantheon.

Foucault, M. (2000). Governmentality. In J. Faubion (ed.), *Essential Works of Foucault 1954*–1984. Vol 3. New York: New Press.

Frankfurt, H. (1988). *The Importance of What We Care About*. Cambridge: Cambridge University Press.

Frazer, J. G. (1960). *The Golden Bough: A Study in Magic and Religion*, Vol. I. London: Macmillan.

Friedman, B. and P. Kahn. (April 2000). New directions: A value-sensitive design approach to augmented reality. In *Designing Augmented Reality Environments (DARE)*, 163–4. Denmark: Interactive Design Foundation. Retrieved May 5, 2019, from www.interaction-design.org/about.

Frumkin, Howard, Lawrence Frank, and Richard Jackson. (2004). *Urban Sprawl and Public Health: Designing, Planning and Building for Healthy Communities*. Washington, DC: Island Press.

Fryberg, S. A., H. R. Markus, D. Oyserman, and J. M. Stone. (2008). Of warrior chiefs and Indian princesses: The psychological consequences of American Indian mascots. In *Basic and Applied Psychology*, 30, 208–18.

Frye, Northrop. (1963). *Fables of Identity: Studies in Poetic Mythology*. New York: Harcourt, Brace and World.

Frye, N. (1976). *The Secular Scripture: A Study of the Structure of Romance*. Cambridge, MA: Harvard University Press.

Frye, N. (2015). *The Anatomy of Criticism*. Princeton, NJ: Princeton University Press.

Georgakopoulou, A. (2006). Thinking big with small stories in narrative and identity analysis. In *Narrative Inquiry*, 16(1): 120–30.

Giddens, A. (1987). *Social Theory and Modern Sociology*. Cambridge: Polity Press.

Gilroy P. (2004). *After Empire: Melancholia or Convivial Culture?* New York: Routledge.

Gilroy P. (2006). Multiculture in times of war (an inaugural lecture given at the London School of Economics). In *Critical Quarterly*, 48(4), 27–45. Retrieved from https://onlinelibrary.wiley.com/doi/abs/10.1111/j.1467–8705.2006.00731.x

Goffman, E. (1972). *Relations in Public*. London: Penguin.

Goffman, E. (1981). *Forms of Talk*. Pennsylvania, PA: University of Pennsylvania Press.

Goh, Robbie B. H. (2001). Ideologies of "upgrading" in Singapore Public Housing: Postmodern style, globalisation and class construction in the built environment. In *Urban Studies*, 38(9), 1589–604.

Goh, R. B. H. (2014). *The Lord of the Rings* and New Zealand: Fantasy tourism, pilgrimages, imaginative transnationalism. In *Social Semiotics*, 24(2), 263–82.

Goldberg, A. (1995). *Constructions: A Construction Grammar Approach to Argument Structure*. Chicago, IL: University of Chicago Press.

Gorter, D. (2013). Linguistic landscapes in a multilingual world. In *Annual Review of Applied Linguistics*, 33, 190–212.

Graham, E. (2013). *Between a Rock and a Hard Place: Public Theology in a Post-Secular Age*. London: SCM Press.

Gu, Y. (1990). Politeness phenomenon in Modern Chinese. In *Journal of Pragmatics*, 14, 237–57.

Guichard, Michael and Lionel Marti. (2013). Purity in ancient Mesopotamia: The Paleo-Babylonian and Neo-Assyrian periods. In Christian Frevel and Christophe Nihan (eds.), *Purity and the Forming of Religious Traditions in the Ancient Mediterranean World and Ancient Judaism*, 47–114. Leiden: Brill.

Guidelines and Procedures of the Social Committee [PDF file]. In *Discovery Harbor*. Retrieved March 31, 2018 from http://discoveryharbour.net/wp-content/uploads/2014/03/Social-Committee-Procedures.pdf.

Harvey, D. (1989). *The Condition of Postmodernity: An Enquiry into the Origins of Cultural Change*. Oxford: Basil Blackwell.

Harvey, D. (2009). *Social Justice and the City*, Rev edn. Athens, GA: University of Georgia Press.

Harvey, K. and C. Shalom. (2002). *Language and Desire*. London: Routledge.

Hauseit. (2017). How to ace a co-op board interview in NYC. Posted June 2. Online at: www.hauseit.com/co-op-board-interview/

Hauseit. (2018). NYC coop board package purchase application. Posted March 6. Online at: www.hauseit.com/nyc-coop-board-package-purchase-application/

Haxel, C. (March 3, 2011). The r-word: Missing the point. In *The Diamond Back*. Retrieved August 8, 2011, from www.diamondbackonline.com.

Heal, Bridget (2007). *The Cult of the Virgin Mary in Early Modern Germany: Protestant and Catholic Piety, 1500–1648*. Cambridge: Cambridge University Press.

Henseler, Christine. (2013). Introduction: Generation X goes global – tales of accelerated cultures. In Christine Henseler (ed.), *Generation X Goes Global: Mapping a Youth Culture in Motion*, 1–29. New York: Routledge.

Hill, J. (2008). *The Everyday Language of White Racism*. Oxford: Blackwell.

Hobbiton Movie Set. In *Hobbiton Tours*. Retrieved March 31, 2018 from www.hobbitontours.com/en/.

Hochschild, A. R. (1979). Emotion work, feeling rules, and social structure. In *American Journal of Sociology*, 85(3), 551–75.

Hochschild, A. R. (1983). *The Managed Heart: Commercialization of Human Feeling*. Berkeley, CA: University of California Press.

Hochschild, A. R. (1990). Ideology and emotion management: A perspective and path for future research. In T. D. Kemper (ed.), *Research Agendas in the Sociology of Emotions*, 117–44. Albany, NY: State University of New York Press.

Holmes, J. (1995). *Women, Men and Politeness*. London: Longman.

Hoopes, J. (ed.). (1991). *Pierce on Signs: Writings on Semiotics by Charles Sanders Pierce*. Chapel Hill, NC: University of North Carolina Press.

Horii, M. and A. Burgess. (2012). Constructing sexual risk: "Chikan," collapsing male authority and the emergence of women-only train carriages in Japan. In *Health, Risk & Society*, 14(1), 41–55.

House, Laura. (2016). The Peak: Secluded luxury high above Hong Kong. *South China Morning* Post October 8. Online at: www.mansionglobal.com/articles/42153-the-peak-secluded-luxury-high-above-hong-kong

How to Ace a Co-op Board Interview in NYC. (June 2, 2017). In *Hauseit*. Retrieved from www.hauseit.com/co-op-board-interview/.

Howe, Neil and William Strauss. (2000). *Millennials Rising: The Next Great Generation*. New York: Vintage Books.

Hughes, C. J. (2011). Getting into NYC's strictest co-ops. *The Real Deal* (June issue). Online at: https://therealdeal.com/issues_articles/getting-across-the-moat-at-the-top-cooperatives/

Hürzeler, C. and T. Frey. (November 17, 2017). *Seeing the invisible – augmented reality in urban planning*. Paper presented at the Urban Knowledge Visualization Series, Singapore-ETH Centre.

Hutcheon, L. (1988). *A Poetics of Postmodernism: History, Theory, Fiction*. New York: Routledge.

Imrie, R. (2014). Space, place and policy regimes: The changing contours of disability and citizenship. In K. Soldatic, H. Morgan, and A. Roulstone (eds.), *Disability, Spaces and Places of Policy Exclusion*, 13–30. New York: Routledge.

Jameson, F. (1991). *Postmodernism: Or, the Cultural Logic of Late Capitalism*. Durham, NC: Duke University Press.

Jasper, J. M. (2014). *Protest: A Cultural Introduction to Social Movements*. London: Polity.

Jaworski, A. and D. Galasiński. (2002). The verbal construction of non-verbal behavior: British press reports of President Clinton's grand jury testimony video. In *Discourse & Society*, 13(5), 629–49.

Jaworski, A. and C. Thurlow. (eds.). (2010). *Semiotic Landscapes: Language, Image, Space.* London: Continuum.

Jeffers, Thomas L. (2005). *Apprenticeships: The Bildungsroman from Goethe to Santayana.* New York: Palgrave Macmillan.

Jennifer Aniston blasted for using the word "retard". (August 19, 2010). In *US Weekly.* Retrieved February 20, 2013, from www.usmagazine.com/celebrity-news/news/jennifer-aniston-blasted-for-using-the-word-retard-2010198.

Johnson, L. (July 4, 2016). How a sweet, simple instagram photo gave rise to a sweeping global travel brand. In *Adweek.* Retrieved from www.adweek.com/digital/how-sweet-simple-instagram-photo-gave-rise-sweeping-global-travel-brand-172124/.

Julia. (April 15, 2010). Response to "Unethical website: www.r-word.org." Retrieved August 12, 2011.

Jung, Carl. (1971). *The Portable Jung.* Joseph Campbell (ed.). Harmondsworth: Penguin.

Kadouf, Hunud Abia. (2013). *Law, Custom and Property Rights among the Āma/ Nyimaŋ of the Nuba Mountains of the Sudan: An Analysis of Traditional Property Concepts in a Historical Perspective.* Singapore: Partridge.

Kaye, L. K., S. A. Malone, and H. J. Wall, (2017). Emojis: Insights, affordances, and possibilities for psychological science. In *Trends in Cognitive Sciences*, 21(2), 66–8, doi:10.1016/j.tics.2016.10.007.

Keat, R. (1991). Introduction. In R. Keat and N. Abercrombie (eds.), *Enterprise Culture*, 1–17. London: Routledge.

Kennedy, R. (2002). *Nigger: The Strange Career of a Troublesome Word.* New York: Pantheon.

Khan, N. (2007). Inter-cultural arts policy – challenge paper. Retrieved June 23, 2008, from www.interculturaldialogue.eu/web/files/64/en/CP-Khan-03.doc. (Cited in McDermott 2012).

Kincaid, C. (September 7, 2014). What is *Kawaii*? In *Japan Powered.* Retrieved January 25, 2016, from www.japanpowered.com/japan-culture/what-is-kawaii.

Kindaichi, H. and T. Kokubo. (eds.). (2014). *Zenyaku Kogo Jiten* [Translated Dictionary of Archaisms], 2nd edn. Tokyo: Gakken.

Kinsella, S. (1995). Cuties in Japan. In L. Skov and B. Moeran (eds.), *Women, Media, and Consumption in Japan*, 220–54. Richmond, VA: Curzon.

Kramsch, C. (2007). The uses of communicative competence in a global world. In Jun Liu (ed.), *English Language Teaching in China*, 55–74. London: Continuum.

Kulick, D. and B. Schieffelin. (2004). Language socialization. In A. Duranti (ed.), *A Companion to Linguistic Anthropology*, 349–68. Cambridge: Cambridge University Press.

Kymlicka, W. (1995). *Multicultural Citizenship.* Oxford: Oxford University Press.

Kymlicka, W. (2007). *Multicultural Odysseys: Negotiating the International Politics of Diversity.* Oxford: Oxford University Press.

Labov, W. (1963). The social motivation of a sound change. In *WORD*, 18, 1–42.

Lam, Adam and Nataliya Oryshchuk (eds.). (2007). *How We Became Middle-Earth: A Collection of Essays on* The Lord of the Rings. Zollikofen: Walking Tree.

Lash, S. (2000). Risk culture. In B. Adam, U. Beck, and J. Van Loon (eds.), *The Risk Society and Beyond*, 47–62. London: Sage.

Lazarus, Z. (April 25, 2017). The experience economy: Key trends for 2017. In *Campaign*. Retrieved December 3, 2017, from www.campaignlive.co.uk/article/exp erience-economy-key-trends-2017/1431150.

Leeman, J. and G. Modan. (2009). Commodified language in Chinatown: A contextualized approach to linguistic landscape. In *Journal of Sociolinguistics*, 13(3), 332–62.

Lefebvre, H. (1991). *The Production of Space*. (D. Nicholson-Smith, Trans.). Oxford: Blackwell. (Original work published 1974.)

Lefebvre, H. (1996). *Writings on Cities*. E. Kofman and E. Lebas (eds.). Oxford: Blackwell.

Levitin, Michael. (2015). The Triumph of Occupy Wall Street. *The Atlantic* June 10. Online at: www.theatlantic.com/politics/archive/2015/06/the-triumph-of-occupy -wall-street/395408/

Lewis, M., J. Haviland-Jones, and L. Barrett. (eds.). (2008). *Handbook of Emotions*. New York: Guilford Press.

Lien Foundation (2016). "Forget Us Not". Retrieved November 5, 2017, from https:// forgetusnot.sg/about.html.

Light, Richard and Louise Kinnaird. (2002). Appeasing the gods: Shinto, sumo and "true" Japanese spirit. In Tara Magdalinski and Timothy J. L. Chandler (eds.), *With God on Their Side: Sport in the Service of Religion*, 139–59. London and New York: Routledge.

Liszka, J. J. (1996). *Introduction to the Semiotics of Charles Sanders Pierce*. Bloomington, IN: Indiana University Press.

Logan, G. (February 4, 2010). Response to "Unethical website: www.r-word.org." Retrieved August 12, 2011.

Loveridge, Kathryn. (2013). The curse of Christ's Wound: Christ's Blood as Anti-relic. *Hortulus*, 9(1). Online at: https://hortulus-journal.com/journal/volume-9-number-1- 2013/loveridge/

Manning, P. and I. Gershon. (2013). Animating interaction. In *Journal of Ethnographic Theory*, 3(3), 107–37.

Marshall, J. (2010). Unethical website: www.r-word.org. In *Ethics Alarms*. Retrieved August 12, 2011 from, https://ethicsalarms.com/2010/02/04/unethical-website-www -r-word-org/.

Marx, K. (1967). *Capital: A Critique of Political Economy*. Vol I. (S. Moore and E. Aveling, Trans.). New York: International Publishers. (Original Work Published 1867).

Massey, D. (2005). *For Space*. London: Sage.

Massumi B. (1995). The autonomy of affect. In *Cultural Critique*, 31, 83–109.

Massumi B. (2002). *Parables for the Virtual: Movement, Affect, Sensation*. Durham, NC: Duke University Press.

Matsumoto, Y. (1988). Reexamination of the universality of face: Politeness phenomena in Japanese. In *Journal of Pragmatics*, 11, 721–36.

Mautner, G. (2012). Language, space and the law: A study of directive signs. In *International Journal of Speech, Language, and the Law*, 19(2), 189–217.

McAdam, D. (1994). Culture and social movements. In E. Larana, H. Johnston, and J. R. Gusfield (eds.), *New Social Movements: From Ideology to Identity*, 36–57. Philadelphia, PA: Temple University Press.

McDermott, P. (2012). Cohesion, sharing and integration? Migrant languages and cultural spaces in Northern Ireland's urban environment. In *Current Issues in Language Planning*, 13(3), 187–205.

McElhinny, B. (2010). The audacity of affect: Gender, race and history in linguistic accounts of legitimacy and belonging. In *Annual Review of Anthropology*, 39, 309–28.

McKirdy, E. (May 12, 2014). Japanese cuteness overload could result in mascot cull. In *CNN*. Retrieved July 26, 2017, from https://edition.cnn.com/2014/05/12/world/asia/osaka-mascot-cull/index.html.

McLaughlin, Katy. (2017). Charity begins at your new home. *Mansion Global* December 28. Online at: www.mansionglobal.com/articles/84695-charity-begins-at-your-new-home

McVeigh, B. J. (2000). How hello kitty commodifies the cute, cool, and camp: "Consumotopia" versus "control" in Japan. In *Journal of Material Culture*, 5, 225–45.

McWhorter, J. (2013). Is texting killing the English language? In *Time Magazine Online*. Retrieved February 5, 2017, from http://ideas.time.com/2013/04/25/is-texting-killing-the-english-language/.

Mendisu, S. B., D. Malinowski, and E. Woldemichael. (2016). Absence from the linguistic landscape as de facto language policy: The case of two local languages in southern Ethiopia. In R. Blackwood, E. Lanza, and H. Woldemariam (eds.), *Negotiating and Contesting Identities in Linguistic Landscapes*, 117–30. London: Bloomsbury.

Meyer, Z. (December 4, 2017). 5 amazing facts about the world's largest Starbucks. In *USA Today*. Retrieved December 7, 2017, from www.usatoday.com/story/money/2017/12/05/5-amazing-facts-worlds-largest-starbucks/920281001/.

Miller, L. (2010). Japan's zoomorphic urge. In *ASIANetwork Exchange: A Journal for Asian Studies in the Liberal Arts*, 17(2), 69–82.

Miller, T. (March 5, 2010). Why you shouldn't use the R-word. In *Redneck Mommy*. Retrieved September 18, 2011, from www.tanismiller.com/redneckmommy/2010/3/5/why-you-shouldnt-use-the-r-word.html.

Ministry of Foreign Affairs of Japan. (2009). Commission of trend communicator of Japanese pop culture in the field of fashion. Retrieved January 29, 2017, from www.mofa.go.jp/announce/event/2009/2/1188515_1152.html.

Monnier, D. (1989). *Langue d'accueil et langue de service dans les commerces à Montreal*. Notes et documents, Conseil de la langue française 70. Quebec: Service des communications, Conseil de la langue française.

Morrison, A. (2017). A typology of places in the knowledge economy: Towards the fourth place [PDF file]. In *Smart Innovation, System and Technologies*, 100, 444–51 (forthcoming). Retrieved December 3, 2017, from https://ssrn.com/abstract=3056754.

Moss, L. (2013). 5 ways communities persuade dog owners to pick up poo. Posted June 18, 2013, *Mother Nature Network*. Retrieved February 22, 2015, from www.mnn.com/family/pets/stories/5-ways-communities-persuade-dog-owners-to-pick-up-poo.

Muth, S. (2012). The linguistic landscapes of Chişinău and Vilnius: Linguistic landscape and the representation of minority languages in two post-Soviet capitals. In

D. Gorter, H. F. Marten, and L. Van Mensel (eds.), *Minority Languages in the Linguistic Landscape*, 204–24. Basingstoke: Palgrave Macmillan.

Myrvoll, Marit. (2017). Gosa Bassi Varit Leat Javkan? Where have all the sacred mountains gone? In Leena Heinamaki and Thora Martina Herrmann (eds.), *Experiencing and Protecting Sacred Natural Sites of Sami and Other Indigenous Peoples*, 101–16. Cham: Springer Nature.

Neild, B. 2013. "Margaret Thatcher's death greeted with street parties in Brixton and Glasgow". April 8, 2013. *The Guardian*. Retrieved May 5, 2015, from www .theguardian.com/politics/2013/apr/08/margaret-thatcher-death-party-brixton-glasgow.

Newman, D. (November 24, 2015). What is the experience economy, and should your business care? In *Forbes*. Retrieved December 3, 2017, from www.forbes.com/sites/da nielnewman/2015/11/24/what-is-the-experience-economy-should-your-business-care /#319b89281d0c.

Ninivaggi, Frank John. (2010). *Envy Theory: Perspective on the Psychology of Envy*. Lanham: Rowman and Littlefield Publishers.

Nittono, H., M. Fukushima, A. Yano, H. Moriya. (September 26, 2012). The power of *Kawaii*: Viewing cute images promotes a careful behavior and narrows attentional focus. In *PLoS One*, 7(9), doi:10.1371/journal.pone.0046362.

Nittono, H. (2016). The two-layer model of "*kawaii*": A behavioural science framework for understanding kawaii and cuteness. In *East Asian Journal of Popular Culture*, 2(1), 79–95, doi:10.1386/eapc.2.1.79_1.

Norris, C. (2004). Saussure, linguistic theory, and philosophy of science. In C. Sanders (ed.), *The Cambridge Companion to Saussure*, 219–39. Cambridge: Cambridge University Press.

Nowicka, M. and S. Vertovec. (2014). Comparing convivialities: Dreams and realities of living-with-difference. In *European Journal of Cultural Studies*, 17(4), 341–56.

NYC Coop Board Package Purchase Application. (March 6, 2018). In *Hauseit*. Retrieved from www.hauseit.com/nyc-coop-board-package-purchase-application/.

Oborne, P. (2013). Margaret Thatcher: This is a state funeral and that's a mistake. The Daily Telegraph.

Occhi, D. (2012). Wobbly aesthetics, performance, and message: Comparing Japanese Kyara with their anthropomorphic forebears. In *Asian Ethnology*, 71(1), 109–32.

Octia, J. and J. Berlinger. (June 28, 2017). Philippines bill proposes jail time for unenthusiastic anthem singers. In *CNN*. Retrieved July 2, 2017, from http://edition .cnn.com/2017/06/28/asia/philippines-anthem-bill/index.html.

Okabe, C. (2004). Josei senyô sharyô ni kansuru ichikôsatsu: Chikan higai no jittai to tomoni [Study of the "Carriage for Women Only"]. In *Kurume Shin-ai Women's College Bulletin*, 27, 57–66.

Okonkwo, Uche. (2007). *Luxury Fashion Branding: Trends, Tactics, Techniques*. Houndmills: Palgrave Macmillan.

Oldenburg, R. (1997). *The Great Good Place*, 2nd edn. New York: Marlowe & Company.

Oldenburg, R. (2000). *Celebrating the Third Place: Inspiring Stories about the "Great Good Places" at the Heart of Our Communities*. New York: Marlowe & Company.

Oldenburg, R. (2015). Q+A with Ray Oldenburg. In *360 Magazine*, Issue 6. Retrieved November 2, 2017, from www.steelcase.com/research/articles/topics/design-q-a/q -ray-oldenburg/.

Ong, Cheryl. (2013). Sembawang's Beachfront "Kampung". *Singapore Property News* June 3. Online at: www.stproperty.sg/articles-property/singapore-property-news/sem bawangs-beachfront-kampung/a/121330.

Ousby, Ian. (2016). *The Englishman's England: Taste, Travel and the Rise of Tourism*. London: Thistle Publishing.

Parekh, B. (2000). *The Future of Multi-Ethnic Britain: The Parekh Report*. London: Runnymede Trust.

Park, C. C. (1994). *Sacred Worlds: An Introduction to Geography and Religion*. London: Routledge.

Parrish, Helen L. (2005). *Monks, Miracles and Magic: Reformation Representations of the Medieval Church*. London: Routledge.

Parry, Hannah. (2015). Rothschild family estate . . . goes on the market for £24 Million. *Mail Online* May 1. Online at: www.dailymail.co.uk/news/article-3064443/Rothsch ild-family-estate-boasting-34-homes-award-winning-stud-farm-two-reservoirs-goes -market-24MILLION.html.

Passino, Carla. (2013). For sale and fit for royalty: Manors, estates and castles with royal connections. *Forbes* July 22. Online at: www.forbes.com/sites/carlapassino/2013/07/22/ for-sale-and-fit-for-royalty-manors-estates-and-castles-with-royal-connections /#3281d1c23e42

Peck, A., Q. Williams, and C. Stroud. (eds.). Special issue title: Visceral landscapes. In *Sociolinguistic Studies*, 13(1) (forthcoming).

Peirce, C. S. (1955). *Philosophical Writings of Peirce*. J. Buchler (ed.). New York: Dover Publications.

Peirce, C. S. (1958). *Values in a Universe of Chance: Selected Writings of Charles Sanders Peirce*. P. P. Weiner (ed.). Stanford, CA: Stanford University Press.

Peirce, C. S. (1980). *The Collected Papers of Charles S. Peirce*. 8 vols. Vols. 1–6, C. Hartshorne and P. Weiss (eds.); Vols. 7–8, A. Burks (ed.). Cambridge, MA: Harvard University Press.

Peirce, C. S. (1998). *The Essential Peirce: Selected Philosophical Writings*. Vol 2. Bloomington, IN: Indiana University Press.

Pennycook, A. (2008). Linguistic landscape and the transgressive semiotics of graffiti. In E. Shohamy and D. Gorter (eds.), *Linguistic Landscapes: Expanding the Scenery*, 302–12. New York: Routledge.

Pennycook, A. (2010). Spatial narrations: Graffscapes and city souls. In A. Jaworski and C. Thurlow (eds.), *Semiotic Landscapes: Language, Image, Space*, 137–50. London: Continuum.

Piller, I. and J. Cho. (2013). Neoliberalism as language policy. In *Language in Society*, 42, 23–44.

Pinchefsky, C. (December 14, 2012). The impact (economic and otherwise) of Lord of the Rings/The Hobbit on New Zealand. In *Forbes*. Retrieved February 14, 2018, from www.forbes.com/sites/carolpinchefsky/2012/12/14/the-impact-economic-and-otherwise-of-lord-of-the-ringsthe-hobbit-on-new-zealand /#235d3a7d31b6.

Pine, B. J. and J. H. Gilmore. (1998). Welcome to the experience economy. In *Harvard Business Review*, July–August issue. Retrieved December 3, 2017, from https://hbr .org/1998/07/welcome-to-the-experience-economy.

Pine, B. J. and J. H. Gilmore. (1999). *The Experience Economy: Work is Theatre and Every Business a Stage*. Boston, MA: Harvard Business School Press.

Pinsent, Pat. (2002). The education of a wizard: Harry Potter and his predecessors. In Lana A. Whited (ed.), The Ivory Tower and Harry Potter: Perspectives on a Literary Phenomenon, 27–52. Columbia, MO: University of Missouri Press.

Piper, G. (August 29, 2016). Angry-looking Iowa mascot promotes "aggressivity and even violence", aediatrics prof says. In *The College Fix*. Retrieved January 9, 2017, from www.thecollegefix.com/post/28679/.

Pledge your support. In *R-Word*. Retrieved September 18, 2011, from www.r-word.org /r-word-pledge.

Polletta, F. (1999). 'Free spaces' in collective action. In Theory and Society, 28(1): 1–38.

Postrel, V. (September 17, 2011). What price kindness at Harvard? (from Bloomberg). *The Straits Times.*

Powell, K. A. (2008). Remapping the city: Palimpsest, place and identity in art education research. In *Studies in Art Education*, 50(1), 6–21.

Radimilahy, Chantal. (1994). Sacred sites in Madagascar. In David L. Carmichael, J. Hubert, B. Reeves, and A. Schanche (eds.), *Sacred Sites, Sacred Places*, 82–8. Abingdon: Routledge.

Rainer, Thom S. and Jess W. Rainer. (2011). *The Millennials: Connecting to America's Largest Generation*. Nashville, TN: B&H Publishing.

Rawa, J.M. (2005). *The Imperial Quest and Modern Memory from Conrad to Greene*. New York: Routledge.

Red Carpet Tours. (n.d.) 14 Day Lord of the Rings Tour. Retrieved November 7, 2017, from www.redcarpet-tours.com/lotr-tours/14-day-lord-of-the-rings-tour.

Reddy, W. (2001). *The Navigation of Feeling*. Cambridge: Cambridge University Press.

Richards, Tim. (2014). Top 10 Literary walking tours of the World. Lonely planet, October 2014. Retrieved November 16, 2017, from www.lonelyplanet.com/travel-tips-and-articles/top-10-literary-walking-tours-of-the-world/40625c8c-8a11-5710-a 052-1479d2767dd9.

Richey, L. A. and S. Ponte. (2011). *Brand Aid: Shopping Well to Save the World*. Minnesota, MN: University of Minnesota Press.

Roberts, Joanne and John Armitage. (2016). Knowing luxury: From socio-cultural value to market price? In John Armitage and Joanne Roberts (eds.), *Critical Luxury Studies: Art, Design, Media*, 25–46. Edinburgh: Edinburgh University Press.

Robinson, D. T., L. Smith-Lovin, and A. K. Wisecup. (2006). Affect control theory. In J. E. Stets and J. H. Turner (eds.), *Handbook of the Sociology of Emotions*, 179–202. New York: Springer.

Robson, Julia. (2006). Second string, first class. *The Telegraph* April 3. Online at: http:// fashion.telegraph.co.uk/news-features/TMG3352570/Second-string-first-class.html

Roitman, Sonia. (2006). Who segregates whom? The analysis of a gated community in Mendoza, Argentina. In Rowland Atkinson and Sarah Blandy (eds.), *Gated Communities*, 112–30. Abingdon: Routledge.

Rosaldo, M. (1981). The things we do with words. In Language in Society, 11, 203–37.

Roulstone, A., K. Soldatic, and H. Morgan. (2014). Introduction: Disability, space, place and policy. In K. Soldatic, H. Morgan, and A. Roulstone (eds.), *Disability, Spaces and Places of Policy Exclusion*, 1–9. New York: Routledge.

Rubdy, R. (2015). Conflict and exclusion: The linguistic landscape as an arena of contestation. In R. Rubdy and S. Ben Said (eds.), *Conflict, Exclusion and Dissent in the Linguistic Landscape*, 1–24. Houndmills: Palgrave Macmillan.

Rubdy, R. and Ben Said, S. (eds.). (2015). *Conflict, Exclusion and Dissent in the Linguistic Landscape*. Houndmills: Palgrave Macmillan.

Rudzitis, G., D. Marcouiller, and P. Lorah. (2011). The rural rich and their housing: spatially addressing the "haves." In D. Marcouiller, M. Lapping, and O. Furuseth (eds.), *Rural Housing, Exurbanization, and Amenity-Driven Development: Contrasting the "Haves" and the "Have Nots."* London: Routledge.

Rules and Regulations [PDF file]. In *Tidewater Plantation*. Retrieved from March 31, 2018 http://bwws-assets.s3.amazonaws.com/ironhorseauction/assets/content/auctions/184/2011–09-05-rules-appd.pdf.

Rutherford, D. (2016). Affect theory and the empirical. In *Annual Review of Anthropology*, 45, 285–300.

R-word: Spread the Word to End the Word. Retrieved multiple times between August and September 2011 from http://r-word.org.

Sachchidananda. (1988). *Social Change in Village India*. New Delhi: Concept Publishing.

Sanctuary Cove. Social Committee Charter. Retrieved March 29, 2018 from http://sanctuarycoveca.com/committees/

Scheff, T. J. (1990). *Microsociology: Discourse, Emotion and Social Structure*. Chicago, IL: University of Chicago Press.

Schwarz-Friesel, M. (2015). Language and emotion: The cognitive linguistic perspective. In U. M. Lüdtke (ed.), *Emotion in Language: Theory-Research-Application*, 157–74. Amsterdam: John Benjamins.

Sea Island Company. (2004). A special place: Sea Island. *Architectural Digest March* 2004.

Sengstock, Mary. (2009). *Voices of Diversity: Multi-Culturalism in A*merica. New York: Springer.

Sentosa Cove Real Estate. Sentosa Cove. Retrieved February 3, 2018 from http://sentosacoverealestate.com/sentosa-cove/

Sernau, Scott. (2014). *Social Inequality in a Global Age*, 4th ed. Thousand Oaks, CA: Sage.

Scollon, R., S. B. K. Scollon, and S. Wong Scollon. (2003). *Discourses in place*. London: Routledge.

Scollon, R. and S. Wong Scollon. (2004). *Nexus Analysis: Discourse and the Emerging Internet*. London: Routledge.

Scollon, R. and S. Wong Scollon. (2007). Nexus analysis. In *Journal of Sociolinguistics*, 11(5), 608–25.

Seacombe, Mark. (2011). *Going forward, let's consign this inane phrase to history* [online] MindYourLanguage Blog, August 30, 2011. Retrieved June 5, 2013, from www.guardian.co.uk/media/mind-your-language/2011/aug/30/mind-your-language-going-forward.

Sebeok, T. (1994). *Signs: Introduction to Semiotics*. Toronto: University of Toronto Press.

Sedgwick E. K. (2003). *Touching Feeling: Affect, Pedagogy, Performativity*. Durham, NC: Duke University Press.

Sengstock, M. (2009). *Voices of Diversity: Multi-Culturalism in A*merica. New York: Springer.

Sharpley, Richard. (2009). *Tourism Development and the Environment: Beyond Sustainability?* London: Earthscan.

Shinohara, M. (2012). Kawaii no kouzou [Structure of kawaii]. In *Aida/Seisei* [Between/Becoming], 2, 1–11.

Shogakukan. (2000). *Nihon kokugo daijiten* [the unabridged Japanese dictionary], 2nd edn. Tokyo: Shogakukan.

Shohamy, E. and D. Gorter. (eds.). (2008). *Linguistic Landscape: Expanding the Scenery*. New York/London: Routledge.

Sifianou, M. (1992). *Politeness Phenomena in England and Greece: A Cross-Cultural Approach*. Oxford: Oxford University Press.

Silverstein, M. (1976). Shifters, linguistic categories and cultural description. In K. H. Basso, H. A. Selby (eds.), *Meaning in Anthropology*, 11–55. Albuquerque, NM: University of New Mexico Press.

Silverstein, M. (2003). Indexical order and the dialectics of sociolinguistic life. In *Language and Communication*, 23, 193–229.

Silverstein, M. and Urban, G. (1996). The natural history of discourse. In M. Silverstein and G. Urban (eds.), Natural Histories of Discourse, 1–17. Chicago, IL: University of Chicago Press.

Slater, D. and G. Ritzer. (2001). Interview with Ulrich Beck. In *Journal of Consumer Culture*, 1(2), 261–77.

Smith-Lovin, L. (1995). The sociology of affect and emotion. In K. S. Cook, G. A. Fine, and J. S. House (eds.), *Sociological Perspectives on Social Psychology*, 118–48. Boston, MA: Allyn and Bacon.

Snoek, G. J. C. (1995). *Medieval Piety from Relics to the Eucharist: A Process of Mutual Interaction*. Leiden: E. J. Brill.

Social Committee Charter. In *Sanctuary Cove*. Retrieved March 29, 2018 from http://sanctuarycoveca.com/committees/.

Soja, E. W. (1989). *Postmodern Geographies: The Reassertion of Space in Critical Social Theory*. London: Verso.

Sotheby's International Realty. Fisher Island. Retrieved February 3, 2018 from www.onesothebysrealty.com/communities/fisher-island/?ibp-adgroup=26&utm_source=Google&utm_campaign=26&gclid=EAIaIQobChMIjJOqsbTC2AIVAyQrCh2C3wZ4EAAYAyAAEgKakfD_BwE

Spolsky, B. (2009). *Language Management*. Cambridge: Cambridge University Press.

Spolsky, B. and R. Cooper. (1991). *The Languages of Jerusalem*. Oxford: Clarendon.

Starr, R. (2015). Sweet voice: The role of voice quality in a Japanese feminine style. In *Language in Society*, 44(1), 1–34.

Stein, J. (April 24, 2017). A new tell-all about the Clinton campaign …. In *Vox*. Retrieved from www.vox.com/2017/4/24/15369452/clinton-shattered-campaign.

Stets, J. E. and J. H. Turner. (eds.). (2006). *Handbook of the Sociology of Emotions*. New York: Springer.

Stop using the R-word, please!. (March 2, 2011). In *Zara's Blog*. Retrieved September 18, 2011, from http://community.cbs47.tv/blogs/zarablog.

Stroud, C. and S. Mpendukana. (2009). Towards a material ethnography of linguistic landscape: Multilingualism, mobility and space in a South African township. In *Journal of Sociolinguistics*, 13(3), 363–86.

Sullivan, M. (October 9, 2017). Hillary Clinton thinks the news media was unfair to her ... In *Independent*. Retrieved from www.independent.co.uk/voices/hillary-clinton-media-criticism-what-happened-book-donald-trump-us-presidential-eleciton-2016-a7990086.html.

Suryadinata, L. (2015). *The Making of Southeast Asian Nations: State, Ethnicity, Indigenism and Citizenship*. Singapore: World Scientific.

Suzuki, S. and K. Yohei. (2017). An analysis of tweets by local mascot characters for regional promotions, called yuru-charas, and their followers in Japan. In R. Schegg and B. Stangl (eds.), *Information and Communication Technologies in Tourism*, 711–24. Cham: Springer.

Swaddling, Judith. (1999). *The Ancient Olympic Games*, 2nd edn. Austin, TX: University of Texas Press.

Talbot, M. (1995). A synthetic sisterhood: False friends in a teenage magazine. In K. Hall and M. Bucholtz (eds.), *Gender Articulated*, 143–65. New York: Routledge.

Tang, H. K. (2018). Linguistic landscaping in Singapore: Multilingualism or the dominance of English and its dual identity in the local linguistic ecology? *International Journal of Multilingualism*. DOI:10.1080/14790718.2018.1467422.

Tardiff, Sara. (2017). 5 Frank Lloyd Wright Houses for Sale Right Now. *Elle Décor* November 15. Online at: www.elledecor.com/celebrity-style/luxury-real-estate/g9917182/frank-lloyd-wright-houses/

Tate, Karen. (2006). *Sacred Places of Goddess: 108 Destinations*. San Francisco, CA: Consortium of Collective Consciousness.

Taylor, Ralph B. (1988). *Human Territorial Functioning: An Empirical, Evolutionary Perspective on Individual and Small Group Territorial Cognitions, Behaviors, and Consequences*. Cambridge: Cambridge University Press.

This is Anfield. Retrieved July 19, 2017, from www.thisisanfield.com/clubinfo/anfield/songs/.

Thomas, Dana. (2007). *Deluxe: How Luxury Lost Its Luster*. New York: Penguin.

Thoufeekh, S. (August 8, 2017). Cat cafes in Singapore: Purrfect spots for coffee, snacks and cute kitties. Retrieved November 21, 2017, from http://thehoneycombers.com/singapore/cat-cafes-in-singapore-purrfect-spots-for-coffee-snacks-and-cute-kitties/.

Thurlow, Crispin and Adam Jaworski. (2010). Silence is golden: The "anti-communicational" linguascaping of super-elite mobility. In A. Jaworski and C. Thurlow (eds.), *Semiotic Landscapes: Language, Image, Space*, 187–218. London: Continuum.

Thurlow, Crispin and Adam Jaworski. (2011). Tourism discourse: Languages and banal globalization. In *Applied Linguistics Review*, 2, 285–312.

Tidewater Plantation. Rules and Regulations. Retrieved March 31, 2018 from www.tidewaterplantation.org/documents/2012–07-05%20Rules%20&%20RegulationsAPPD.pdf

Toda, S., A. Fogel, and M. Kawai. (1990). Maternal speech to three-month-old infants in the United States and Japan. In *Journal of Child Language*, 17(2), 279–94.

Tokyo Metropolitan Government Bureau of Transportation. (2012). Minkuru no kobeya [Minkuru's small room]. Retrieved February 5, 2017, from www.kotsu.metro.tokyo.jp /fan/minkuru/minkurutowa.html.

Tomkins, S. S. (1962). *Affect Imagery Consciousness: Volume I, The Positive Affects*. London: Tavistock.

Tomkins, S. S. (1991). *Affect Imagery Consciousness Volume III. The Negative Affects: Anger and Fear*. New York: Springer.

Top Social Media Influencers of 2018. In *CBS*. Retrieved from www.cbsnews.com/pic tures/social-media-influencers-influential-2018/2/.

TripAdvisor. (n.d.). Lord of the Rings Twizel Tour. Retrieved November 3, 2017, from www.tripadvisor.com.sg/Attraction_Review-g612499-d1463625-Reviews -Lord_of_the_Rings_Twizel_Tour-Twizel_Mackenzie_District_Canterbury_Re gion_South_I.html.

TripAdvisor. (n.d.). Millennium Walking Tour Reviews. Retrieved November 16, 2017, from www.tripadvisor.com.sg/Attraction_Review-g189852-d5993711-Reviews-The _Millennium_Tour-Stockholm.html.

Trousselard, M., A. Jean, F. Beiger, F. Marchandot, B. Davout, and F. Canini. (2014). The role of an animal-mascot in the psychological adjustment of soldiers exposed to combat stress. In *Scientific Research*, 5(15), 1821–36.

Turner, J. H. and J. E. Stets. (2005). *The Sociology of Emotions*. Cambridge: Cambridge University Press.

Twitchell, James B. (2002). *Living It Up: Our Love Affair with Luxury*. New York: Columbia University Press.

Van Dam, Raymond. (1993). *Saints and Their Miracles in Late Antique Gaul*. Princeton, NJ: Princeton University Press.

Van Doorn, N. (2014). The neoliberal subject of value: Measuring human capital in information economies. In *Cultural Politics*, 10(3), 354–75.

Veblen, Thorstein. (2000). *The Theory of the Leisure Class*. New Brunswick: Transaction Publishers.

Vertovec, S. (2007). Super-diversity and its implications. In *Ethnic and Racial Studies*, 30(6), 1024–54.

Von Scheve, C. (2013). *Emotion and Social Structure: The Affective Foundations of Social Order*. London: Routledge.

Walgrave, S. and J. Verhulst. (2006). Towards "new emotional movements"? A comparative exploration into a specific movement type. In *Media, Movements & Politics*, 5(3), 275–304.

Wan, W. and S. Denyer. (2014). "In Tiananmen Square, no trace of remembrance on 25th anniversary of protests". *The Washington Post* June 4, 2014. Retrieved May 11, 2015, from www.washingtonpost.com/world/security-tight-as-china-represses-tiananmen-anniversary/2014/06/04/4d1c39e9-84c4-475c-a07a-03f1d2dd9cdf_story.html.

Watts, R. (2003). *Politeness*. Cambridge: Cambridge University Press.

Wee, L. (2015). Mobilizing affect in the linguistic cyberlandscape: The R-word campaign. In R. Rubdy and S. Ben Said (eds.), *Conflict, Exclusion and Dissent in the Linguistic Landscape*, 185–206. Basingstoke: Palgrave.

Wee, L. (2016). Situating affect in linguistic landscapes. In *Linguistic Landscape*, 2(2), 105–26.

Weinswig, Deborah. (2016). Millenials go minimal: The decluttering lifestyle trend that is taking over. *Forbes* September 7. Online at: www.forbes.com/sites/deborah weinswig/2016/09/07/millennials-go-minimal-the-decluttering-lifestyle-trend-that -is-taking-over/#15a96e4e3755

Weller, Chris. (2016). Dubai's wildly ambitious "The World" islands could finally be coming to life. *Business Insider* March 4. Online at: www.businessinsider.com/dubai-the-world-islands-are-slowly-coming-back-to-life-2016-2/?IR=T

Wetherell, M. (2015). Trends in the turn to affect: A social psychological critique. In *Body & Society*, 21(2), 139–66.

What Is Matatabi-kun? (January 30, 2017). In *Tokyo City Air Terminal*. Retrieved February 5, 2017, from www.tcat-hakozaki.co.jp/company/matatabi.html.

Wikipedia. (2013). Hiragana katakana chimei [Hiragana katakana place names]. Retrieved January 30, 2017, from https://ja.wikipedia.org/wiki.

Wilce, J. (2009). *Language and Emotion*. Cambridge: Cambridge University Press.

Williams, S. J. and G. Bendelow. (1998). Introduction: Emotions in social life. In G. Bendelow and S. J. Williams (eds.), *Emotions in Social Life: Critical Themes and Contemporary Issues*, xv–xxx. London: Routledge.

Willis, P. (1990). *Common Culture*. Milton Keynes: Open University Press.

Winograd, Morley and Michael D. Hais. (2011). *Millennial Momentum: How a New Generation Is Remaking America*. New Brunswick: Rutgers University Press.

Winterfell Tours. (n.d.). Home. Retrieved November 6, 2017, from www.gameofthrones-winterfelltours.com/.

Wissinger, E. (2007). Always on display: Affective production in the modelling industry. In P. T. Clough and J. Halley (eds.), *The Affective Turn: Theorizing the Social*, 1–33. Durham, NC: Duke University Press.

Wong, Lisa. (2007). Theme/Film Tour: The Disappearing of Illusion into Integral Reality. In Adam Lam and Nataliya Oryshchuk (ed.), *How We Became Middle-Earth: A Collection of Essays on* The Lord of the Rings, 87–106. Zollikofen: Walking Tree.

Works for me Wednesday – Watching my words. (March 2, 2010). In *The Diaper Diaries*. Retrieved September 18, 2011, from http://thediaperdiaries.net.

Xie, Q. (May 1, 2016). Are these the world's worst journeys to work? Footage reveals daily hell faced by commuters – from Japan's "sardine trains" to China's open-top cable cars. In *Daily Mail*. Retrieved January 8, 2017, from www.dailymail.co.uk/travel/travel_news/article-3565424/Are-world-s-worst-journeys-work-Extraordinary-footage-reveals-daily-hell-faced-commuters-including-rats-sardine-train-conditions-Japan-open-cable-car-China.html.

Yomota, I. (2006). *"Kawaii" Ron [The Theory of Kawaii]*. Tokyo: Chikuma Shobo.

Yoshikawa, Saeko. (2016). *William Wordsworth and the Invention of Tourism, 1820–1900*. Milton Park: Routledge.

Yuva-Davis, N. (1994). Women, ethnicity and empowerment. In K. Bhavnani and A. Phoenix (eds.), *Shifting Identities, Shifting Racisms: A Feminism and Psychology Reader*, 179–98. London: Sage.

Zorach, Rebecca and Michael W. Phillips. (2016). *Gold: Nature and Culture (Earth)*. London: Reaktion Books.

Zuboff, S. (1988). *In The Age of the Smart Machine: The Future of Work and Power*. New York: Basic Books.

Index

For EU product safety concerns, contact us at Calle de José Abascal, 56–1°,
28003 Madrid, Spain or eugpsr@cambridge.org.

www.ingramcontent.com/pod-product-compliance
Ingram Content Group UK Ltd.
Pitfield, Milton Keynes, MK11 3LW, UK
UKHW020352140625
459647UK00020B/2418